# LEGACY OF THE ANCIENT HEBREWS

## UNVEILS THE TRUTH OF BLACK HISTORY AND THE BIBLE

By DELANEY E. SMITH JR., PHARM.D., M.D.

Truth In Publishing

Los Angeles, California

Dedicated to my wife Stephanie, my sons Michael and Daniel, as well as my mother, and the sons and daughters of the almost forgotten Ancient Hebrews.


Library of Congress Catalog Card #95-09478

ISBN: 0-9646568-1-7
Printed in The United States of America.

CONTENTS

**Acknowledgements**

I would like to thank the Ministry of Culture Supreme Council of Antiquities of the Egyptian Museum, and the Egyptian Museum of Cairo, for their cooperation, which made it possible to include some photographs of the most highly treasured objects of their collection in this text. Many of the objects on display in the museum were deliberately buried by the conquering Greeks more than 2,000 years ago, and remained hidden until the beginning of the 20th century.

A special thanks to Jim Kregel of Kregel Publications, the publisher of The Complete Works of Josephus, an ancient work which has survived since shortly after the time of Christ until today. It is the first hand account offered in his comprehensive work which provided special insight into the historic period in question, and was only second to the Bible in that regard, thus accordingly as an eye witness to some to the events described, I heavily relied upon the writings of Flavius Josephus.

I cannot thank my transcriptionist enough for her dedication, and inspiration she offered while relating that the mere typing of this manuscript changed her life in a very positive way. I respect her request to remain an anonymous, and therefore I simply say thanks.... for your commitment to this project.

The transformation of this manuscript into a book was possible through the technology of computers and an "angel." Faced with deadlines which were considered impossible by many of his contemporaries in the field of Graphics and Printing, Angel Gonzalez of Pyramid Press rolled up his sleeves and persevered until not only the project was completed, but at the same time adhering to his own high standard which approached perfection. As a result the reader is in for a pleasurable experience from the time the cover is first viewed, until the assimilation of the last page of the text. Needless to say there is a long list of people that have helped to make this project a success, that extends well beyond those mentioned, to whom again I say... thanks!

Last but not least, I must thank my wife Stephanie, and sons for their patience, although it has grown to be a bit fragile over the past few weeks. Such may be expected as this has been a time consuming endeavor costing three years.... a marathon inwhich we can finally now all focus on the finish line that is clearly in view at this time.

# LEGACY OF THE ANCIENT HEBREWS

Origin, Analysis and Fate of the Ancient Hebrews

SIGMUND FREUD'S CONFESSION

by Delaney E. Smith, Jr., Pharm.D., M.D.

## INTRODUCTION

One day, during a search in a university library for a reference text that would lead me to the authors and place of origin of the first calendar, I stumbled onto a somewhat intriguing statement. However, during the course of my study that day, I reviewed approximately a dozen texts and, therefore, I don't specifically recall the exact source of the statement which left an indelible impression on my memory.

The text had pointed out that the first calendar was developed in the area of Babylon, more specifically, by a nation that was at its southern tip, called Chaldea. The text went on to say that the ancient Chaldeans, including some of its inhabitants who were referred to as "Hebrews" were very advanced in mathematics and astronomy and that the first attempt was fraught with error, in that, it was based upon their observations using a lunar model which resulted in the calendar being several days short of the 365 days actually required for the earth to fully complete its orbit around the sun. These ancient Chaldeans or Hebrews were able to identify the problem and correct it, determining that there were 365 days in a year, and thereby giving us the modern day calendar as we still know it today, although the calculations were done in approximately 3000 B.C.

The point of intrigue came, however, when the text went on to report that almost nothing else was known of these people aside from the fact that they spoke the Hebrew language. My curiosity further peaked when I later discovered that most of the original texts of the Bible "Old Testament" were written by the Hebrews. Given the mass appeal and influence of the Bible upon its billions of readers over the centuries and the wealth of knowledge that exists concerning much more obscure people of the ancient past, it seemed inexplicable that the identity of the people who wrote the Bible could be lost.

Now having determined that the Hebrews were a distinct people who had a written language and had not only given us the calendar, but the holy scriptures, as well, the next logical question seemed to be, what relationship did these ancient people have to the Jews or Jewish religion? I specifically remembered being taught that the term "Jewish" referred to a religion only and that there was no such thing as a Jewish race. However, I did recall that they studied the Hebrew language, which now seemed all the more confusing. It was sometime later that I discovered that the world renowned psychiatrist, Sigmund Freud, had wrestled with some of the same questions as early as the 1930s. His first two manuscripts on the subject were published in German in 1937, but only received limited circulation. Much of what Freud wrote in his manuscript entitled, "Moses and Monotheism", Part I and Part II, well coincided with my own study of these matters up to a certain point, at which time Freud seemed unable to go any further in this process of elucidation, even though he later wrote Part III, which was not published for more than twenty years following his death in 1939. I had not discovered Freud's work in this area until nearly two years after initiating my own independent study of this small, but seemingly neglected component of religious philosophy. By that time, I had reached a point at which my work was nearing its conclusion, but I found it gratifying that for a time, at least, we were on the same path, and more importantly, I knew at once why Sigmund Freud was seemingly unable to take his work to the next highest level, although until reaching that point, he had cut a clear and incontrovertible path.

It is this author's intent to take us well beyond Moses and monotheism and to bring into full focus the origin, historical analysis and fate of the authors of the Old Testament that we know as the Hebrews.

# PART I
# METHODOLOGY

The Hebrew religion was the original Judeo-Christian religion, in that, its teachings encompassed not only the principles within the Old Testament, but also looked to the fulfillment of the scriptural prophecies and the coming of the Messiah. It is written that Christ came not to change the Old Testament, not even so much as to dot an "i" or to cross a "t", but rather to fulfill the prophecies of the scriptures. The New Testament, which was largely written by the disciples of Christ following the crucifixion, did not exist as a compiled text at the time of Christ. Through his teachings, Christ offered an interpretation of the scriptures which were in existence at that time, and thus, such teachings were largely based upon the Old Testament. The original text of the Old Testament was written in Hebrew, yet from a historical perspective, little had been written and reportedly known about these ancient people. There has been much more written by modern-day authors on obscure tribes in South America than on the Hebrews, who are the authors of the world's most respected and revered text.

In a series of manuscripts written by Sigmund Freud late in life, entitled "Moses and Monotheism", this unlikely source, at least for religious works, opened the door to such insight over fifty years ago in an obscure, poorly circulated text which, as he related, was somewhat of a troubling experience for him. While the writing of the manuscript might have been a troubling experience, Freud made it quite clear that he was compelled to do so, and was unwilling to compromise or to set aside the truth at any cost. Much of the text of "Moses and Monotheism" was written prior to the 1938 German invasion of Vienna, which caused Freud to leave his home, thereafter moving to England where he continued to refine his text. Although his profession as a psychiatrist, who was considered by many to be the "Father of Psychoanalysis," seemed far removed from religious philosophy, Freud wrote that he feared that publication of his manuscript on Moses "Might cause psychoanalysis to be forbidden in a country where its practice is still allowed."[1] In spite of any concerns that Freud may have had concerning his professional career or what might happen to the practice of psychoanalysis, he felt that these concerns should take a second seat to the noble cause of truth and enlightenment.

Thereby, in Part I, entitled, "Moses as an Egyptian," Freud reflects, "To deny a people the man whom it praises as the greatest of its sons is not a deed to be undertaken lightheartedly especially by one belonging to that people. No consideration, however, will move me to set aside the truth in favour of supposed national interest. Moreover, the elucidation of the mere facts of the problem may be expected to deepen our insight into the situation with which they are concerned."[2]

The first part of the statement is quite clear and speaks for itself. However, the last part of the statement seems to hold a special significance and perhaps a deeper meaning, which is only known to Freud himself. In elucidating the matter of Moses as an Egyptian, Freud's path seemed to be quite clear and soundly based, until he reached a certain point, at which time he seemed to be hindered, and as I will later point out, the source of this hindrance stemmed from semantics which could only be overcome through a gymnastic exercise in amphiboly. "Amphiboly" is defined by Funk and Wagnalls Encyclopedic Edition as "An ambiguous construction of language; a group of words admitting two meanings."

There is clear evidence which will be presented that suggests a great deal of mystery and perhaps some confusion was deliberately interjected into the Greek translation of the Hebrew text of the Old Testament which dates back to the Hellenistic period which followed the conquest of the Mediterranean and Northern Africa, including the Egyptian empire, by Alexander "the Great." It was during that period that the names of individuals, as well as those of geographical locations were changed for the reasons to be discussed later on in this text.

It is the careful investigation of purposely introduced error which when fully elucidated will then clearly point the way to the truth that Freud had begun to ascertain. But more importantly, it will be shown that such errors were deliberately introduced at a particular place in time in antiquity in an attempt to forever veil a concealed truth.

As it has been written in the scriptures...and the truth shall set you free, would seem to infer that a segment of mankind has not and will not be free until the truth visits them. However, the truth must be actively sought, since it has been camouflaged since the ancient times and has only now begun to surface, although on the other hand, I suspect that much of what will be reflected in this manuscript does not come as a surprise to a small circle of scholars who, with few exceptions, such as Martin Bernal, have chosen to remain close-lipped.

In spite of any negative impact that the Hellenistic period may have exerted upon the Greek translation of the Old Testament, few would deny the fact that if one truly seeks the truth, the best starting place is, indeed, the Holy Bible. In addition to being the word of God, archeological confirmation has shown that the scriptures represent the most comprehensive historical text covering the period beginning with the creation of the earth and mankind extending to and beyond the time of Jesus with predictions or prophecies which continue well into our future. The problem in unlocking some of the truths and mysteries contained within the scriptures is at least twofold, in that, as previously indicated, there was a deliberate effort to change the names or geographical markings of the biblical lands from their original or Hebrew designations to a Greek "nom de plume" and the pseudonyms in most cases had no traceable roots and bore no identifiable relationships to other words as had been a characteristic of Hebrew and other languages of the period. In addition, further confusion stems from reading the scriptures without any time markers or coordinates, by which we can easily date or chronologize such events.

It is only when events in the Bible are placed in the context of time and the geographical and historical correlates are clearly identified that the reader will then be able to unlock some of these otherwise hidden mysteries that will, in turn, shed forth the truth. Despite the best efforts of wicked men to conceal God's truth from the masses, the truth can be hidden, but it is difficult, if not impossible to completely destroy, particularly in this case since there are cross references available from extra biblical sources, thus making it possible to assemble pieces just as one would put together a jigsaw puzzle. I would like to reiterate the fact that especially when considering its longevity which dates back thousands of years, any changes in the text of the scriptures have been few, and this has been verified by relatively recent archeological finds which have shown, for example, that the original Hebrew text of Isaiah compares remarkably well to the text of today. It just so happens that the point of my focus is to elucidate at least some of those subtle changes by introducing the reader to a method of biblical study that will allow him to see the truth clearly as long as he has an open heart and mind, for only those with an open heart and mind will ever recognize the truth.

I found it to be somewhat intriguing that Sigmund Freud employed a somewhat similar method of elucidation which led him to proclaim the possibility that Moses was an Egyptian in his manuscript, Moses as an Egyptian, which was published in Imago in 1937 with the final section of the manuscript not being published until more than twenty years after his death.

As has been previously stated, much of our inability to comprehend all that is written in the scriptures is the result of a calculated effort dating back to antiquity, and more specifically, the Hellenistic period of Greek domination of the Mediterranean and Northern Africa following the conquest of Alexander "the Great."

While much of the documentary evidence from this period remains remarkably well intact, there are no surviving eye-witnesses, as this was a point in time that dates back a couple of hundred years before the time of Christ. Therefore, the most practical method of elucidation involves taking from the traditional and period specific written materials what seems useful, then rejecting that which is unsuitable, and then assembling the pieces together according to their psychological probability, to which Freud did not seem to disagree. This method of investigation was employed in this particular manuscript, predominantly relying upon the text of the Bible itself in conjunction with a biblical encyclopedia and the comprehensive works of a few ancient historians, including Josephus, and Herodotus, as well as the more traditional works of the English author, Breasted, who was considered by some to be the foremost authority of Egyptian history. As alluded to earlier, an understanding of the location of such events or the geography of ancient times is key to understanding the Bible.

Since the text of the Bible is largely centered around the descendants of Abraham, it is important for us to know the identity of Abraham and his descendants, as well as the other key groups of people discussed in the Old Testament. God's original promise regarding the inheritance of the "promised land" was made to Abram, whose name was later changed to Abraham by God, as set forth in Genesis, Chapter 12. Abram or Abraham was originally from Chaldea, that is, the southern portion of Babylon, and was the individual to whom "Hebrew" was first applied in Genesis (14:13). "Jew" is the Greek term for "Yehumdim," a Hebrew word which meant originally, descendants of the tribe of Judah; however, this was subsequently applied to those who inhabited the land of Judah (the latter of which was later changed to Judea), the area claimed by them. So the Greek term "Jew" is the first amphiboly or word which admittedly has two or more meanings that is discussed in this text. Judah was the son of Jacob (whose name was changed to Israel after he wrestled with an angel). Jacob's father was Isaac, who was the son of Abraham, thus making Judah the great grandson of Abraham. Due to its double meaning, the Greek term "Jew" is very loosely used in the Greek translation of the original Hebrew text of the Old Testament, as well as in the New Testament. Judah, who was one of the twelve sons of Jacob (Israel) gave rise to one of the twelve tribes of Israel. As Abraham was described as a Hebrew in the 12th chapter of Genesis, it followed that his son, his grandson and descendants thereafter, including Judah, were considered to be

Hebrews. Information which will be introduced later in this manuscript will point to the fact that the terms "Hebrew" and "Jew" are not synonymous.

But for now, let's turn to the book of Genesis and the description of the promise made to Abraham and his descendants in:

Genesis (12:1-3):

> **"Now the Lord had said unto Abram, 'Get thee out of they country, and from thy kindred, and from thy father's house, unto a land that I will shew thee: And I will make of thee a great nation, and I will bless thee, and make thy name great; and thou shalt be a blessing: And I will bless them that bless thee, and curse them that curseth thee: And in thee shall all families of the earth be blessed.'"**

Genesis (12:7):

> **"And the Lord appeared unto Abram, and said, Unto thy seed will I give this land: and there builded he an altar unto the Lord who appeared unto him."**

In various places throughout the Old Testament, there are repeated references to the original covenant with Abraham, as well as subsequent renewals of such with his descendants.

Psalms (105:8):

> **"He hath remembered his covenant forever, the word which he commanded to a thousand generations."**

Psalms (105:9-11):

> **"Which covenant he made with Abraham and his oath unto Isaac; and confirmed the same unto Jacob for a law and to Israel for an everlasting covenant: Saying, unto thee will I give the land of Canaan, the lot of your inheritance."**

The Old Testament books of both Genesis and Chronicles

make it clear that Abraham was the descendant of Shem, who was one of the sons of Noah. Although Genesis 14:13 clearly describes Abraham as a Hebrew, it is not clear from the Greek Translation of Genesis or the remainder of the Old Testament why Abraham was designated as such. In looking up the term "Hebrew" in the biblical encyclopedia, it was defined as a descendant of Eber.

Flavius Josephus was one of the few outstanding historians who lived shortly after the time of Christ whose work has survived to this day. He has been described by some as a Roman citizen who belonged to the Jewish sect of the Pharisees. His in depth knowledge of the traditions and historical accounts of the Hebrews would seem to point to the fact that Josephus himself was a Hebrew. Further in Book III, Chapter V of his classic work, "Antiquities of the Jews," it is written, "When this was done, the Hebrews conquered the Amalekites by main force; indeed, they had all perished, unless the approach of the night had not obliged the Hebrews to desist from killing anymore. So our forefathers obtained a most signal and most seasonable victory; for they not only overcame those that fought against them, but terrified also the neighboring nations, and got great and splendid advantages, which they did obtain of their enemies by their hard pains in this battle." The above is only a small segment of the writings of Josephus which pertain to this one battle against the Amalekites which was led by Moses after he had led their escape from slavery in Egypt as they journeyed toward the "promised land." In the aforementioned passage, Josephus clearly indicates that his forefathers were the Hebrews. It, therefore, seemed appropriate to look to Josephus for insight as to the origin of the ancient Hebrews, which once again, was not clear from the Greek translation of the Old Testament.

In Josephus, "Antiquities of the Jews" in Book I, Chapter VI, it became clear that the name "Eber" as written in the Greek translation of the Old Testament was actually "Heber," and it was from Heber "from whom they originally called the Jews, Hebrews." He went on to say that Heber begat Joctan and Phaleg, and the descendants of Heber were further traced to Abraham within this same chapter. The lineage of Eber (Heber) was then verified by turning back to the biblical text I Chronicles. More specifically, it was pointed out in Chronicles (1:4) that Noah's sons were named Shem, Ham, and Japheth; Chronicles (1:17) the sons of Shem: Elam, and Asshur, and Arphaxad, and Lud, and Aram and Uz, and Hul, and Gether, and Meshech. Chronicles (1:18-19) continues, And Arphaxad begat Shelah, and Shelah begat Eber. And unto Eber were born two sons: The name of the one was Peleg; because in his days, the earth was divided: and his brother's name was Joktan.

Thus, it was verified that the Heber described by Josephus, who gave rise to the Hebrews, was, indeed, the same Eber described in Chronicles as being the son of Arphaxad, or the grandson of Shem, wnose father was Noah. Clearly the connections between the Hebrews and Heber would have been much more apparent, had not the Greek translation recorded the name as Eber. And so the next logical question which would seem to follow would be was this a mere oversight of the Greeks, or was the omission of the "H" deliberate?

For this answer, once again, we can turn to Josephus, "Antiquities of the Jew", Book I, Chapter V, which was entitled, "After What Manner the Posterity of Noah Sent Out Colonies, and Inhabited the Whole Earth," where it was described that at the time of his writing, which was shortly after the time of Christ, "Some of those nations do still retain the denominations which were given them by their first founders; but some have lost them also; and some have only admitted certain changes in them, that they might be more intelligible to the inhabitants; and they were the Greeks who became the authors of such mutations; for when and after ages, they grew potent, they claimed to themselves the glory of antiquity, giving names to nations that sounded well (in Greek) that might be better understood among themselves; and setting agreeable forms of government over them, as if they were people derived from themselves." In such a strong condemnation, Josephus left little to the imagination as he clearly stated that the Greeks were responsible for various changes or mutations in nomenclature as they tried to take credit for all of antiquity and claim it as their own.

Now armed with this additional insight, let us go back to **Chronicles (1:18): "And Arphaxad begat Shelah and Shelah begat Eber."** And in tracing the genealogy to **Chronicles (1:27),** and then again to **Chronicles (2:1)** in which the names of the sons of Israel (Jacob) are described as Reuben, Simeon, Levi, and Judah, Issachar, and Zebulun, which continues to name Dan, Joseph, Benjamin, Naphtali, Gad, and Asher. This exercise points out that the Hebrews were in existence prior to the time of Abraham and his great grandson, Judah, both of whom, themselves, were Hebrews, as has been shown.

The order of the sequence of events which follow are of paramount importance to our understanding and a key component of the elucidation method which must be employed in our quest to obtain the deepest level of insight into these matters. While the sequence of events is important, of equal importance is the dating of these sequential biblical events. Since the text of the Bible itself offers only limited clues by which we can associate extra biblical events, those clues, limited as they might be, for the same reason take on even greater significance as we attempt to match biblical events with specific points in time in history.

The extra-biblical gold standard which is often used as a reference point for time during the ancient period is the Egyptian Chronological Table which lists the kings of each dynasty and the dates in which they reigned with reasonable accuracy dating back to 3000 B.C. While there are frequent references to Egypt throughout the writings of the Old Testament, rarely are the names of the kings specifically mentioned, therefore synchronizing biblical events even against the chronological table of the Egyptian Dynasties is a difficult task.

However, other methods can be employed with reasonable accuracy. One such method would include using a well known biblical event, whose date is known, as a reference point. Using the relatively few clues available through the Bible, other events can be roughly dated. For instance, it is known that Solomon reigned over the area of Israel and Judah for a forty year period and according to the Old Testament Survey, page 253, this period of reign extended from (ca. 971-931). Solomon, one of the younger sons of his father, King David, was appointed king as King David lay on his death bed, which would have placed the time of his death at the approximate year of 971 B.C. **I Kings (6:1)** states:

> **"And it came to pass in the four hundred and eightieth year after the children of Israel were come out of the land of Egypt, in the fourth year of Solomon's reign over Israel, and in the month of Zif, which is the second month that he began to build the house of the Lord."**

This reference is to the great temple that was constructed during the reign of Solomon and, accordingly, construction would have begun in the year 967 B.C. On the other hand, from the same passage, it can be shown that the Hebrew exodus from bondage in Egypt, also marked by the crossing of the Red Sea, would have occurred 480 years prior to the date on which construction of the temple began, or the year 1447 B.C. Using the year of 1447 B.C. as the time of exodus, which is then applied to the chronological table of the Egyptian Dynasties, we find that this date falls within the period of the New Kingdom which spans from 1550 B.C. to 1070 B.C. and includes the 18th Dynasty, the 19th Dynasty, and the 20th Dynasty. More specifically, it refers to the reign of Thutmose III whose reign extended from 1479 to 1425 B.C.

According to the British Museum Book of Ancient Egypt[3], Thutmose I was succeeded by a son, Thutmose II, who married his half sister, Hatshepsut. Following the death of Thutmose II, because of the young age of Thutmose III, Hatshepsut took the position of regent and then in the second year of this new reign, she became the first woman since Sobekneferu to be crowned King of Egypt. As the years passed, Thutmose III seems to have reigned alongside Hatshepsut, during which time he conducted many well documented military campaigns. Hatshepsut insisted that she was King of Egypt and not Queen until the time of her death, after which time, her image and name as King were erased from every monument. The period of reign for Hatshepsut extended from 1473 to 1458 B.C. and was eclipsed by the co-reign of Thutmose III, which as previously mentioned, extended from 1479 to 1425 B.C.

As confirmation of the time line that we have created and the fact that Thutmose was, indeed, the Pharaoh at the time in which the Hebrew captives were released from bondage in Egypt, we once again turn to the ancient Hebrew historian, Josephus, who in turn, quotes even the more ancient Egyptian historian Manetho.

"But now I shall produce the Egyptians as witness to the antiquity of our nation. I shall, therefore, here bring in Manetho again, and what he writes as to the order of the times in this case, and thus he speaks; 'When this people or shepherds were gone out of Egypt to Jerusalem, Tethmosis, the king of Egypt, who drove them out, reigned afterward 25 years and four months and then died...'"[4] (See Thutmose III, plate.)

This cross reference offered by Josephus and Manetho confirms the accuracy of the method dating based upon time correlates offered in the Bible itself. The reign of young Thutmose III extended for a 54 year period from the year 1479 to 1425 B.C., and using our date of 1447 B.C. as the date in which the Exodus began out of Egypt, Thutmose died 22 years later. This is a very important point since there were four different Pharaohs who bore this name, beginning with Thutmose I, whose reign began 1504 B.C. to Thutmose IV whose reign ended at the time of his death in 1391 B.C. In the account given by Josephus in which Manetho was quoted, in confirming that Thutmose was, indeed, the king at the time of the Exodus, there was no further clarification as to which Thutmose Manetho was referring to in his historical text. This in itself might leave room for doubt, in that it could be argued that the Exodus may have been anywhere from 1504 through 1391 B.C. However, once again, we return to Josephus and his quote of Manetho,

"When this people or shepherds were gone out of Egypt to Jerusalem, Tethmosis, the king of Egypt, who drove them out, reigned afterward twenty five years and four months and then died."

Although there was a three year difference between our computation of the time between the Exodus and the death of Thutmose and that which is offered in Josephus' quote of Manetho, by referring to the log of the New Kingdom Pharaohs, we find that we can only be speaking of Thutmose III. None of the other Thutmose Pharaohs reigned for twenty five years or even twenty two years.

Thus, in Manetho's account of Thutmose being Pharaoh at the time the Hebrews gained their freedom from Egypt, he could only be referring to Thutmose III, as has been previously described in this text.

Moses was eighty years old at the time he appealed to Pharaoh to release the Hebrews from bondage, which was eventually granted. **Exodus (7:7):**

> **"And Moses was fourscore years old and Aaron fourscore and three years old when they spake unto Pharaoh." (Eighty years and eighty three years old, respectively.)**

The previous Pharaoh, Thutmose II had already died with his death occurring during the time in which Moses was in exile and shortly after the birth of his first son, Gershom.
**Exodus (2:22-23):**

> **"And she bare him a son, and he called his name Gershom: for he said, I have been a stranger in a strange land. And it came to pass in the process of time, that the king of Egypt died: and the children of Israel sighed by reason of the bondage, and they cried and their cry came up unto God by reason of the bondage."**

Moses, having been adopted by the princess and growing up in the royal palace, would have been a contemporary of Thutmose II and, interestingly enough, Hatshepsut, the wife of Thutmose II, who later declared herself King of Egypt, also would have shared the palace as a youthful contemporary of Moses. Later, Hatshepsut went on to marry her half brother, Thutmose II, although Thutmose III was the product of a union between Thutmose II and a "lesser wife." Photographs of the carved busts of Hatshepsut, as well as several other royal contemporaries of this period are provided in this text. Hatshepsut was the aunt and stepmother, therefore, of young Thutmose III.

According to the biblical text, following the exodus from Egypt, the children of Israel, led by Moses and his brother Aaron, wandered in the wilderness for forty years before finally entering the promised land of Canaan, the area known as Palestine today. According to the scriptures, Moses died at the age of 120 and apparently just prior to the children of Israel finally entering the promised land. Once again, using the year 1447 as the year of the Exodus and then applying the forty-year period in which the tribes of Israel wandered in the wilderness prior to entering the promised land, it can be extrapolated that entry occurred in approximately 1407 B.C. If we add the 120-year life span-of Moses to that date, it can be extrapolated that he was born in the year 1527 B.C. Once again, if we turn to the chronology table of the Egyptian Dynasties, we find that the birth of Moses in 1527 would correspond to the reign of Ahmose which extended from the period 1550 to 1525 B.C. Ahmose would have been in the last two years of his reign when the infant Moses was found in a cradle by the Nile by the young Egyptian princess who later named him Moses. Pharaoh Amenhotpe I (1525-1504 B.C.), sometimes referred to as Amenophis 1, married the "princess" and daughter of Ahmose I, that this author believes was the adoptive mother of Moses.
**Exodus (2:5-6):**

> **"And the daughter of Pharaoh came down to wash herself at the river; and her maidens walked along the river's side; and when she saw the ark among the flags, she sent her maid to fetch it. And when she had opened it, she saw the child: and behold, the babe wept. She had compassion on him, and said, This is one of the Hebrews' children."**

Exodus (2:9-10):

**"And Pharaoh's daughter said unto her, Take this child away and nurse it for me, and I will give thee thy wages. And the woman took the child, and nursed it. And the child grew, and she brought him unto Pharaoh's daughter, and he became her son. And she called his name Moses: and she said, Because I drew him out of the water."**

This, once again returns us to Sigmund Freud's observation in his manuscript, Part I, Moses as an Egyptian, when he points out...

"I am a little surprised, however, that Breasted in citing related names should have passed over the analogous theophorous names in the list of Egyptian kings, such as Ah-mose, Thut-mose (Thotmes), and Ramose (Rameses)."[5] Freud continues, "It might have been expected that one of the many authors who recognized Moses to be an Egyptian name would have drawn the conclusion, or at least considered the possibility, that the bearer of an Egyptian name was himself an Egyptian." We will revisit this topic as we will review significant events within the Bible which point to the identity of the Hebrews.

At this time, however, we will continue our attempt to date significant events in the Bible as we will later show their relationship to the Hebrews as a people. For this, once again, we turn to God's promise to Abraham, which we find at this point in

Genesis (15:13-14):

**"And he said unto Abram, Know of a surety that thy seed shall be a stranger in a land that is not theirs, and shall serve them; and they shall afflict them four hundred years; And also that nation, whom they shall serve, will I judge: and afterward shall they come out with great substance."**

Genesis (15:18):

**"In the same day the Lord made a covenant with**

**Abram, saying, Unto thy seed have I given this land, from the river of Egypt unto the great river, the river Euphrates."**

Once again, if we take the year in which the Hebrews were freed from their bondage in Egypt to be 1447, as previously calculated, and add four hundred years of servitude as set forth in

Genesis 15:13, this establishes the point in time in which the Hebrews entered bondage in Egypt to be approximately the year 1847 B.C.

Once again, turning to the chronology tables of the Egyptian Dynasties, we find that the period 1847 B.C. corresponds with the 12th dynasty which extended from the period 1991-1783. More specifically, this would have occurred under the reign of Senwosret III, who reigned from 1878-1842 B.C. Still an earlier date for which a time marker is convenient is the biblical appearance of the Hebrew, Abraham, with whom the Lord established the covenant. And according to the scriptures, Genesis (11:27-28):

**"Now these are the generations of Terah: Terah begat Abram, Nahor and Haran; and Haran begat Lot. And Haran died before his father Terah in the land of his nativity, in Ur of the Chaldees."**

Genesis (11:31) continues:

**"And Terah took Abram, and Lot the son of Haran his son's son and Sarai his daughter-in-law, his son Abrams wife; and they went forth with them from Ur of the Chaldees, to go into the land of Canaan; and they came unto Haran and dwelt there."**

The call of Abraham followed in Genesis (12:1-2:

**"Now the Lord said unto Abram, Get thee out of thy country, and from thy kindred, and from thy father's house, unto a land that I will show thee. And I will make thee a great nation, and I will bless thee and make thy name great; and thou**

**shalt be a blessing:"**

Genesis (12:4):

> **"So Abram departed, as the lord had spoken unto him; and Lot went with him: and Abram was seventy and five years old when he departed out of Haran."**

And according to the scriptures, he lived a long life, dying at the age of one hundred and seventy-five years.

Genesis (25:7):

> **"And these are the days of the years of Abraham's life which he lived, and hundred three score and fifteen years."**

Thus, there was a hundred-year period between the time in which Abram received the word of the Lord and departed out of Haran for Canaan. Following their journey to Canaan, Sarai, Abraham's wife, designated her handmaid, an Egyptian woman whose name was Hagar, to bear Abraham's first child.

Genesis (16:3):

> **"And Sarai, Abram's wife took Hagar, her maid, the Egyptian, after Abram had dwelt ten years in the land of Canaan and gave her to her husband Abram to be his wife. And he went unto Hagar and she conceived: and when she saw that she had conceived, her mistress was despised in her eyes."**

Genesis (16:15) continues:

> **"And Hagar bear Abram a son: And Abram called his son's name, which Hagar bare, Ishmael."**

Genesis continues, and Sarai, whose name has now been changed to Sarah, herself then went on to bear Abraham a son.

Genesis (21:2-3):

> **"For Sarah conceived, and bare Abraham a son in his old age, at the set time of which God**

**had spoken to him. And Abraham called the name of his son that was born unto him, whom Sarah bare to him, Isaac."**

Genesis (21:5):

**"And Abraham was an hundred years old, when his son Isaac was born unto him.**

And as recorded in I Chronicles (1:34):

**"And Abraham begat Isaac. The sons of Isaac; Esau and Israel."**

As has been previously recorded in this text, the prior name of Israel had been Jacob, but his name was later changed. It was the twelve sons of Israel who went on to establish the twelve tribes of Israel, the youngest of whom was Joseph.

Genesis (50:26):

**"So Joseph died being an hundred and ten years old: and they embalmed him, and put him in a coffin in Egypt."**

And as recorded in Exodus (1:6):

**"And Joseph died, and all his brethren and all that generation."**

As Exodus continues, it is pointed out that the descendants of the children of Israel were fruitful, but as a new king rose up over Egypt who did not know Joseph, they were subjected to task masters who pressed them into servitude. Based upon our earlier calculations, we know that this occurred in approximately 1847 B.C. This would have placed the journey of Abraham into the land of Canaan, at which time he was reported to be 75 years old, at approximately the year 2000 B.C.

According to the Old Testament Survey, page 103, "Abraham's journey from Northwest Mesopotamia (Haran) to Canaan accords well with a number of conditions known to pertain during

MB II A (2000/ 1950-1800). Now from an extra-biblical perspective, the years 2000-1500 B.C. were known as the Patriarchal Age as it pertained to Mesopotamia and surrounding areas, the beginning of which period was known to be a time of peace and prosperity.

Once again, turning to the Egyptian Chronological Table, we find that this also corresponds with the beginning of the period of the middle kingdom of Egypt.

Now that we have set the appropriate time markers for the most ancient period of the Old Testament, it is now time that we begin to address the issues which will allow us to identify the ancient Hebrews, their contributions and fate.

## CHRONOLOGIC TABLE OF THE PHARAOHS

Egyptian Culture dates back to 5000 B.C., which is sometimes referred to as the "Nagada Culture." The late Predynastic Period began 3000 B.C., and many of the statues of the Pharaohs, which were buried during the Greco-Roman period, have been identified at this time as a result of archeological expeditions, which occurred at the turn of this century.

| | |
|---|---|
| **MIDDLE KINGDOM PERIOD** | **2040-1640 B.C.** |
| **SECOND INTERMEDIATE PERIOD** | **1640-1550** |
| **15th-17th Dynasty**<br>*(Hyksos or Shephard Kings were from Phoenicia) | |
| **NEW KINGDOM PERIOD** | **1550-1070** |
| **18th Dynasty** | |
| **AHMOSES I**<br>(Nebpehtire) | **1550-1525** |
| **AMENHOTPE I**<br>(Djeskare) | **1525-1504** |
| **THUTMOSE I**<br>(Akheperkare) | **1504-1492** |
| **THUTMOSE II**<br>(Akheperenre) | **1492-1479** |
| **THUTMOSE III**<br>(Menkheperre) | **1479-1425** |
| **HATSHEPSUT**<br>(Ma atkare) | **1473-1458** |
| **AMENHOTPE II**<br>(Akheprure) | **1427-1401** |
| **THUTMOSE IV**<br>(Menkheprure) | **1401-1391** |
| **AMENHOTPE III**<br>(Nebma atre) | **1391-1353** |
| **AMENHOTPE IV (AKHENATEN)**<br>(Neferkheprure) | **1353-1335** |

* "This statement of the Phoenician origin of the Hyksos kings

has generally been discredited until recently: now the Ras esh-Shamra tablets, which imply a pantheon strikingly similar to that of the Hyksos, have shown that the Hyksos were closely related to the Phoenicians."

(Manetho, p. 90)

The focus of our attention is largely the period of time involving the New Kingdom Pharaonic Era, as reflected by the Table of Pharaohs.

---

## Part I notes:

[1] Moses and Monotheism, Sigmund Freud

[2] Ibid., p. 3

[3] British Museum Book of Ancient Egypt,

[4] The Complete Works of Josephus, translated by William Whiston, p. 6II.

[5] Moses and Monotheism, Sigmund Freud, p. 5.

PHARAOH **SENWOSRET I** (SESOSTRIS I) **1971 - 1926 B.C.**
COURTESY OF THE EGYPTIAN MUSEUM, CAIRO

**PHARAOH SENWOSRET III (SESOSTRIS III) 1878 - 1842 B.C.**

THE PHARAOH THAT INITIATED THE EGYPTIAN CAPTIVITY OF THE HEBREWS.
COURTESY OF THE EGYPTIAN MUSEUM, CAIRO

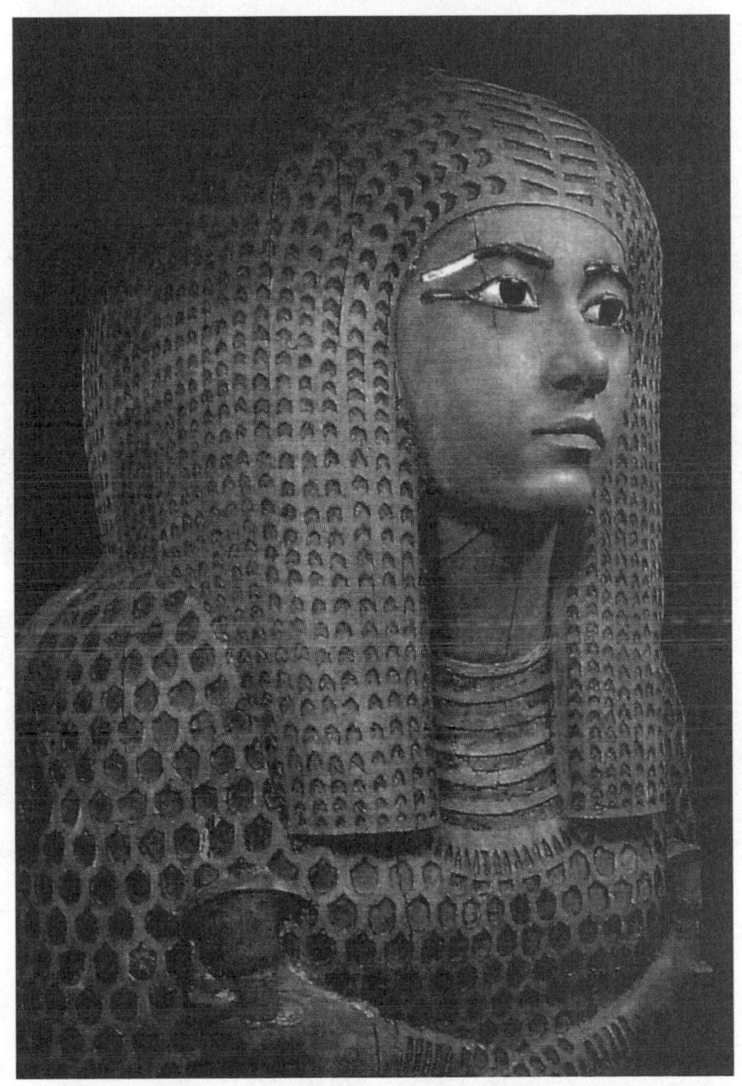

**Queen Ahmose Merit-Amon 1550 B.C.**

Daughter of Ahmose I

Princess and probable adoptive mother of Moses.

Coffin with funerary mask was found at El-Dair El-Bahari.

Courtesy of the Egyptian Museum, Cairo

PHARAOH (**QUEEN HATSHEPSUT**) 1473 -1458 B.C.
STEP MOTHER AND REGENT OF THUTMOSE III
FOUND AT EL-DAIR EL-BAHARI
COURTESY OF THE EGYPTIAN MUSEUM, CAIRO

PHARAOH **THUTMOSE III 1479- 1425 B.C.**

PHARAOH DURING THE EXODUS OF THE HEBREWS FROM CAPTIVITY

COURTESY OF THE EGYPTIAN MUSEUM, CAIRO

**QUEEN ISIS,** MOTHER OF PHARAOH **THUTMOSE III**
FOUND AT KARNAK
COURTESY OF THE EGYPTIAN MUSEUM, CAIRO

# PART II

## FATE OF THE HEBREWS

Now that we have established reference points in time for various events in the oldest part of the Old Testament, we will now re-explore such events in a chronologic order, using extra-biblical sources where necessary to present a full portrait of the ancient Hebrew people. In this process of elucidation whereby the facts are oftentimes scattered amongst various reference materials and thereby must be reassembled piece by piece to form a composite picture of the ancient times and the people therein, repetition is unavoidable; however, it is hoped this will be viewed as constructive reinforcement rather than a distraction.

Throughout the ages, the Bible is considered to be the golden standard of truth which continues to this day and the archeological and historical expeditions of the past one-hundred years have served only to add to the validity of the Bible as an accurate historical text. When extra-biblical texts do not agree with the Bible, more oftentimes than not, it is the Bible that will point the way to the truth. Sometimes when biblical descriptions are not complete, we must then rely upon extra-biblical sources to complete the picture, and more times than not, they are excellent for such a purpose. One such case was as previously mentioned, Flavius Josephus, whose writings were largely based upon the Bible itself. However, since he was a contemporary of the era immediately following the crucifixion of Christ, he had access to other sources, which are not available today, as he prepared his comprehensive text. Even still, when held against the gold standard of the Bible, the flaws are readily seen.

It was Josephus in his text, "Antiquity of the Jews," who pointed out that Abram, a Chaldean, was a righteous man, great, and skillful in the celestial science. In Chapter Eight, Josephus continues, "Now after this, when a famine had invaded the land of Canaan and Abram had discovered that the Egyptians were in a flourishing condition, he was disposed to go down to them, both to partake of the plenty they enjoyed and to become an auditor of their priests, and to know what they said concerning the gods, designing either to follow them, if they had better notions than he, or to convert them into a better way, if his notions proved to be the truest." Commenting on Abram's sojourn into Egypt, "He communicated them arithmetic and delivered to them the science of astronomy; for before Abraham came into Egypt, they were unacquainted with those parts of learning; for that science came from the Chaldeans into Egypt, and from thence to the Greeks also." In further describing Abraham, Josephus seemingly flawed when he described him as "The first that ventured to publish this notion, that there was but one God, the creator of the universe; and that as to the other [gods] if they contributed anything to the happiness of men, that each of them afforded it only according to his appointment and not by their own power." While according to Josephus, it was these doctrines which caused the Chaldeans and other people of Mesopotamia to raise a tumult against him, which contributed to his leaving that country, aside from the fact that he was called by God, the Bible points out that there was one to whom even Abraham paid tithes, and that was the high priest, Melchizedec, who was priest and king of Salem, the city whose name was later changed by the Greeks to Jerusalem.

**Genesis (14:18-20):**

> **"And Melchizedec, king of Salem, brought forth**
> **bread and wine: and he was a priest of the most high God.**
> **And he blessed him, and said, Blessed be**
> **Abram of the most high God, possessor of**
> **heaven and earth:**
> **And blessed be the most high God, which hath**
> **delivered thine enemies into thy hand.**
> **And he gave him tithes of all."**

In **Hebrews (5:6-7)**, there is another reference to Melchizedec which states: **"So also Christ glorified not himself to be made**
**an high priest; but he that said unto him, thou**

**art my son, today have I begotten thee.**
**As he saith also in another place, thou art a priest forever after the order of Melchizedec. Melchizedec and Abraham both worshiped one true God."**

Hebrews Chapter Seven continues **(Hebrews 7: 1-7)** and offers even insight into Melchizedec, as follows:

**"For this, Melchizedec, king of Salem,**
**Priest of the most high God, who met Abraham returning from the slaughter of the kings, and blessed him;**
**To whom also Abraham gave a tenth part of all; first being by interpretation King of righteousness, and after that also King of Salem, which is King of peace;**
**Without father, without mother, without descent, having neither beginning of days, nor end of life; but made like unto the Son of God; abideth a priest continually.**
**Now consider how great this man was unto whom even the patriarch Abraham gave the tenth of the spoils.**
**And verify they that are of the sons of Levi, who receive the office of the priesthood, have commandment to take tithes of the people according to the law, that is of their brethren, though they come out of the loins of Abraham:**
**But he whose descent is not counted from them received tithes of Abraham, and blessed him that had the promises.**
**And without all contradiction the less is blessed of the better."**

Once again, I would like to point out to the reader one I important fact which is alluded to in **Genesis (28:1):**

**"And Isaac called Jacob, and blessed him and charged him, and said unto him, Thou shalt not take a wife out of the daughters of Canaan."**

This admonishment referring to the daughters of Canaan refers to the women descendants of Canaan who lived in the land of Canaan and thereby called themselves Canaanites and were considered to be the descendants of Ham, who were largely considered to be pagan worshipers. The fact that Melchizedec was a high priest in Salem or in Jerusalem, which is also located in "the Land of Canaan" which later became known as the "Promised Land," obviously not all Canaanites or people living in Canaan were pagan worshipers, although this, of course, assumes that Melchizedec had followers in his ministry. It would seem to follow that even under the leadership of the high priest, Melchizedec, there was a failure of the Canaanites to embrace the concept of monotheism and its principles and therefore, they fell from favor with God who ultimately promised the Land of the Canaanites, "the Promised Land" to the seed of Abraham which went on to become the twelve tribes of Israel with Moses himself being a descendant and member of the tribe of Levi.

Biblical or classical Hebrew belongs to the Northwest Semitic branch of Semitic languages which includes Ugaritic, Phoenician, Moabite, Edomite, and Ammonite. This linguistic group is referred to commonly as Canaanite, although some prefer not to call Ugaritic a Canaanite dialect. "The affinities for Hebrew and the other Canaanite languages are recognized by the Old Testament itself, for one of the names applied to it is literally lip of Canaan" (Isaiah 19:18). [1] The Pentateuch is a Greek term for the first five books of the Old Testament Hebrew text, "The common Jewish arrangement calls the first five books of the Hebrew Bible Torah, Law, or Teaching.[2] The first translation of the Hebrew text into Greek occurred in approximately 200 B.C., and as previously indicated, the use of the term "Jewish" did not come into being until after the conquest of North Africa by Alexander "the Great," which preceded the great influx of Greeks and other Europeans into the area which prior to that time had been predominantly occupied by the twelve tribes which at least partially displaced the Canaanites during the period of exodus. The Hebrews, in turn, fell into disfavor with God as they violated his covenant, as explained in Judges chapters two and three. **Judges (2:20-22):**

> **"And the anger of the Lord was hot against**
> **Israel; and he said, Because that this people**
> **hath transgressed my covenant, which I commanded**

**their fathers, and have not harkened**
**unto my voice;**
**I also will not henceforth drive out any from**
**before them of the nations which Joshua left**
**when he died:**
**That through them I may prove Israel, whether**
**they will keep the way of the Lord to walk**
**therein, as their fathers did keep it, or not."**

Judges (3:5-7):

**"And the children of Israel dwelt among the**
**Canaanites, Hittites, and Amorites, and**
**Perizzites, and Hivvites, and Jebusites:**
**And they took their daughters to be their**
**wives, and gave their daughters to their**
**sons, and served their gods.**
**And the children of Israel did evil in the**
**sight of the Lord, and forgat the Lord their**
**God, and served Baalim and the groves."**

Josephus himself was aware of Melchizedec and in "Antiquity of the Jews," page 33, "Now the king of Sodom met him at a certain place, which they called the king's dale where Melchizedec, king of the city of Salem, received him. The name signifies the righteous king: and such he was without dispute insomuch that, on this account he was made the priest of God: however, they afterwards called Salem, Jerusalem." It continues, "And when Abram gave him the tenth of his prey, he accepted the gift."[3]

It is interesting to note that the city of Salem which we now call Jerusalem was located in the Land of Canaan which was to become the Promised Land or the area of Palestine as we know it today. In the time of Abraham and Melchizedec, the Land of Canaan was largely occupied by the Canaanites who have been largely portrayed as idol worshipers; however, the presence of Melchizedec would seem to point to the presence of at least a segment of this population acknowledging the true God, a point which I have not seen raised during the course of my research.

As previously mentioned, Abraham's first son was ishmael, the product of a union between Abraham and an Egyptian handmaid. Josephus, in Chapter Twelve, adds further insight as to what happened to Ishmael when he states, "When the lad was grown up, he married a wife, by birth an Egyptian, from whence the mother herself was derived originally. Of this wife were born to Ishmael twelve sons; these inhabited all the country from Euphrates to the Red Sea, and called it Navatene."4 They are an Arabian nation. It was Abraham's second son, Isaac, who was the father of Esau and Jacob, an d out of Egyptian bondage by Moses and eventually went on to inherit the Promised Land (Land of Canean). It is the story of Joseph, the youngest son of Israel, that offers us the first clue as to the physical appearance of the Hebrews, which we will examine, but first it is probably more appropriate to, once again, offer an overview of the genealogical span of the Hebrews which is traced back to one of the sons of Noah, Sem, whose name was later changed to Shem in the Greek translation of the Old Testament. Thusly, the Hebrews are also referred to as Semitic people, some of whose descendants, as previously mentioned, include Moses, King David, King Solomon, Mary the mother of Jesus whose genealogy traces back to Judah, one of the sons of Israel. Although he has been described by the Greek term "Jew," a more accurate description would be that he was a Hebrew, and the two are not synonymous, as will be clearly shown.

Let us now turn to the story of Joseph which we find in Chapter 37 of **Genesis (37:3-4):**

> **"Now Israel loved Joseph more than all his children, because he was the son of his old age: and he made him a coat of many colors. And when his brethren saw that their father loved him more than all his brethren, they hated him and could not speak peaceably unto him."**

An overview of Chapter 37 reveals that his brothers,

because of their jealousy and their concern that their father favored Joseph, the youngest of the sons conspired to slay him.

Genesis (37:18):

> **"And when they saw him afar off, even before he came near unto them, they conspired against him to slay him."**

Genesis (37:23-24)

> **"And it came pass, when Joseph was come unto his brethren, that they stript Joseph out of his coat, his coat of many colours that was on him: And they took him and cast him into a pit: And the pit was empty, there was no water in it."**

Genesis (37:26-27):

> **"And Judah said unto his brethren, what profit is it if we slay our brother, and conceal his blood? Come and let us sell him to the Ishmaelites and not let our hand be upon him; for he is our brother and our flesh. And his brethren were content."**

Joseph was eventually sold to an officer of Pharaoh in Egypt. He eventually came to the attention of Pharaoh himself due to an ability to interpret dreams. He fell into favor with Pharaoh after accurately interpreting Pharaoh's dream which revealed that there would be seven years of famine. By making such a prediction and allowing the Egyptians to prepare by placing into storage a large portion of their food, he saved the country during the period of the great famine. Joseph was made the ruler of Egypt.

Genesis (41:40-45):

> **"Thou shalt be over my house, and according unto thy word shall all my people be ruled: only in the throne will I be greater than thou. And Pharaoh said unto Joseph, See I have set thee over all the land of Egypt. And Pharaoh took off his ring from his hand, and put it upon Joseph's hand and arrayed him**

**in vestures of fine linen and put a gold chain about his neck;**
**And he made him to ride in the second chariot which**
**he had; and they cried before him, Bow the knee:**
**And he made him ruler over all the land of Egypt.**
**And Pharaoh said unto Joseph, I am Pharaoh, and**
**without thee shall no man lift up his hand or**
**foot in all the land of Egypt.**
**And Pharaoh called Joseph's name Zaphnath-paaneah;**
**and gave him to wife Asenath, the daughter of**
**Potipherah, priest of On. And Joseph went out**
**over all the land of Egypt."**

When the period of the famine was upon them, all the countries came to Egypt to Joseph, for the famine was described as being over all the face of the earth. Jacob (Israel) sent his sons to Egypt to buy corn and as **Genesis (42:5-8)** describes:

**"And the sons of Israel came to buy corn,**
**among those that came: for the famine was in**
**the Land of Canaan.**
**And Joseph was the governor over the land,**
**and he it was that sold to all the people of**
**the land: and Joseph's brethren came, and**
**bowed down themselves before him with their**
**faces to the earth.**
**And Joseph saw his brethren, and he knew them,**
**but made himself strange unto them, and spake**
**roughly unto them; and he said unto them,**
**Whence come ye? And they said, From the Land**
**of Canaan to buy food.**
**And Joseph knew his brethren, but they knew not him.**

Genesis (43:32):

**"And they set on for him by himself, and for**
**for them by themselves, and for the Egyptians,**
**which did eat with him, by themselves: because**
**the Egyptians might not eat bread with the**
**Hebrews; for that is an abomination unto the Egyptians."**

Joseph spoke to his brothers through an interpreter to further conceal his Hebrew identity, seemingly appearing to be Egyptian.
**Genesis (42:23):**

> **"And they knew not that Joseph understood them; for he spake unto them by an interpreter."**

As Genesis continues, eventually Joseph admits that he is their brother and invites them, along with his father, Jacob (Israel) to live in Egypt, as **Genesis (45:17-18)** records

> **"And Pharaoh said unto Joseph, Say unto they brethren, This do ye; lade your beasts, and go, get you unto the land of Canaan. And take your father and your households, and come unto me: and I will give you the good land of Egypt, and ye shall eat the fat of the land."**

**Genesis (47:27-28):**

> **"And Israel dwelt in the land of Egypt, in the country of Goshen; and they had possessions therein, and grew, and multiplied exceedingly. And Jacob lived in the land of Egypt seventeen years: so the whole age of Jacob was an hundred forty and seven years."**

Joseph's brethren and their offspring continued to prosper until, as recorded in **Genesis (50:26):**

> **"So Joseph died, being an hundred and ten years old: and they embalmed him, and he was put in a coffin in Egypt."**

It was following the death of Joseph that the period of servitude began, and as was previously calculated, would have been approximately the year 1847 B.C. with Joseph being born one hundred and ten years prior to that, and would have placed him at his height of rule in approximately 1900 B.C., during the reign of Senwosret II and Senwosret III, the period of rule being 1897 to 1878, and 1878 to 1841 B.C., respectively. (See plate of bust of

Senwosret I.) His reign was consistent with the period of time in which Joseph's brothers had mistaken him as being Egyptian.

It is the death of Joseph that brings us to the end of the book of Genesis and the beginning of the second book of the Bible called Exodus. Exodus offers only a brief account of the period of enslavement which is covered in Chapter One, while the second chapter begins with the birth of Moses and offers a recounting of those events which were described in Genesis concerning his adoption by the daughter of Pharaoh, but then suddenly jumps to the point at which Moses is a man and apparently aware himself that he was a Hebrew. **Exodus (2:11-12)** reflects:

> **"And it came to pass in those days, when**
> **Moses was grown, that he went out unto his**
> **brethren, and looked on their burdens: and**
> **he spied an Egyptian smiting an Hebrew, one**
> **of his brethren.**
> **And he looked this way and that way, and when**
> **he saw that there was no man, he slew the**
> **Egyptian, and hid him in the sand."**

**Exodus (2:15)** continues:

> **"Now when Pharaoh heard this thing, he sought**
> **to slay Moses. But Moses fled from the face of Pharaoh, and**
> **dwelt in the land of Midian:**
> **and he sat down by a well."**

It was shortly after that time that Moses encountered the burning bush and that God called out to him, offering instructions as to how he was to set about freeing the children of Israel from their bondage in Egypt.

For deeper insight into the ancestry of Alexander the Great of Greece and surrounding area Europeans, we once again turn to Josephus, Book I, Chapter 6, which indicates that the genealogy begins with Japhet, the son of Noah: "Now as to Javan and Madai, the sons of Japhet; from Madai came the Madeans, who are called Medes by the Greeks; but from Javan, Ionia and all the Grecians are derived." Josephus earlier described, in Chapter 6, that Japhet, son of Noah, had seven sons: "They inhabited so, that, beginning at the mountains Taurus and Amanus, they proceeded along Asia, and as far as the river Tanais and along Europe to Cadiz; and settling themselves on the lands which they light upon, which none had inhabited before, they called the nations by their own names; for Gomer founded those whom the Greeks now call Galations (Galls); but were then called Gomerites. Magog founded those that from him were named Magogites, but who are by the Greeks, called Scythians."

At this point, we have discussed the origin of the Hebrews as being from Sem, which the Greeks changed to Shem. We have traced the lineage of the Greeks and other Europeans back to the line of Japhet. We now look to the genealogy of Ham, who gave rise to the Egyptians, although it should be noted that these are both Greek terms which found application during the Hellenistic period after the conquest of Alexander of North Africa. Josephus continues:

Book I, Chapter 6, "The children of Ham possessed the land from Syria and Amanus, and the mountains of Lebanus, seizing upon all that was at sea coast, and as far as the ocean, and keeping it as their own. Some, indeed, of its names are utterly vanished away; others of them being changed, and another sound given them, are hardly to be discovered: Yet, a few there are which have kept their denominations entire: For of the four sons of Ham, time has not at all hurt the name of Cush; for the Ethiopians over whom he reigned, or even at this day by themselves and by all men in Asia, called Cushites. The memory also of the Mesraites is preserved in their name; for all we who inhabit this country (of Judea) call Egypt, Mestre and the Egyptians, Mestreans. Phut was also the founder of Libya and called the inhabitants 'Phutites' from himself: There is also a river in the country of the moors which bears that name." "We will inform you presently of what has been the occasion, why it has been called Africa also."

Canaan, the fourth son of Ham, inhabited the country now called Judea, and called it from his own name, Canaan. Josephus goes on to tell us that the great son of Canaan, Judads, "settled the Judadeans, a nation of the Western Ethiopians, and left them his name." Josephus goes on to tell us that all the children of Meshram, being eight in number, possessed the country from Gaza to Egypt, through it retained the name of one only, the Philistines; for the Greeks called that part of the country Palestine. [5] Mizraim is described as the "Hebrew word for Egypt; number one son of Ham." As has been previously indicated, Egypt is a Greek term which was applied during the Hellenistic period to the area known as Mizraim, a Hebrew term; however, its inhabitants refer to the land as Kemet meaning "The Black Land."

The British Museum Book on Ancient Egypt, on page 11, points out that "the ancient Egyptians called themselves the Remet-Kemet, people of Egypt, and there language, Medet-Remet-En-Kemet, speech of the people of Egypt. However, it would seem that the more accurate translation would be Kemet, meaning people of the black land, and Medet-Remet-En-Kemet meaning speech of the people of the black land. As previously alluded to, the Pentateuch or the first five books of the Hebrew Bible, most scholars agree, were written partially, if not totally by Moses. This would have occurred shortly after the Exodus from Egyptian bondage, which we calculated to be 1447 B.C. by the method we described within this text.

The first transcription of the Old Testament did not appear until approximately 200 B.C., which is a well-documented fact. Stated another way, the Greeks did not have the Old Testament in their language until nearly 1200 years after the time it was written. Therefore, the insertion of the Greek word "Jew" was interjected into the scriptures for the first time during or after this first Greek translation. Accordingly, the first Jewish sects were formed during the same period and embraced certain aspects of the Old Testament as the basis for this new religion. While the double meaning of the word "Jew" in itself constituted and amphibology, one such meaning was those from the region of Judah or Judea, which allowed this group to then not only assimilate the religion of the Hebrews, but very importantly, it allowed them to eclipse the Hebrew people to such an extent that even the ancient history of the Hebrew people through this process of assimilation became their own history. The carved reliefs, however, inside the ancient tombs which depicted the slaves revealed no evidence that they were at all European. To the contrary, they showed the dark-skinned Hebrew people as being slaves in Egypt, a fact which is confirmed by physical evidence which will be presented later in this text.

I should point out, once again, that the Hebrew people can perhaps be best described as a Judeo-Christian people, in that they looked to the fulfillment of the prophecies, the pinnacle of which was to be the coming of the Messiah or Christ. Therefore, it would follow that the word "Jew" as it appears throughout the Old Testament would more accurately read "Hebrew;" that the word "Egypt" would exist by its Hebrew name, "Mizraim." The Greek word "synagogue" would be replaced with "tabernacle" or "temple." No form of the Greek word "synagogue" appears in any of the Old Testament, except Psalms (74:8). "Jerusalem" would be "Salem." The Greek word "Ethiopia" would be "Cush."

"Confusion has arisen between the names 'Ethiopia' and 'Cush.' The Old Testament Hebrew (and Egyptian) name for the region was 'Cush.' The ancient Greek translation of the Old Testament, the Septuagint, rendered 'Cush' by the Greek word 'Ethiopia,' except where it could be taken as a personal name." It continues,

"The biblical Ethiopia should not be confused with the modern nation of the same name that is somewhat further to the Southeast. In biblical times, Ethiopia was equivalent to Nubia, <u>the region beyond the first cataract of the Nile south or upstream of Egypt</u>."[6]

During the period of 1550-1070 B.C., Ethiopia was part of the Egyptian empire and was ruled from the North. However, Nubian kings gained power as Egypt weakened and by 715 B.C. established themselves as Pharaohs over Egypt as the late period of the 25th Dynasty which included Egypt and all of Nubia, as opposed to the beginning of the 25th Dynasty which included Nubia and the Theban areas. Thereafter, the Egyptian empire was overrun by the Persians until the Greco-Roman period which lasted from 332 B.C. to 395 A.D.

The tongue spoken by the Jews in Christ's time (John 19:13)

was related to a semitic language, Aramaic, though Hebrew itself was not dead.[7] Although most of the Old Testament text was written in Hebrew, three sections of the Old Testament were written in Aramaic: Ezra 4:8-6:18; 7:12-26; Jeremiah 10:1 1; Daniel 2:4-7:28.[8] As the Hebrews had fallen under first Greek and then Roman oppression, the Hebrew language was discouraged in favor of the national language, Aramaic. The reason why the language was suppressed is clear, particularly under Roman rule which began 30 B.C. after the Romans had defeated the Greeks, "sedition" was punishable by death. Sedition can be defined as "(1) Language or conduct directed against public order and the tranquility of the state; (2) the incitement of such disorder tending toward treason, but lacking in overt act; (3) dissension, revolt."[9]

Thus, since the Romans did not speak or write in Hebrew, its use, particularly among the oppressed Hebrews, if allowed, would have constituted a secret language whose employ would allow seditious comments to go undetected. In these ancient times, sedition was considered to be a crime that was punishable by death. This is perhaps best demonstrated by the New Testament itself, in which the Jewish leaders from the sects of the Pharisees and Sadducees tried time and time again to entice Jesus into making statements which could be considered seditious and for which he would have been immediately arrested by the centurions of the Roman army. According to **Luke (11:53-54):**

> **"And as he said these things unto them, the Scribes and the Pharisees began to urge him vehemently, and to provoke him to speak of many things: Laying wait for him and seeking to catch something out of his mouth, that they might accuse him."**

As previously discussed, Jesus himself was a Hebrew and therefore it would have been an easy matter for him to speak in that tongue to the poor and oppressed who followed his ministry, and much of what was said would have escaped the Romans and the Pharisees. Christ himself may have been forced, therefore, to speak in Aramaic which was the language of the time. He often spoke in parables in response to questions and to express his point of view. "Parable" can be defined as "A comparison; simile; specifically, a short narrative making a moral or religious point by comparison natural or homely things: the New Testament parables."[10] Such parables proved to be an effective means of demonstrating the point in which Christ attempted to convey, but at times, the meaning which was to be conveyed may not always have been crystal clear, but more direct language might have been construed as sedition.

**John (16:25):**

> **"These things have I spoken unto you in proverbs: but the time cometh, when I shall speak no more unto you in proverbs, but I shall shew you plainly of the Father."**

For further insight as to what happened to the Hebrew people and their language, we must turn to a more recent discovery, that being the "Dead Sea Scrolls" whose content, except for bits and pieces had long been suppressed by the scholars who were assigned to reassemble and decipher these ancient documents. The discovery of the Scrolls, which were found in the mountainous area and caves of Qumran, generated a lot of interest at the time of their discovery since the documents date back to the period of the time of Christ and were thereby expected to offer a deeper perspective into the events which occurred at that time. However, mystery rapidly enshrined these scrolls, whose full content has yet to be revealed, even though the discovery took place nearly fifty years ago. As was written in the book, Dead Sea Scrolls Deception, Preface, Page 12, "In tracing the progress of the Dead Sea Scrolls from their discovery in the Judean Desert to various institutions that hold them today, we've found ourselves confronting a contradiction we had faced before - the contradiction between the Jesus of history and the Christ of faith."[11]

It should be pointed out that of the relatively limited information contained within the scrolls which has been published to date, it is possible to unravel some of the mystery which the scrolls themselves have generated, but to aid us in elucidating some of these mysteries, it is necessary to turn to still another text which was translated into

English for the first time only a hundred years ago, although the texts within, once again, date back to the time of Christ and are referred to as the "lost books" of the bible.

Before we turn to the controversies generated by the Dead Sea Scrolls, which directly shed light on what happened to the Hebrew language and the people, it is necessary to look at the more modern day history of the area of Palestine and the formation of the Jewish state of Israel. The area of Palestine and its people had long been dominated by British imperialism, which allowed England to drain the country of its resources, predominantly oil, until the people began to revolt. The area was clearly about to fall from the hands of British control as the British mandate was to expire on May 15, 1948, when the Jewish Peoples Consul met in the Tel Aviv Museum and declared their own independent state of Israel based upon the need for a Jewish homeland and the promise made by God to Abraham, as has been discussed, which occurred nearly four thousand years ago. This was all sanctioned following an emergency meeting of the United Nations. The response from the neighboring Arab states was almost immediate and the area was engaged in fighting until January 7, 1949, when a cease-fire took effect. As part of that agreement, Palestine was then divided between the Arabs and the Jews as the boundaries of Israel were redefined.

As previously discussed, the Greek word "Jew" or "Jewish" is an amphibology which due to multiple meanings has allowed Funk and Wagnall to define Israel (page 677) as "Jewish people, traditionally regarded as descended from Israel (Jacob)" who, of course is the descendant of the Hebrew, Abraham, and as we have shown, the two are not synonymous. By 1954, there were two groups working on the scrolls independently and included the Palestine Archeological Museum in East Palestine, which was also known as the Rockefeller Museum as it was built in 1938 during the British Mandate by funds donated by John D. Rockefeller; and in Jerusalem, the Israelis were at work. In a communication dated January 16, 1990, it was revealed that in the '50s, Moshe Dayan had devised a plan to raid the Rockefeller Museum through Jerusalem's sewer system, which ultimately never materialized. In 1966, the Jordanian government nationalized the Rockefeller Museum and the scrolls contained within. Thus, they became Jordanian property. In the Six-Day War which followed in June of 1967, during which Israel fought against Egypt, Jordan and Syria, the area of the museum became occupied by the Israelis who were victorious in this war for which the arms were largely provided by the United States. Thus, the bulk of the Qumran Scrolls fell under Israeli control where control has remained until the recent release of the photographs from the Huntington Memorial Library in Pasadena, which finally gave all scholars access to the scrolls.

Although we were told that the Essenes (a faction of the Hebrews) were the most likely authors of the scrolls, still another faction, the Zealots, made perhaps even a greater contribution as is supported by references within the scrolls themselves, many of which were written in Hebrew, some of the remaining being written in Aramaic. To identify the true authors, it is important that we take a careful look at certain areas of the scrolls, as well as the clues found in the area of the Qumran caves, including the grave sites. But before we do that, it is first necessary to identify the origin of the various Jewish sects, all of which formed during the Hellenistic period in time, and the relationship between the Greeks, the Hebrews and finally the, Romans. It is only after these various groups and their relationships have been clearly defined that we can put the final pieces of the puzzle of this exercise in place.

To define these interrelationships, we must first go back to the beginning for which the key source, once again, is the Bible, to determine who the original caretakers and protectors of the Covenant or Law that was given to Moses by God, who later went on to appoint a specific tribe within the Hebrews to undertake this task.

———

## Part II notes:

[1] Holman Bible Dictionary, p. 623.

[2] Holman Bible Dictionary, p. 1088.

[3] The Complete Works of Josephus, Translated by William Whiston, p. 33.

[4] The Complete Works of Josephus, Translated by William Whiston, p. 36.

[5] Holman Bible Dictionary, p. 982.

[6] Holman Bible Dictionary, p. 444.

[7] Scriptural Directory of the Holy Bible, p. 17.
J.G. Ferguson Publishing Company.

[8] Ibid., p. 4.

[9] Funk and Wagnalls New Comprehensive International Dictionary of the English Language - 1973.

[10] Ibid

[11] Dead Sea Scrolls Deception, Michael Paget, preface pg. 12

## PART III

## IDENTIFICATION OF THE HEBREWS

As previously stated, it is the story of Joseph, the youngest son of Israel, that offers the first clue as to the physical appearance of the Hebrews, and to initiate the process of elucidation in this case, once again we turn to the book of Genesis. As has been previously mentioned, when the period of famine was upon them, all the countries came to Egypt to Joseph, for the famine was described as being all over the face of the earth. Jacob (Israel) sent his sons to Egypt to buy corn and as **Genesis (42:5-8)** describes:

> **"And the sons of Israel came to buy corn, among those that came: for the famine was in the land of Canaan.**
> **And Joseph was the governor over the land, and he it was that sold to all the people of the land: And Joseph's brethren came, and bowed down themselves before him with their faces to the earth.**
>
> **And Joseph saw his brethren, and knew them, but made himself strange unto them, and spake roughly unto them; and he said unto them, Whence come ye? And they said, From the land of Canaan to buy food. And Joseph knew his brethren, but they knew not him."**

Joseph, who was now governor of Egypt, second only to Pharaoh himself, continued to conceal his identity from his brothers who thought that Joseph, indeed, was an Egyptian. Accordingly, he spoke to his brothers through an interpreter. **Genesis (42:23)**:

> **"And they knew not that Joseph understood them; for he spake unto them by an interpreter."**

After inviting his brothers to eat, in following the Egyptian tradition, he and the Egyptians sat apart from the Hebrews, as described in **Genesis (43:32):**

> **"And they sat on for him by himself and for them by themselves and for the Egyptians, which did eat with him, by themselves: Because the Egyptians might not eat bread with the Hebrews; for that is an abomination unto the Egyptians."**

As has been previously established, the period of the famine and the time in which Joseph's brothers first visited him would have been in approximately the year 1948 B.C. We, indeed, have an idea of the physical appearance of the Egyptians during this period which can perhaps be best demonstrated by examining a photograph of the bust of Pharaoh himself. This is, indeed, possible as a result of some rather remarkable archeological finds which have occurred over the past 150 years. In one such find, the excavation of the floor of the so-called Cachett Court, more than two-thousand statues of kings, deities and private individuals, dating from Dynasty XI to as late as the Ptolemaic period. Ironically, it was during the period of Ptolemy, the self-appointed family of Greek Pharaohs in Egypt which came to power immediately following the conquest of Alexander the Great of Macedonia, that the royal palaces were swept clean of every remnant of their Black past. During this period of approximately 300 B.C., the statues of Pharaohs going back to nearly 3,000 B.C. were collected together and buried, only now to resurface as the greatest monument to the Black presence in Egypt as its founding fathers. Genesis points out that throughout the land of Egypt, Joseph was only second to Pharaoh himself.

Extra-Biblical sources tell us that this same Senwosret I was perhaps the greatest conqueror in history and that his military quest extended into lands vastly exceeding those of even Alexander the Great.

In his book, Black Athena, the linguist, Martin Bernal, writes, "Herodotus and later authors wrote at length about the widespread conquests of a Pharaoh he called Sesostris, whose name has been identified with S-n-Wsrt or Senwosret, that of a number of 12th Dynasty pharaohs."[1]

The ancient Greek historian, Herodotus, writes, "Sesostris, the priest said, sailed first with a fleet of warships from the Arabian Gulf along the coast of the Indian Ocean, subduing the coastal tribes as he went, until he found that shoal water made further progress impossible; then on his return to Egypt (still according to the priest's account) he raised a powerful army and marched across the continent, reducing to subjection every nation in his path. Whenever he encountered a courageous enemy who fought valiantly for freedom, he erected pillars on the spot inscribed with his own name and country, and a sentence to indicate that by the might of his armed forces he had won the victory; if however, a town fell easily into his hands without a struggle, he made an addition to the inscription on the pillar, for not only did he record upon it the same facts as before, but added a picture of a woman's genitals, meaning to show that the people of that town were no braver than women. Thus his victorious progress through Asia continued, until he entered Europe and defeated the Scythians, and the Thracians; this, I think, was the farthest point the Egyptian Army reached for the memorial columns are to be seen in this part of the country but not beyond."

Herodotus continues, "The Egyptians did, however, say that they thought the original Colchians were men from Sesostris' army. My own idea on this subject was based first on the fact that they have black skins and wooly hair (not that that amounts to much, as other nations have the same) and secondly and more specially, on the fact that the Colchians and Egyptians and Ethiopians are the only races from which ancient times have practiced circumcision."[2]

Herodotus was writing from the perspective of his time, in that he lived from approximately 490 to 425 B.C. and is known as the European "father of history." His comments here hold special significance since the ritual of circumcision was practiced by the

Hebrews, dating back to 2000 B.C. when Abraham himself was circumcised. Genesis 17:8-12:

> **"And I will give unto thee, and to thy seed after thee, the land wherein thou art a stranger, and all the land of Canaan, for an everlasting possession; and I will be their God.**
>
> **And God said unto Abraham, thou shalt keep my covenant therefore, thou, and thy seed after thee in their generations.**
>
> **This is my covenant, which ye shall keep, between me and you and thy seed after thee; every man child among you shall be circumcised.**
>
> **And ye shall circumcise the flesh of your fore-skin; and it shall be a token of the covenant betwixt me and you.**
>
> **And he that is eight days old shall be circumcised, among you, every man child in your generations, he that is born in the house, or bought with money of any stranger, which is not of thy seed.**
>
> **He that is born in thy house, and he that is bought with thy money, must needs be circumcised: and my covenant shall be in your flesh for an everlasting covenant."**

Genesis (17:24):

> **"And Abraham was ninety years old and nine, when he was circumcised in the flesh of his foreskin."**

Genesis (17:25):

> **"And Ishmael, his son, was thirteen years old, when he was circumcised in the flesh of his foreskin."**

Genesis (17:26):

**"And the selfsame day was Abraham circumcised, and Ishmael his son."**

Genesis (17:27):

**"And all the men of his house, born in the house, and bought with money of the stranger, were circumcised with him."**

It should be pointed out that Abraham's circumcision followed his stay in Egypt as Genesis points out, chapter 13, verse 1:

**"And Abraham went up out of Egypt, he and his wife, and all that he had, and Lot with him into the south."**

Genesis (13:15-16):

**"For all the land which thou seest, to thee I will give it, and to thy seed forever. And I will make thy seed as dust of the earth: so that if a man can count the number of dust of the earth, then shall thy seed also be numbered."**

God's covenant with Abraham continues:

Genesis (15:18-21):

**"In the same day, the Lord made a covenant with Abraham, saying, Unto thy seed I have given this land, from the river of Egypt unto the great river, the River Euphrates:**

**The Kenites and the Kenizzites and the Kadmonites, And the Hittites and the Perizzites and the Rephaims,**

**And the Amorites and the Canaanites and the Girgashites and the Jebusites."**

God had chosen to give the lands of these people which dwelled in the land of Canaan, the promised land, today known as Palestine, to the Hebrews because they had become pagan worshipers and had fallen. To better identify these Canaanite families, we turn once again to the book of Genesis and we find that of Noah's three sons, Ham, Shem and Japheth, that Ham had several sons.

**Genesis (10:6):**

> **"And the sons of Ham; Cush, and Mizraim, and Phut and Canaan."**

**Genesis (10:15-18):**

> **"And Canaan begat Sidon his firstborn, and Heth, And the Jebusite, and the Amorite, and the Girgasite, and the Hivite, and the Arkite, and the Sinite, And the Arvadite, and the Zemarite, and the Hamathite: and afterward were the families of the Canaanites spread abroad."**

The other sons of Ham, it should be pointed out, gave rise to the nation of Cush or the Cushites, whose country was later renamed by the Greeks as Ethiopia. His son Mizraim gave rise to land which the Hebrews referred to as Mizraim, but to which the occupants themselves referred to as being from the land of Kemet, which literally means "the black land." There are many other lines which are derived from Mizraim, including the Philistines.

**Genesis (10:14):**

> **"And Pathrusim, Casluhim (out of whom came Philistim) and Caphtorim."**

But note, Philistim - the alternate form of Philistine.[3] One of the most famous Philistines was the giant, Goliath that battled David. Now as we turn to the Hebrew, Joseph, the great grandson of Abraham whose own brothers thought this governor to Pharaoh was, indeed, Egyptian, as Joseph spoke to them through an interpreter, there would seem to be little doubt as to his physical appearance as we have attempted to demonstrate, using both biblical and extra-biblical sources as the basis for our portrait of the Hebrews.
The limbs of the genealogical trees of the Hebrew Semites (descendants of Shem) and those of the descendants of Ham have

been intertwined since the time of Abraham and probably earlier. And in that regard, Abraham's first son, Ishmael, was born to the Egyptian woman, Hagar, who was the servant of his wife, Sarah.

Genesis (16:3):

> **"And Sarah, Abram's wife, took Hagar her maid the Egyptian, after Abram had dwelt ten years in the land of Canaan, and gave her to her husband Abram, to be his wife."**

Genesis (16:4):

> **"And he went unto Hagar, and she conceived: and when she saw that she had conceived, her mistress was despised in her eyes."**

Genesis (16:15):

> **"And Hagar bare Abram a son: Abram called his son's name, which Hagar bare, Ishmael."**

Genesis (16:16):

> **"And Abram was four-score and six when Hagar bare Ishmael to Abram."**

According to Genesis, Abram's name was changed to Abra-ham by God Himself.

Genesis (17:5):

> **"Neither shall thy name anymore be called Abram, but thy name shall be Abra-ham; for a father of many nations I have made thee."**

Joseph, whose Egyptian name was Zaphnath-paaneah, was also married to an Egyptian.

Genesis (41:44):

> **"And Pharaoh said unto Joseph, I am Pharaoh, and without thee shall no man lift up his hand or foot in all the land of Egypt.**

Genesis (41:45):

> **"And Pharaoh called Joseph's name Zaphnath- paaneah; and he gave him to wife Asenath, the daughter of Pontipherah, priest of On. And Joseph went out over all the land of Egypt."**

Joseph and his wife went on to have two sons, Ephraim and Manasseh. When Joseph later revealed his identify to his brothers and he summoned his father, Jacob, to also come into Egypt where they all lived happily ever after. Jacob so loved Joseph and his two sons that he adopted them as his own and consequentially, as a result, instead of there being twelve tribes from the twelve sons of Jacob, there were, indeed, thirteen tribes since from Joseph, Ephraim and Manasseh gave rise to two distinct tribes.

Genesis (48:5):

> **"And now thy two sons, Ephraim and Manasseh, which were born unto the in the land of Egypt before I came unto thee in Egypt, are mine; as Reuben and Simeon, they shall be mine."**

Genesis (48:6):

> **"And thy issue, which thou shall begettest after them, shall be thine and shall be called after the name of their brethren in their inheritance."**

Genesis (48:20):

> **"And he blessed them that day, saying, In thee shall Israel bless, saying, God make thee as Ephraim and as Manasseh: and he said Ephraim before Manasseh."**

This gesture by Jacob (Israel) in which he placed the blessing of the younger Ephraim before his older brother, Manasseh, was done in spite of the objection raised by Joseph, who suggested that according to tradition, the older Manasseh should have received the first or greatest of the blessings. The blessing of Ephraim in the manner performed by Jacob proved to be prophetic, since as described in the next chapter, it was the Egyptian, Joshua, of the tribe of Ephraim, who was to replace the much older Moses following his death.

In addition to having been born in Egypt, Joshua, as the descendant of Ephraim, was of Egyptian genealogy through the wife of Joseph, who was daughter of the priest of On. On was a city in Egypt whose name was changed by the Greeks to Heliopolis. It was Joshua who led the Hebrews into the land of Cannan. He went on to conquer the city of Jericho, when accompanied by priests, and the Arc of the Covenant, he circled the city seven times and after blowing the trumpet on the seventh occasion, the walls of Jericho fell down. Archeologists have, indeed, located the remnant of the fallen walls of Jericho.

To fulfill another portion of the covenant, it was seemingly inevitable that the Hamitic line and Semitic line would have to interconnect.

Genesis (17:2):

> **"And I will make my covenant between me and thee, and will multiply thee exceedingly."**

Genesis (17:6):

> **"And I will make thee exceedingly fruitful and I will make nations of thee, and kings shall come out of thee."**

God's promise to Abraham continues as it pertained to his first son, Ishmael, born to his second wife, the Egyptian, Hagar.

Genesis (17:20):

> **"And as for Ishmael, I have heard thee: Behold, I have blessed him, and will make him fruitful, and will multiply him exceedingly; twelve princes shall he beget, and I will make him a great nation."**

Genesis (17:21):

> **"But my covenant I will establish with Isaac, which Sarah shall bear unto thee at this set time in the next year."**

**Genesis (22:17):**

> **"That in blessing I will bless thee, and in multiplying I will multiply thy seed as the stars of heaven, and as the sand which is upon the sea shore; and thy seed shall possess the gate of his enemies;"**

**Genesis (22:18):**

> **"And in thy seed all the nations of the earth be blessed; because thou hast obeyed my voice."**

Following the death of Sarah, Abraham took a second wife, Keturah.

**Genesis (25:1-2):**

> **"Then again Abraham took a wife and her name was Keturah. And she bare him Zimran and Jokshan and Medan and Midian and Ishbak and Shumah."**

Keturah bore six sons (daughters rarely are listed) to Abraham, the most notable being Midian. The list of Keturah's children substantiates the link between the Hebrews and the tribes which inhabited the areas east and southeast of Palestine. As the children of a second wife, they were viewed as inferior to Isaac, Sarah's son. The Midianites descended from the line of Midian. They occupied an area east or Palestine known as Midian. After Moses killed an Egyptian overseer of the Hebrew slaves, it is pointed out in Exodus that Moses fled to Midian where he later married the daughter of a Midian priest. **(Exodus 2:12-20.)**

The promise continued to Abraham's second son, Isaac.

**Genesis (26:4):**

> **"And I will make thy seed to multiply as the stars of heaven and will give unto thy seed all these countries; and in thy seed all the nations of the earth be blessed;"**

Abraham's son Isaac had twins whom he named Esau and

Jacob, and Esau went on to have two Hittite wives to the displeasure of Isaac and Rebekah.

**Genesis (26: 34-35):**

> **"And Esau was forty years old when he took to wife Judith the daughter of Beeri the Hittite, and Bashemath the daughter of Elon the Hittite: which were a grief of mind to Isaac and to Rebekah."**

Jacob went on to marry his uncle Laban's daughters, Leah and Rachel. After Rachel could not conceive, as was the custom of the day, she gave over her handmaiden, Bilhah, to her husband Jacob, who became his concubine at Rachel's instigation, ultimately becoming the mother of Daniel and Naphtali. His other wife, Leah, went on to mother Reuben the oldest child, Simeon, Levi and Judah. Leah's handmaiden also became Jacob's concubine to whom Gad and Asher were born. Leah herself went on to also bear several otherchildren - Issachar, Zebulun and Dinah the only daughter born to Jacob. Eventually, Rachel conceived and bore Jacob's two youngest sons, Joseph and Benjamin; however, following the birth of Benjamin, the youngest, Rachel died in childbirth. The sons of Jacob (Israel) intermarriage with the Hamitics continued.

**Genesis (38:2-5):**

> **"And Judah saw there a daughter of a certain Canaanite, whose name was Shuah; and he took her, and went in unto her. And she conceived, and bare a son; and he called his name Er. And she conceived again and bare a son; and she called his name Onan. And she yet again conceived, and bare a son; and called his name Shelah; and he was at Chezib when she bare him."**

Judah went on to have five sons in all, as his daughter-in-law, Tamar bare him Pharez and Zerah. **(I Chronicles 2:4.)**

As previously mentioned, Joseph married the daughter of the Egyptian priest of On. The Egyptian, Moses (born in Egypt), descended from the tribe of Levi **(Exodus 2: 1-10)** was adopted by the Egyptian princess and was raised in the house of Pharaoh. Moses was referred to as an Egyptian by the daughters of the Midianite priest, Reuel, who would later become his father-in-law.

**Exodus (2:19)**

> **"And they said, an Egyptian delivered us out of the hand of the shepherds, and also drew water enough for us, and watered the flock."**

Exodus (2:20):

> **"And he said unto his daughters, And where is he? Why is it that ye have left the man? Call him, that he may eat bread."**

Exodus (2:21):

> **"And Moses was content to dwell with the man: and he gave Moses Zipporah, his daughter."**

As was the Egyptian/Hebrew tradition, Zipporah circumcised her son. **(Exodus 4:25)**

It should be pointed out that Zipporah, the wife of Moses who was a descendant of Midian (the son of Abraham by Keturah) was herself an "Ethiopian." We will later examine how the Greek word "Ethiopian" was applied generically to nearly all the natives of the biblical lands, except the Hebrews and Egyptians. So in summary, Moses, the Egyptian, was married to an "Ethiopian" woman who has heretofore only been described as a Midianite. The book of **Numbers (12:1)** clarifies this issue.

> **"And Miriam and Aaron spake against Moses because of the Ethiopian woman whom he had married: For he had married an Ethiopian woman."**

Although only described as a Midianite up until this point, if we look further, we find that the Midianites are traced back to the second wife of Abraham, and as has been previously discussed, Abraham's lineage can be traced back to Heber (Eber), a relative of Noah, from whom all Hebrews are derived. Furthermore, it should be added that while all Israelites are then Hebrews, it does not necessarily follow that all Hebrews are Israelites.

Just as the brother of Moses, Aaron, was a priest, more specifically, a Hebrew priest, the father of Zipporah, the Midianite-Hebrew, was also a priest and his name was Reuel. (Exodus 2:16-21) Reuel is the Hebrew name for "God is my friend."[4] Reuel, Moses' father-in-law, was also sometimes referred to by a second name, Jethro, in Hebrew the name is Excellence.[5] **(See Genesis 3:1):**

> **"Now Moses kept the flock of Jethro, his father-in-law, the priest of Midian: And led the flock to the back side of the desert, and came to the Mountain of God, even to Horeb."**

Another reference to Moses' father-in-law being called Jethro can be found in Exodus (18:1):

> **"When Jethro, the priest of Midian, Moses' father-in-law, heard of all that God had done for Moses and for Israel his people, and that the Lord had brought Israel out of Egypt; "**

Exodus (18:2):

> **"Then Jethro, Moses' father-in-law, took Zipporah, Moses' wife, after he had sent her back..."**

Exodus (18:3-4):

> **"And her two sons of which the name of one Gershom; for he said, I have been an alien in a strange land: And the name of the other was Eliezer; for the God of my father, said he, was mine help, and delivered me from the sword of Pharaoh:"**

Exodus (18:5-12):

> **"And Jethro, Moses' father-in-law, came with his sons and his wife unto Moses into the wilderness, where he encamped at the mount**

**of God:**

**And he said unto Moses, I thy father-in-law Jethro am come unto thee, and thy wife, and her two sons with her.**

**And Moses went out to meet his father-in-law, and did obeisance, and kissed him; and they asked each other of their welfare; and they came to meet into the tent.**

**And Moses told his father-in-law all that the Lord had done unto Pharaoh and to the Egyptians for Israel's sake, and all the travail that had come upon them by the way, and how the Lord had delivered them.**

**And Jethro rejoiced for all the goodness which the Lord had done to Israel, whom he had delivered out of the hands of the Egyptians.**

**And Jethro said, Blessed be the Lord, who hath delivered you out of the hand of the Egyptians, and out of the hand of Pharaoh, who hath delivered the people from under the hand of the Egyptians.**

**Now I know that the Lord is greater than all gods: for in the thing wherein they dealt proudly he was above them.**

**And Jethro, Moses' father-in-law, took a burnt offering and sacrifices for God: and Aaron came, and all the elders of Israel, to eat bread with Moses' father-in-law before God."**

Moses' father-in-law, the Ethiopian, Reuel (Jethro) gave

counsel to Moses **(Exodus 18:19-26).** And then Moses let his father-in-law depart and he went his way into his own land **(Exodus 18:27).**

The Egyptian, Moses, invited Hobab, the Ethiopian brother of his wife Zipporah to join the Israelites in their journey to the promised land, but Hobab declined the invitation, indicating that he would return to his own homeland. It is interesting to note that in the account offered in **Numbers (10:29-30)** that Reuel is referred to as Raguel, which perhaps represents an error in the Greek translation of the original Hebrew text.

> **"And Moses said unto Hobab, the son of Raguel, the Midianite, Moses' father-in-law, We are journeying unto the place of which the Lord said, I will give it you: Come thou with us, and we will do thee good: for the Lord hath spoken good concerning Israel.**
>
> **And he said unto him, I will not go; but I will depart to my own land, and to my kindred."**

At one point during the Exodus from Egypt to the promised land, the brother and sister of Moses, Miriam and Aaron, respectively, spoke against Moses because, as previously mentioned, Moses had married an Ethiopian. As they were descendants of the second wife of Abraham known as Keturah, these Hebrews were the cousins of the "sons of Israel," but not held in as high esteem by the descendants of Isaac and Jacob whose mother was Abraham's first wife, Sarah. Interestingly enough, the same could probably be said concerning the line from Ishmael who was actually Abraham's first- born, born to the Egyptian handmaiden, Hagar, after Sarah had difficulty conceiving a child. Sarah did eventually conceive and was the mother of Isaac who in turn, was the father of Jacob and Esau. As previously stated, the tribes of Israel arose from the twelve sons of Jacob (Israel). On the other hand, as we have previously demonstrated the Egyptian line of Hebrews from the two children of Joseph were granted equal blessings and status by Jacob prior to his death. Thus, there were thirteen tribes. As has been previously discussed, Moses and his family were direct descendants of the priestly tribe of Levi.

In speaking against Moses because of his marrying the Ethiopian woman Zipporah, Aaron and Miriam incurred the wrath of God **(Numbers 12:3-9)**. God in turn punished Miriam, in that she became leprous and white as snow.

> **"And the cloud departed from off the tabernacle; and, behold, Miriam became leprous, white as snow: and Aaron looked upon Miriam, and, behold, she was leprous."**

Subsequently, Moses begged God to heal her, and after seven days of being shut out from the camp, Miriam was brought in again **(Numbers 12:14)**.

The lineage of Jesus can be traced to the line of David and further back to the tribe of Judah. The line of Judah is genetically linked to the Hebrews and Canaanites, in that all five sons of Judah were born to Canaanite women, Shua and her daughter, Tamar. I Chronicles (2:3-4):

> **"The sons of Judah; Er, and Onan, and Shelah: which three were born unto him of the daughter of Shua the Canaanitess. And Er, the first-born of Judah was evil in the sight of the Lord; and he slew him.**
>
> **And Tamar his daughter-in-law bare him Pharez and Zerah. All the sons of Judah were five."**

The lineage of David can be traced to Pharez, the son of Tamar. Ruth (4:18-22):

> **"Now these are the generations of Pharez: Pharez begat Hezron, And Hezron begat Ram, and Ram begat Amminadab, and Amminadab begat Nahshon, and Nahshon begat Salmon, And Salmon begat Boaz, and Boaz begat Obed, And Obed begat Jesse, and Jesse begat David."**

**John (7:42)** alludes to the issue of Christ being of the seed of David:

**"Hath not the scriptures said, That Christ cometh of the seed of David, and out of the town of Bethlehem, where David was?"**

**Psalms(110:1)** King James Version,reflects the following:
**"The Lord said unto my Lord, sit thou at my right hand, until I make thine enemies thy footstool."**

**Psalms (110:1)** Living Bible:
**"Jehovah said to my Lord, the Messiah, Rule as my regent - I will subdue your enemies and make them bow low before you."**

**Psalms (110:4)** King James Version:
**"The Lord hath sworn, and will not repent, thou art the priest forever after the order of Melchizedec."**

Christ raised the issue in the form of a question of how it could be said that Christ was the son of David when it was David who had referred to the Messiah as his **Lord. Luke (20:41-44):**
**"And he said unto them, How say they that Christ is David's son?**

**And David himself saith in the book of Psalms, The Lord said unto my Lord, Sit thou on my right hand,**

**Till I make thine enemies thy footstool. David therefore calleth him Lord, how is he then his son?"**

The question raised by Christ gives rise to two distinct possibilities, the first being that as a high priest forever of the order of Melchizedec, as Melchizedec was able to take human form without mother or father and therefore, presumably, without sharing the genetic pool of any living human being, could the same be said for Christ. However, unlike Melchizedec, Christ did have a mother, Mary, and therefore it was possible that he borrowed from her genetic pool. She, in turn, descended from David. While the lineage of Joseph is traced back to David, there are relatively few clues in the Bible concerning the lineage of Mary. According to the ancient, but non-canonical book of **Mary (1:1,2)**:

> **"The blessed and ever glorious Virgin Mary, sprung from the royal race and family of David, was born in the city of Nazareth, and educated at Jerusalem, in the temple of the Lord. Her father's name was Joachim and mother's Anna. The family of her father was of Galilee in the city of Nazareth. The family of her mother was of Bethlehem."**

The latter case is seemingly supported by **Timothy (2:8)**:

> **"Remember that Jesus Christ of the seed of David was raised from the dead according to my gospel:"**

According to **Revelation (22:16)**:

> **"I Jesus have sent mine angel to testify unto you these things in the churches. I am the root and the offspring of David and the bright and morning star."**

Now returning to Moses, he and the Hebrews continued to wander in the wilderness for a forty-year period, as described in the Bible, the book of Exodus, during which time Miriam, her brothers Aaron and Moses eventually died with only Moses ever actually seeing the promised land after being taken to the top of the mountain by God, however, as his punishment for disobedience to God, Moses never actually entered the promised land.

The Hebrews upon entering Palestine, "Land of Canaan/Land of Milk and Honey," encountered many battles, but they went on to become a nation for the first time. Indeed, by the 10th Century, B.C., beginning with Saul, the first king of this new nation and followed by King David and later his son, Solomon, the Hebrews had gone on to become one of the greatest and wealthiest nations on the face of

**"HOLY MOTHER AND CHILD"**
BYZANTINE PERIOD, RUSSIA, COLLECTION OF DR. & MRS. DELANEY SMITH

the earth and the envy of nearly all other countries of that time.

Saul was the handsome son of Kish from the tribe of Benjamin **(I Samuel 9:1-2, 21)**. As previously mentioned, the lineage of David, who became Saul's successor to the throne, can be traced back to the line of Judah, as is true with his son, King Solomon. Mary, the mother of Jesus, can be traced back to King David in fulfillment of the scriptures in which it was prophesied that Christ would come from the line of King David. **St. Luke (1:31-33):**

> **"And, behold, thou shalt conceive in thy womb, and bring forth a son, and shalt call his name Jesus. He shall be great, and called the son of the highest: And the Lord God shall give unto him the throne of his father David: And he shall reign over the house of Jacob forever; and of his kingdom there shall be no end."**

Due at least partially to the "isolationism" of the eastern block European countries, including Russia, they were spared some of the effects of the iconoclast period which occurred in western Europe and thus they continued to be a source of ancient icons of the "black madonna and child." (See plate.) It is of interest to note that the twelve disciples chosen by Christ were largely, if not all, Hebrew, as well as the Apostle Paul, who is frequently referred to as a Roman Jew in the traditional literature. Jesus directed his twelve disciples not to seek out the gentiles, but instead to seek out "the lost sheep of the house of Israel." **St. Matthew (10:5-6):**

> **"These twelve Jesus sent forth, and commanded them, saying Go not into the way of the gentiles, and into any city of the Samaritans enter ye not. But go rather to the lost sheep of the house of Israel."**

In specifying the "house of Israel," it would seem that Christ was directing his disciples at this time to seek out the Hebrews. As previously indicated, the Pharisees and Sadducees controlled the wealth of the temple and they were perplexed by the ministry of Jesus whose focus was on the masses, particularly the poor and disenfranchised, as reflected by the following: **Mark (7:1-2,5):**

> **"Then came together unto him the Pharisees, and certain of the scribes, which came from Jerusalem. And when they saw some of his disciples eat bread with the defiled, that is to say, with unwashen hands, they found fault.**
>
> **Then the Pharisees and scribes asked him, Why walk not thy disciples according to the tradition of the elders, but eat bread with unwashen hands?"**

**Luke (5:30-31):**

> **"But their scribes and Pharisees murmured against his disciples, saying Why do ye eat and drink with publicans and sinners? And Jesus answering said unto them, They that are whole need not a physician; but they that are sick."**

While Jesus had many disciples, the term "apostle" is most applicable to the twelve disciples which were described in **Luke (6:13-16):**

> **"And when it was day, he called unto him his disciples and of them he chose twelve, whom he named apostles; Simon (whom he also named Peter) and Andrew his brother, James and John, Philip and Bartholomew, Matthew and Thomas, James the son of Alphaeus, and Simon called Zelotes, And Judas the brother of James, and Judas Iscariot which was also the traitor."**

Due to events which are unfolding today, the issue of the priesthood and its relationship to God may take on increasing importance and therefore a chapter of this text has been specifically devoted to "The Priesthood."

In concluding this chapter on the "Identification of the Hebrews," I would be remiss if I did not at least mention the fact that racism was a force prior to and during the time of Christ to such an extent that one biblical dictionary has asserted that, "Mark's gentile audience may explain his omission of the genealogy of Jesus. Perhaps these Gentile readers were Roman Christians." [6] Now having stripped away the cumulative veil afforded by the passage of nearly twenty centuries, we are now in a better position to view the naked root of racism and at its foundation we see the embodiment of an ego which not only lacks the aura of superiority but instead more closely resembles that of one which has stolen something and therefore has something to hide, which manifests in some as a "guilt complex." Finally, that which was thought to have been hidden away in the caches of Egypt which were dug and covered over two-thousand years ago have now ironically surfaced as busts or statues that are largely able to speak for themselves. Accordingly, such physical evidence has provided us with certain keys which have allowed us to unlock many of the mysteries contained within the greatest historical text ever written, that being the Holy Bible.

Concerning modern day Jews, Sigmund Freud wrote, "Jewish tradition, however, behaved later on as if it were pressed by the sequence of ideas we have just developed. To admit that circumcision was an Egyptian custom introduced by Moses would be almost to recognize that the religion handed down to them from Moses was also Egyptian."[7]

---

## Part III notes:

[1]Black Athena, Vol. I, Martin Bernal, p. 19.

[2]The Histories, Herodotus, Translated by Aubrey de Selincourt, pp. 166-167.

[3]Holman Bible Dictionary, page 1108.

[4]Who's Who, The Old Testament, Joan Comay, p. 286.

[5]Ibid., p. 189.

[6]Holman Bible Dictionary, p.920.

[7]Moses and Monotheism, Sigmund Freud, p. 34.

## PART IV

## THE PRIESTHOOD

Truth shall triumph over deceit, as fact will prevail over fiction in all things that pertain to God.

**Luke (12:2,3):**

> **"For there is nothing, covered, that shall not be revealed; neither hid, that shall not be known.**
> **Therefore, whatsoever ye have spoken in darkness shall be heard in the light; and that which ye have spoken in the ear in closets shall be proclaimed upon the housetops."**

The conveyance of the word of God in the ancient period of the old testament was entrusted to the tribe of Levi by God himself as he called upon Aaron, the brother of Moses to enter the ministry.

**Exodus (28:1-3):**

> **"And take thou unto thee Aaron thy brother, and his sons with him, from among the children of Israel, that he may minister unto me in the priest's office, even Aaron, Nadab and Abihu, Eleazar and Ithamar, Aaron's sons.**
>
> **And thou shalt make holy garments for Aaron thy brother for glory and for beauty.**
>
> **And thou shalt speak unto all that are wise hearted whom I have filled with the spirit of wisdom, that they make Aaron's garments to consecrate him, that he may minister unto me in the priest's office."**

A detailed account of the garments to be worn by the

priest was provided in **Exodus (28:4):**

**"And these are the garments which they shall make: A breast plate, and an ephod, and a robe, and a broidered coat, a mitre and a girdle: and they shall make the holy garments for Aaron thy brother, and his sons, that he may minister unto me in the priest's office."**

The Bible continues in explicit detail as to the colors and construction of the priestly garments. Exodus (28:5-43). Special attention should be given to the last two verses.

**"And thou shalt make them linen breeches to cover their nakedness; from the loins even unto the thighs they shall reach:**

**And they shall be upon Aaron, and upon his sons, when they come unto the tabernacle of the congregation, or when they come near unto the altar to minister in the holy place; that they bear not iniquity, and die: it shall be a statute, forever unto him and his seed after him."**

The construction of the golden altar is described in Exodus (30:1-6). The construction of the laver is described in Exodus (30:17-21):

**"And the Lord spake unto Moses, saying, Thou shalt also make a laver of brass, and his foot also of brass, to wash withal: and thou shalt put it between the tabernacle of the congregation and the altar, and thou shalt put water therein.**

For Aaron and his sons shall wash their hands and their feet thereat:

**When they go into the tabernacle of the congregation, they shall wash with water, that they die not;**

**or when they come near to the altar**
**to minister, to burn offerings made by fire**
**unto the Lord."**

The construction of the tabernacle or holy tent of worship can be found in **Exodus (26:1-37).** Prior to building the tabernacle, Moses had an encounter with God which resulted in his being given the Law and Commandments written by God in tablets of stone. That account can be found in **Exodus (24:1-18).** Moses was later instructed to place the stone tablets that he had been given into a specially constructed container known as the "Ark of the Covenant" which was to become the central symbol of God's presence with the people of Israel. **Exodus (25:22):**

**"And there I will meet with thee, and I will**
**commune with thee from above the mercy seat,**
**from between the two cherubims which are upon**
**the ark of the testimony, of all things which**
**I will give thee in the commandment unto the**
**children of Israel."**

The Ark of the Covenant has been described as the most beautiful object ever to exist on the face of the earth, as its construction was inspired by God himself as described in **Exodus (25:10-22):**

**"And they shall make an ark of shittim wood: two**
**cubits and a half shall be the length thereof,**
**and a cubit and a half the breadth thereof, and**
**a cubit and a half the height thereof.**

**And thou shalt overlay it with pure gold, within**
**and without shalt thou overlay it, and shalt make**
**upon it a crown of gold round about.**

**And thou shalt cast four rings of gold for it**
**and put them in the four corners thereof; and**
**two rings shall be in the one side of it, and**
**two rings on the other side of it.**
**And thou shalt make staves of shittim wood and**

overlay them with gold.

And thou shalt put the staves into the rings by
the sides of the ark and the ark may be borne
with them.

The staves shall be in the rings of the ark:
they shall not be taken from it.

And thou shalt put into the ark the testimony
which I shall give thee.

And thou shalt make a mercy seat of pure gold:
two cubits and a half shall be the length thereof, and a cubit
and a half the breadth thereof.

And thou shalt make two cherubims of gold, of
beaten work shalt thou make them, in the two
ends of the mercy seat.

And make one cherub on the one end, and the
other cherub on the other end: even of the
mercy seat shall ye make the cherubims on the
two ends thereof.

And the cherubims shall stretch forth their
wings on high, covering the mercy seat with
their wings, and their faces shall look one
to another; toward the mercy seat shall the
faces of the cherubims be.

And thou shalt put the mercy seat above upon
the ark; and in the ark thou shalt put the
testimony that I shall give thee.

And there I will meet with thee, and I will
commune with thee from above the mercy seat,
from between the two cherubims which are upon

**the ark of the testimony, of all things which I will give thee in commandment unto the children of Israel."**

A specific individual was called and filled with the spirit of wisdom in workmanship in the metals - gold, silver and brass, and "all manner of workmanship." Exodus (31:1-5):

**"And the Lord spake unto Moses saying, See, I have called by name Bezaleel the son of Uri, the son of Hur, of the tribe of Judah:**

**And I have filled him with the spirit of God, in wisdom, and in understanding, and in knowledge, and in all manner of workmanship,**

**To devise cunning works, to work in gold, and in silver, and in brass, And in cutting of stones, to set them, and in carving of timber, to work in all manner of workmanship."**

Bezaleel was given an assistant by the name of Aholiab. Exodus (31:6):

**And I, behold, I have given him Aholiab, the son of Ahisamach, of the tribe of Dan: and in the hearts of all that are wise hearted I have put wisdom, that they may make all that I have commanded thee;"**

The construction of the Ark of the Covenant and other furniture of the tabernacle can be found in Exodus 37, and 39. And upon completion of all the work which was to be done, as the Lord commanded Moses, Exodus (40:20-21):

**"And he took and put the testimony into the ark, and set the staves on the ark, and put the mercy seat above upon the ark:**

**And he brought the ark into the tabernacle and set up the vail of the covering, and covered the**

**ark of the testimony; as the Lord commanded Moses."**

Moses and his brother. Aaron were of the tribe of Levi and it was this specific tribe which was entrusted with the priesthood. Numbers (3:6-12):

**"Bring the tribe of Levi near, and present them before Aaron the priest, that they may minister unto him.**

**And they shall keep his charge, and the charge of the whole congregation before the tabernacle of the congregation, to do the service of the tabernacle.**

**And they shall keep all the instruments of the tabernacle of the congregation, and the charge of the children of Israel, to do the service of the tabernacle.**

**And thou shalt give the Levites unto Aaron and to his sons: they are wholly given unto him out of the children of Israel.**

**And thou shalt appoint Aaron and his sons, and they shall wait on their priest's office: and the stranger that cometh nigh shall be put to death.**

**And the Lord spake unto Moses saying, And I, behold, I have taken the Levites from among the children of Israel instead of all the firstborn that openeth the matrix among the children of Israel: therefore the Levites shall be mine;"**

Numbers (3:32):

**"And Eleazar the son of Aaron the priest shall be the chief over the chief of the Levites, and have the oversight of them that keep the charge of the sanctuary."**

The term of service of the priests was described as follows: Numbers (8:23-26):

**"And the Lord spake unto Moses, saying, This is it that belongeth to the Levites: from twenty and five years old and upward they shall go in to wait upon the service of the tabernacle of the congregation:**

**"And from the age of fifty years they shall cease waiting upon the service thereof, and shall serve no more:**

**But shall minister with their brethren in the tabernacle of the congregation, to keep the charge, and shall do no service. Thus shalt thou do unto the Levites touching their charge."**

The tabernacle was a holy place in which God made his appearance to Moses and the priests and only those that were cleansed and appropriate could enter the tabernacle, and if not appropriately clothed, death could ensue. Exodus (28:31, 34-35):

**"And thou shalt make the robe of the ephod all of blue. A golden bell and a pomegranate, a golden bell and a pomegranate, upon the hem of the robe round about. And it shall be upon Aaron to minister: and his sound shall be heard when he goeth in unto the holy place before the Lord, and when he cometh out, that he die not."**

Exodus (28:42-43):

**"And thou shalt make them linen breeches to cover their nakedness; from the loins even**

**unto the thighs they shall reach.**

**And they shall be upon Aaron, and upon his sons when they come in unto the tabernacle, or when they come near unto the altar to minister in the holy place: that they bear not iniquity and die: it shall be a statute for ever unto him and his seed after him."**

As previously discussed, only those that were appropriate could enter the tabernacle or approach the Ark of the Covenant. No one was allowed to touch the Ark itself and it was therefore transported by the golden staves or poles that were inserted in the rings on each side, and even then only the priestly Levites were allowed to carry it.

It came to pass that Moses died just prior to the time in which the Hebrews entered the promised land and as described in the book of Joshua, Joshua became the new leader and later went on to lead the assault on Jericho. **Joshua (1:1-2):**

**"Now after the death of Moses the servant of the Lord it came to pass, that the Lord spake unto Joshua the son of Nun, Moses' minister saying, Moses my servant is dead; now therefore arise, go over this Jordan, thou and all this people, unto the land which I do give to them, even to the children of Israel."**

To enter Jericho, it was necessary to cross the Jordan River. While the Red Sea crossing in which the sea split to allow the passage of the Hebrews, only to later close on the Egyptian army which was in pursuit is widely known, to a lesser extent it is known that the Jordan also parted to allow the Hebrew crossing. **Joshua (3:13-17):**

**"And it came to pass as soon as the soles of the feet of the priests that bear the ark of the Lord, the Lord of all the earth, shall rest in the waters of the Jordan, that the waters of the Jordan shall be cut off from the waters that**

**come down from above; and they shall stand upon an heap.**

**And it came to pass, when the people removed from their tents to pass over the Jordan, and the priests bearing the ark of the covenant before the people;**

**And as they that bare the ark were come unto the Jordan, and the feet of the priest that bare the ark were dipped in the brim of the water, (for Jordan overfloweth all his banks all the time of harvest,)**

**That the waters which came down from above stood and rose up upon an heap very far from the city Adam, that is beside Zaretan: and those that came down toward the sea of the plain, even the salt sea, failed, and were cut off: and the people passed over right against Jericho.**

**And the Priests that bare the ark of the covenant of the Lord stood firm on dry ground in the midst of the Jordan, and all the Israelites passed on dry ground until the people were passed clean over the Jordan."**

In the siege of Jericho, armed men marched before the priests that blew the trumpets and carried the ark as the city was circled seven times. Joshua 6:16-20):

**"And it came to pass at the seventh time, when the priests blew with the trumpet, Joshua said unto the people, Shout; for the lord hath given you the city.**

**And the city shall be accursed even it, and all that are therein, to the Lord: only Rahab the**

**harlot shall live, she and all that are with her in the house, because she hid the messengers that we sent.**

**And ye, in any wise keep yourselves from the accursed thing, lest ye make yourselves accursed thing and make the camp of Israel a curse and trouble it.**

**But all the silver, and gold, and vessels of brass and iron are consecrated unto the Lord: they shall come into the treasury of the Lord.**

**So the people shouted when the priests blew with the trumpets: and it came to pass, when the people heard the sound of the trumpet and the people shouted with a great shout, that the wall fell down flat, so that the people went up to the city, every man straight before him, and they took the city."**

The success of the Hebrews continued and it came to pass that just as God had promised, the land of Canaan was inherited by the Hebrews who were the seed of Abraham. However, the Hebrews failed to heed the instructions of God and did evil in his sight, as they began serving Baalim, the god of the Canaanites.

**Judges (2:1-3, 11, 12, 13):**

**"And an angel of the Lord came upon Gilgal to Bochim and said, I made you go up out of Egypt, and have brought you unto the land which I sware unto your fathers; and I said, I will never break my covenant with you.**

**And ye shall make no league with the inhabitants of this land; ye shall throw down their altars: but ye have not obeyed my voice: why have ye done this?**

**Wherefore I also said, I will not drive them**

**out from you; but they shall be as thorns in your sides, and their gods shall be a snare unto you.**

And the children of Israel did evil in the sight of the Lord and served Baalim.

And they forsook the Lord God of their fathers, which brought them out of the land of Egypt, and followed other gods of the gods of the people that were round about them, and bowed themselves unto them, and provoked the Lord to anger.

And they forsook the Lord, and served Baal and Ashtaroth." **Judges (6:1):**

**"And the children of Israel did evil in the sight of the Lord: and the Lord delivered them into the hand of Midian seven years."**

After being inspired by God, the Hebrew, Gideon, first cut down the altar Baal **(Judges 6:28)**, and then went on to defeat the Midianites in battle **(Judges 8:28):**

**"Thus was Midian subdued before the children of Israel, so that they lifted up their heads no more. And the country was in quietness forty years in the days of Gideon."**

Unfortunately, the children of Israel once again turned to idolatry. **Judges (8:33-34):**

**"And it came to pass as soon as Gideon was dead, that the children of Israel turned again and went to whoring after Baalim, and made Baal-berith their god.**

**And the children of Israel remembered not the Lord their God, who had delivered them out of the hands of all their enemies on every side:"**

**Judges (10:7-8)**
**"And the anger of the Lord was hot against Israel, and he sold them into the hands of the Philistines, and into the hands of the children of Ammon.**

**And that year, they vexed and oppressed the children of Israel: eighteen years, all the children of Israel that were on the other side of the Jordan in the land of the Ammorites, which is Gilead."**

And the oppression of the Hebrews by the Philistines did not end until the lords of the Philistines and a multitude of people were killed by Samson when he pushed the two middle support pillars of a great building, causing its collapse.

In a later battle against the Philistines, as recorded in the book of Samuel, chapter 4, the Ark of the Covenant was captured **(I Samuel 4:11).** Following the capture of the Ark by the Philistines, they took it to the temple of their god Dagon and set it by Dagon, only to awake and find that it was cut to pieces **(I Samuel 5:1-5).** The Philistines decided to remove the Covenant from the temple of Dagon located in Ashdod, thereafter placing it in the city of Gath. Once again, great destruction came to the city and this time the Philistines decided to move the Ark to the city of Ekron. **I Samuel (5:10-12):**

**"Therefore they sent the ark of God to Ekron. And it came to pass, as the ark of God came to Ekron, that the Ekronites cried out, saying, They have brought about the ark of the God of Israel to us, to slay us and our people.**

**So they sent and gathered together all the lords of the Philistines, and said, Send away the ark of the God of Israel, and let it go again to his own place, that it slay us not,**

**and our people: for there was a deadly destruction throughout all the city; the hand of God was very heavy there.**

**And the men that died not were smitten with the emerods: and the cry of the city went up to heaven."**

The Philistines returned the Ark of the Covenant to the Levites who were awaiting in the city of Beth-shemesh. The city of Beth-shemesh also suffered destruction as some of its inhabitants attempted to look inside the ark. **I Samuel (6:19-21):**

**"And he smote the men of Beth-shemesh because they had looked into the ark of the Lord, even he smote of the people fifty thousand and three-score and ten men: and the people lamented, because the Lord had smitten many of the people with a great slaughter.**

**And the men of Beth-shemesh said Who is able to stand before this holy Lord God? And to whom shall he go up from us?**

**And they sent messengers to the inhabitants of Kirjath-jearim, saying, The Philistines have brought again the ark of the Lord; come ye down, and fetch it up to you."**

**I Samuel (7:1-4):**

**"And the men of Kirjath-jearim came and fetched up the ark of the Lord, and brought it into the house of Abinadab in the hill, and sanctified Eleazar his son to keep the ark of the Lord.**

**And it came to pass, while the ark abode in Kirjath-jearim, that the time was long; for it was twenty years: and all the house of Israel lamented after the Lord.**

**And Samuel spake unto all the house of Israel saying, If ye do return unto the Lord with all your hearts, then put away the strange gods and Ashtaroth from among you, and prepare your hearts unto the Lord, and serve him only: and he will deliver you out of the hand of the Philistines.**

**Then the children of Israel did put away Baalim and Ashtaroth, and served the Lord only."**

The Philistines were defeated. **I Samuel (7:11-13):**

**"And the men of Israel went out of Mizpeh, and pursued the Philistines, and smote them until they came under Beth-car.**

**Then Samuel took a stone, and set it between Mizpeh and Shen, and called the name of it Ebenezer, saying, Hitherto hath the Lord helped us.**

**So the Philistines were subdued and they came no more to the coast of Israel: and the hand of the Lord was against the Philistines all the days of Samuel."**

There continued to be, however, occasional battles with the Philistines. One of the most noteworthy was that which involved the giant Goliath, who stood over nine feet tall, in one of the most celebrated accounts in the Bible in which the young David slays the giant. The biblical account of this event can be found in **I Samuel (17:1-54).** David, a Hebrew from the line of Judah was later anointed king of Judah, but the son of King Saul continued to reign over Israel. There was a long war between the house of Saul and the house of David, but David prevailed. **(II Samuel, chapter 3)**

King David arose with thirty thousand from Judah and removed the Ark of the Covenant from the house of Abinadab and they placed the Ark of the Covenant upon a new cart which was driven by the sons of Abinadab. And all of Israel rejoiced. **(II Samuel 6:12-17.)** He then went on to place the Ark of the Covenant in a tabernacle which he had prepared; however, the permanent resting place for the Ark of the Covenant was not built until the reign of his son, King Solomon. Zadok was the high priest during the time of David, and his son, Azariah, was the high priest under **Solomon (I Kings 4:2),** also known as Ahimaaz, the son of Zadok **(II Samuel 15:27).**

The Ark of the Covenant was once again entrusted to the care of the high priest from the God appointed priestly tribe of the Levites.

David, the King of Judah, after capturing the Ark of the Covenant and moving it into the city of Jerusalem, made this city the capitol, and he became king of both Judah and of Israel, thereby uniting all of Israel under his rule.

Solomon, whom David appointed King on his death bed, was actually the tenth son of David and the second son of Bathsheba. Bathsheba was the daughter of Eliam and former wife of Uriah the Hittite, who was killed in battle, with David subsequently taking her as his wife.

As king over Israel, both the wealth and wisdom of King Solomon grew, as he has been described as the wealthiest and the wisest king of all times. Zadok and his son were the high priests at the time of Solomon, who behind Saul and David, became the third king of Israel. Solomon enjoyed a forty-year reign of prosperity, 971-931 B.C. The temple which was to be the permanent resting place of the Ark of the Covenant was constructed in the reign of Solomon, beginning in the year 967 B.C., 480 years after the Hebrews were freed from bondage and came out of Egypt.

**I Kings (6:1):**

> **"And it came to pass in the four hundred and eightieth year after the children of Israel were come out of the land of Egypt, in the**

**fourth year of Solomon's reign over Israel, in the month Zif, which is the second month, that he began to build the house of the Lord."**

Up until the time of Solomon, there had never been an undertaking of the magnitude of the planned temple of God. Both in size and expense, it exceeded all others. (Full description is provided in I Kings 6, 7.) In the dedication of the temple which followed, the priests brought in the Ark of the Covenant and placed it in the holiest place in the temple known as the Holy of Holies.

I Kings (8:10-13):

> **"And it came to pass, when the priests were out of the holy place, that the cloud filled the house of the Lord, So that the priests could not stand to minister because of the cloud: for the glory of the Lord filled the house of the Lord.**
>
> **Then spake Solomon, The Lord said that he would dwell in the thick darkness.**
>
> **I have surely built thee an house to dwell in, a settled place for thee to abide in for ever."**

God went on to establish a covenant with Solomon.

I Kings (9:4-8):

> **"And if thou wilt walk before me, as David thy father walked, in integrity of heart, and in uprightness to do according to all that I have commanded thee, and wilt keep my statutes and my judgments:**
>
> **Then I will establish the throne of thy kingdom upon Israel for ever, as I promised to David thy father, saying, There shall not fail thee a man upon the throne of Israel.**

**But if ye shall at all turn from following me, ye or your children, and will not keep my commandments and my statutes which I have set before you, but go and serve other gods, and worship them:**

**Then will I cut off Israel out of the land which I have given them; and this house, which I have hallowed for my name, will I cast out of my sight; and Israel shall be a proverb and a byword among all people:**

**And at this house, which is high, every one that passeth by it shall be astonished, and shall hiss; and they shall say, Why hath the Lord done thus unto this land, and to this house?"**

Meanwhile, King Solomon's wealth and fame continued to grow until such time as it was heard even in the distant land of Arabia. The Queen of Sheba, known as Makeda, in her homeland of Arabia (Ethiopia), after hearing of the great wisdom of Solomon, came to test him and at the same time further develop the trade relationship between their two countries. The queen herself being quite wealthy was accompanied by a train of camels bearing gold, spices and precious stones. Solomon was captivated by the beauty of the great queen which sparked a romance which has been legendary through the ages of time. I Kings (10:1-10):

**"And when the queen of Sheba heard the fame of Solomon concerning the name of the Lord, she came to prove him with hard questions.**

**And she came to Jerusalem with a very great train with camels that bare spices, and very much gold, and precious stones: and when she was come to Solomon, she communed with him of all that was in her heart.**

**And Solomon told her all her questions: there was not any thing hid from the king, which he told her not.**

**And when the queen of Sheba had seen all Solomon's wisdom, and the house that he had built,**

**And the meat of his table, and the sitting of his servants, and the attendance of his ministers, and their apparel, and his cupbearers, and his ascent by which he went up unto the house of the Lord, there was no more spirit in her.**

**And she said to the king, It was a true report that I heard in mine own land of thy acts and of thy wisdom.**

**Howbeit I believed not the words until I came, and mine eyes had seen it: and, behold, the half was not told me; thy wisdom and prosperity exceedeth the fame which I heard.**

**Happy are thy men, happy are these thy servants which stand continually before thee, and that bear thy wisdom.**

**Blessed be the Lord thy God, which delighted in thee, to set thee on the throne of Israel:**

**Because the Lord loved Israel forever, therefore made thee king, to do judgment and justice.**

**And she gave the king an hundred and twenty talents of gold, and of spices very great store, and precious stones: there came no more such abundance of spices as these which the queen of Sheba gave to King Solomon."**

**I Kings (10:13):**

> **"And King Solomon gave unto the queen of Sheba all her desire, whatsoever she asked, beside that which Solomon gave her of his royal bounty. So she turned and went to her own country, she and her servants."**

It is said that, "During her six-month visit, Makeda conferred frequently with King Solomon. She was so impressed with his wisdom that she gave up her religion and adopted Judaism."[1]

I would point out once again at this time that Judaism was the religion of the ancient Hebrews which seemingly took on its name as being the result of the fact that at one time, Judah and Israel were divided; however, Judah was the largest tribe (the kingdom of Judah, an expanse which also included the greater part of that of Benjamin on the northeast, Dan on the northwest, and Simeon on the south). When coupled with the fact of its size and that it was Solomon's father, David, who was the first king of Judah before reuniting it with the rest of Israel, the religion took on the name of the patriarch, Judah, the same name that was also to be shared by the kingdom. The Greek word "Jew" which initially described those from the land of Judah or Jerusalem, was eventually broadened to include the religion (Judaism) of the Hebrews.

The historical period of David and Solomon was approximately the 10th Century B.C., and there was no significant Greek influence in this area prior to the invasion of Alexander the Great which did not occur for nearly another seven centuries. It should come as no surprise to anyone that the original text of the Old Testament was not written in Greek, but rather, nearly all of it was written in Hebrew. The Hebrew language, according to the linguist, Martin Bernal, is a "Canaanite dialect spoken in the kingdom of Israel, Judah and Moab, being between 1500 and 500 B.C. For religious reasons, it is often treated as a distinct language." [2]

While Canaan was a descendant of Ham, the Canaanite language, including Hebrew, is considered to be a West Semitic language. The few verses of the Old Testament which were not written in Hebrew were written in Aramaic which is considered to be a North Semitic language. "Not all Shem's descendants spoke Semitic languages. Elim and Lud, for instance, used non-Semitic languages **(Genesis 10:22)**, while a few descendants of Ham (e.g., Canaan, v.6, and the son's of Cush mentioned in v. 7) spoke Semitic rather than Hamitic languages."[3] Additionally, there was no comprehensive translation of the Old Testament which was a compilation of texts written over a period from the time of Moses, 1500 B.C., until approximately the 4th century B.C. The oldest form of the Greek translation of the ancient text is known as the Septuagint, as previously discussed, but the modern-day definition is problematic for this author, in that once again, it seems to represent still another Greek amphibology, which will be discussed later in this text.

"The language is not called Hebrew in the Old Testament. Rather, it is known as the language (literally 'lip') of Canaan, (Isaiah 19:18) or as Judean (N.A.S.), that is, the language of Judah **(Nehemiah 13:24; Isaiah 36:11)."[4]**

Now returning to the association of Solomon and Sheba, nine months after her return to Ethiopia, Sheba gave birth to Menolik, who was destined to become the first descendant of King David and line of Judah to rule Ethiopia,

Back in Jerusalem, however, things were not going well, largely due to Solomon's appetite for women. "But King Solomon loved many strange women, together with the daughter of Pharaoh, women of the Moabites, the Ammonites, the Edomites, the Zidonians, and the Hittites **(I Kings 11:1).** It should be pointed out that most of these women were of Hamitic and/or Semitic origin, and all in all, Solomon had 700 wives, princesses, and 300 concubines: and his wives turned away his heart **(I Kings 11:3)** Solomon was convinced by some of his women to build temples to their gods **(I Kings 11:4-8).** As a result of his involvement with such idolatry, he incurred the wrath of God. **I Kings (11:9-13):**

**"And the Lord was angry with Solomon, because**

**his heart was turned from the Lord God of Israel, which had appeared unto him twice,**

**And had commanded him concerning this thing, that he should not go after other gods: but he kept not that which the Lord commanded.**

**Wherefore the Lord said unto Solomon, Foras much as this is done of thee, and thou hast not kept my covenant and my statutes, which I have commanded thee, I will surely rend the kingdom from thee, and will give it to thy servant.**

**Notwithstanding in thy days I will not do it for David they father's sake: but I will rend it out of the hand of thy son.**

**Howbeit I will not rend away all the kingdom: but will give one tribe to thy son for David my servant's sake, and for Jerusalem's sake which I have chosen."**

Jeroboam was a very industrious servant of Solomon and accordingly was made ruler over all the charge of the house of Joseph. The prophet Ahijah, the Shilonite, advised Jeroboam.

**I Kings (11:31-37, 40):**

**"And he said to Jeroboam, Take thee ten pieces for thus saith the Lord, the God of Israel, Behold, I will rend the kingdom out of the hand of Solomon, and will give ten tribes to thee:**

**(But he shall have one tribe for my servant David's sake, and for Jerusalem's sake, the city which I have chosen out of all the tribes of Israel:)**

**Because that they have forsaken me, and have worshipped Ashtoreth the goddess of the**

**Zidonians, Chemosh the god of the Moabites and Milcom the god of the children of Ammon, and have not walked in my ways, to do that which is right in mine eyes, and to keep my statutes and my judgments, as did David his father.**

**Howbeit I will not take the whole kingdom out of his hand: but I will make him prince all the days of his life for David my servant's sake, whom I chose, because he kept my commandments and my statutes:**

**But I will take the kingdom out of his son's hand, and will give it unto thee, even ten tribes.**

**And unto his son will I give one tribe, that David my servant may have a light always before me in Jerusalem, the city which I have chosen me to put my name there.**

**And I will take thee, and thou shalt reign according to all that thy soul desireth, and shall be king over Israel."**

**"Solomon sought therefore to kill Jeroboam. And Jeroboam arose, and fled into Egypt, unto Shishak king of Egypt, and was in Egypt until the death of Solomon."**

As previously stated, Solomon reigned for a forty-year period, from 971 to 931 B.C.

Now turning to the Egyptian Chronological Table, we find that the Pharaoh Shishak **(I Kings 11:40),** was the Egyptian Pharaoh whose reign corresponded to the time of Shoshenq I, whose reign was from 945 to 924 B.C. **I Kings (11:43):**

**"And Solomon slept with his fathers, and was buried in the city of David his father: and Rehoboam his son reigned in his stead."**

I Kings (12:1-2):

**"And Rehoboam went to Shechem: for all Israel were come to Shechem to make him king.**

**And it came to pass, when Jeroboam the son of Nebat, who was yet in Egypt, heard of it, (for he was fled from the presence of King Solomon, and Jeroboam dwelt in Egypt;)"**

I Kings (12:20):

**"And it came to pass, when all Israel heard that Jeroboam was come again, that they sent and called him unto the congregation, and made him king over all Israel; there was none that followed the house of David, but the tribe of Judah only."**

So now the tribes of Israel had split into two warring camps.

I Kings (12:21):

**"And when Rehoboam was come to Jerusalem, he assembled all the house of Judah with the tribe of Benjamin, an hundred and fourscore thousand chosen men, which were warriors, to fight against the house of Israel, to bring the kingdom again to Rehoboam the son of Solomon."**

This battle did not materialize; however, Jeroboam became concerned that when followers returned to worship at the temple in Jerusalem they might once again turn to Rehoboam as he was over the house of David **(I Kings 12:27).**

Jeroboam then tempted them to fall into return to idolatry, in that he created two calves of gold and said unto them:

**"It is too much for you to go up to Jerusalem:**

**behold thy gods, O Israel, which brought thee up out of the land of Egypt."**

Jeroboam established a place of worship in two places.

I Kings (12:29-32):

**"And he set the one in Beth-el, and the other he put in Dan.**

**And this thing became a sin: for the people went to worship before the one, even unto Dan.**

**And he made an house of high places, and made priests of the lowest of the people, which were not of the sons of Levi.**

**And Jeroboam ordained a feast in the eighth month on the fifteenth day of the month, like unto the feast in Judah, and he offered upon the altar. So did he in Beth-el, sacrificing unto the calves that he had made: and he placed in Beth-el the priests of the high places which he had made."**

I Kings (13:33-34):

**"After this thing Jeroboam returned not from his evil way, but made again of the lowest of the people priests of the high places: whoever would, he consecrated him, and he became one of the priests of the high places.**

**And this thing became sin unto the house of Jeroboam, even to cut it off, and to destroy it from off the face of the earth."**

I Kings (14:19-22):

**"And the rest of the acts of Jeroboam, how he warred, and how he reigned, behold, they are written in the book of the chronicles of**

**the kings of Israel.**

**And the days which Jeroboam reigned were two and twenty years: and he slept with his fathers, and Nadab his son reigned in his stead.**

**And Rehoboam the son of Solomon reigned in Judah. Rehoboam was forty and one years old when he began to reign, and he reigned seven-teen years in Jerusalem, the city which the Lord did choose out of the tribes of Israel, to put his name there. And his mother's name was Na-amah an Ammonitess."**

**"And Judah did evil in the sight of the Lord, and they provoked him to jealousy with their sins which they had committed, above all that their fathers had done."**

There were two other major events which occurred during this same period. However, first let us return to the Prophet Ahijah the Shilonite who first revealed to Jeroboam that the kingdom would be taken away from the hand of Solomon, that is, following his death.
**I Kings (11:31-32):**

**"And he said to Jereboam, Take thee ten pieces: for thus saith the Lord, the God of Israel, Behold, I will rend the kingdom out of the hand of Solomon, and will give ten tribes to thee:**

**(But he shall have one tribe for my servant David's sake, and for Jerusalem's sake, the city which I have chosen out of all the tribes of Israel:)"**

Given the gravity of such a situation, as would be expected, Ahijah certainly would have told others. Certainly Solomon knew of the impending split and therefore he sought to kill Jeroboam.
**I Kings (11:40):**

**"Solomon sought therefore to kill Jeroboam. And Jeroboam arose, and fled into Egypt unto Shishak, king of Egypt, and was in Egypt until the death of Solomon."**

Zadok, the high priest during the time of David and at least during early in Solomon's reign, and his son, Azariah, was also appointed to the post of high priest by Solomon.

The Bible clearly states that in what would have been the year 926 B.C., that is, five years after the death of Solomon, Shishak (Shoshenq I) invaded Jerusalem and took everything out of the temple of the Lord. While there are scholars that would like to claim that Pharaoh's men never entered the temple but instead were somehow bought off, I am not aware of any evidence to support such a claim which in itself would clearly be inconsistent with the biblical text, the account of which can be found in **II Chronicles (12:1-12).** Still another account can be found in **I Kings (14:25)** which reads:

**"And it came to pass in the fifth year of king Rehoboam, that Shishak king of Egypt came up against Jerusalem:**

**And he took away the treasures of the house of the Lord, and the treasures of the king's house; he even took away all: and he took away all the shields of gold which Solomon had made."**

Now severely lacking resources, the king replaced the golden shields with brass ones. **I Kings (14:27):**

**"And king Rehoboam made in their stead brasen shields, and committed them unto the hands of the chief of the guard, which kept the door of the king's house."**

Apparently not being even able to make enough brass shields for both the temple and the king's house, Rehoboam instead had his guards carry the shields over to the temple when he chose to visit it and then had them bring the same shields back to the guard chamber at his house ... a fact which the Bible explicitly mentions.

**I Kings (14:28):**

> **"And it was so, when the king went into the house of the Lord, that the guard bare them, and brought them back into the guard chamber."**

During all the strife between Jeroboam and Rehoboam, it is interesting to note that while the bible points to the fact that Jeroboam was made king over all Israel and that none followed the house of David, that is, Rehoboam but the tribe of Judah, which was later seemingly also joined by the house of Benjamin **(I Kings 12:20-21).** This raises a very interesting point since Jeroboam had the following of all the tribes of Israel except for Judah and possibly the tribe of Benjamin, why was it necessary for him to choose his priests from the lowest of people which were not even of the tribe of the priestly Levis. In other words, what happened to the high priest?

**I Kings (12:31):**

> **"And he made an house of high places, and made priests of the lowest of the people, which were not of the sons of Levi."**

Under Jeroboam's misdirection, the Hebrew nation had lost its shining glory and as Jeroboam stood before the altar to burn incense at the temple of Bethel, he suffered a withered hand.

**I Kings (13:1, 4):**

> **"And behold, there came a man of God out of Judah by the word of the Lord unto Beth-el: And Jeroboam stood by the altar to burn incense."**
>
> **"And it came to pass, when king Jeroboam heard the saying of the man of God, which had cried against the altar in Beth-el, that he put forth his hand from the altar, saying, Lay hold on him. And his hand, which he put forth against him, dried up, so that he could not pull it in again to him."**

While it was stated that all of the treasures of the temple in Jerusalem were looted, there was no mention of the centerpiece of the Hebrew religion, that is, the Ark of the Covenant. And thereafter, it seems as though it is only mentioned in passing, as is the case in **Jeremiah (3:15-16)**:

> **"And I will give you pastors according to mine heart, which shall feed you with knowledge and understanding.**
>
> **And it shall come to pass, when ye be multiplied and increased in the land, in those days, saith the Lord, they shall say no more, The ark of the covenant of the Lord: neither shall it come to mind: neither shall they remember it; neither shall they visit it; neither shall that be done any more."**

The most coveted object in the temple quietly disappeared from its former place in status as being the protector and showpiece of the Hebrews. The menacing question of what happened to the Ark of the Covenant can perhaps be best answered by returning to days of Solomon.

"At the age of 22, Menelik traveled to Jerusalem to visit his father. He did not need the ring Solomon had given his mother for identification, because when he arrived in Gaza, the people knew by his appearance that he was Solomon's son."[5]

There are two accounts by which, however, Menelik is reported to have left his father's palace to return to Ethiopia. One such account is that, "When Solomon realized that he could not persuade his son to remain in Jerusalem, he anointed Menelik king of Ethiopia, bestowed upon him the name of David, and provided him with counselors and officers for the founding of Israel's new kingdom in Ethiopia."[6]

The other account is offered by perhaps the foremost authority on the Ark of the Covenant, Graham Hancock, who states, "After a

**St. Mary's Church in Axum, Ethiopia**

Believed to be the resting place of the Arc of the Covenant for the past 3,000 years.

**100 Ft. Stele in Axum, Ethiopia**

Where several can be found that date back to the reigns of Sheba and Menolik 930 B.C.

year had passed, however, the elders of the land became jealous of him. They complained that Solomon showed too much favor and they insisted that he must go back to Ethiopia. This, the king accepted on the condition that the first-born sons of all the elders should be sent to accompany him. Amongst these latter was Azarias, son of Zadok, the high priest of Israel, and it was Azarias, not Menelik, who stole the Ark of the Covenant from its place in the Holy of Holies in the Temple."[7]

Although the accounts are different, in one respect they are the same. Menelik did not return to Ethiopia by himself. This author differs with Graham Hancock in that the Ark of the Covenant was removed as a result of the Lord's promise to Solomon.

**I Kings (11:11):**

> **"Wherefore the Lord said unto Solomon, Forasmuch as this is done of thee, and thou hast not kept my covenant and my statutes, which I have commanded thee, I will surely rend the kingdom from thee, and I will give it to thy servant."**

The Lord clearly foretold a split in the house of Israel and by Solomon's sending the high priest, whose primary function is to minister to God and to watch over and transport the Ark of the Covenant, there would be no reason for Azarias, the high priest of Solomon to go to Ethiopia except to assist in the establishment of Israel's new kingdom in Ethiopia from the line of David and Judah. By virtue of Graham Hancock's recent discovery, all evidence at this time would seem to point to the fact that the Ark of the Covenant for hundreds of years has rested in a small church in the city of Axum and it has been watched over by the Zadokite line of priests since the Ark of the Covenant was carried from the temple of Jerusalem nearly three thousand years ago.

Needless to say, the impending attack of Shishak, the Egyptian Pharaoh who removed all items from the temple necessitated that the ark be relocated, thus it was taken to the new kingdom of Israel in Ethiopia, thought to have been established in the year 930 B.C., the year following Solomon's death. The reign of Menolik's mother, Makeda (Queen of Sheba), was from 960 to 930

B.C. Thus, King Solomon died just prior to the establishment of this new kingdom.

Graham Hancock recently discovered that the worship services of the Hebrews in Ethiopia are nearly identical to that which took place thousands of years ago, even to the point that the Ark of the Covenant is the centerpoint of their worship even today. Its removal to Ethiopia was seemingly done with God's blessing, since those of the past that have taken it against the will of God, we know that their fate has been well described in the book of Samuel. In all probability, even today, a similar fate would be suffered by anyone who attempted to move the Ark of the Covenant against the will of God. Biblical history tells us that entire populations suffered with some experiencing mass destruction. The Ark of the Covenant has rested in Ethiopia five to ten times longer than it has rested any other place on earth, and for all but five hundred years of its nearly thirty-five hundred years existence.

In answering the previously posed question concerning the fate of the temple priests at the time of the split of the children of Israel into two nations, with Rehoboam, the son of Solomon remaining the king of the tribes of Judah and Benjamin, while the other ten tribes rebelled to follow Jeroboam, once again we turn to Josephus. "After those thirteen high priests, eighteen took the high priesthood at Jerusalem, one in succession, to another, from the days of Solomon until Nebuchadnezzar, king of Babylon, made an expedition against that city, and burnt the temple, and removed our nation to Babylon, and then took Josadek, the high priest, captive."[8] We know that Jerusalem and the temple remained under the control of Rehoboam, but if, indeed, the priests were also present in Jerusalem, we know through inference that therefore at least a portion of the priestly tribe of the Levis had to also be present along with the tribes of Judah and Benjamin. The fact that a portion of another tribe(s) was also present in Jerusalem at the time of the split is seemingly confirmed by scriptures. **I Kings (12:23):**

> **"Speak unto Rehoboam, the son of Solomon, king of Judah and unto all the house of Judah and Benjamin, and to the remnant of the people,**

**saying"...**

If indeed, the priests were among the "remnant of the people" referred to in the aforementioned passage, that would certainly explain why Jeroboam, who had become a pagan worshiper had no choice but to reappoint others to the priesthood. Given his inclination to worship golden calves, it is highly likely that Jeroboam met with great resistance from the priests, high priests in particular, whom Josephus confirmed continued in succession in Jerusalem. This conclusion is actually confirmed by Josephus himself who writes, "The priests also that were in all Israel, and the Levites, and if there were any of the multitude that were good and righteous men, they gathered themselves together to him, having left their own cities, that they might worship God in Jerusalem; for they were not willing to be forced to worship the heifers which Jeroboam had made; and they augmented the kingdom of Rehoboam for three years."[9]

Josephus goes on to describe how Rehoboam grew dissatisfied when his kingdom did not increase in prosperity and subsequently became wicked and corrupt, as did many of his followers. "But God sent Shishak, king of Egypt to punish them for their unjust behavior towards him; concerning whom Herodotus was mistaken, and applied his actions to Sesostris; for this Shishak, in the fifth year of the reign of Rehoboam, made an expedition [into Judea] with many ten thousand men; for he had one thousand two hundred chariots in number that followed him, and three score thousand horseman, and four hundred thousand footmen. These he brought with him, and they were the greatest part of them Libyans and Ethiopians."[10]

In addition to openly refuting the previous account given by the Greek historian, Herodotus, who had in error attributed this conquest to Sesostris, Josephus lays to rest the notion by some modern-day historians that the temple was never itself actually invaded by Shishak as they contended that he was stopped at the city limits of Jerusalem and bought off. They concluded that this was the reason that the Ark of the Covenant was not taken by Shishak. To the contrary, Josephus states, "So when Shishak had taken the city without fighting, because Rehoboam was afraid, and received him into it, yet did not Shishak stand to the covenants that he had made, but spoiled the temple, and emptied the treasures of God and those of the king, and carried off innumerable tens, thousands of gold and silver, and left nothing at all behind him." [11]

As we now have this extra-biblical source confirming the events which were previously described in the Bible, noting the fact that the temple was completely emptied, needless to say, if the Ark of the Covenant had been present during the invasion of Shishak, there certainly would have been an attempt to take it at that time.

The make-up of Shishak's army was quite interesting. Josephus gives us every impression, especially by referring specifically to the Libyans and the Ethiopians that these were, indeed, distinct nationalities of people that were in alliance with Egypt at that time. It is necessary to point out at this time that the term "Ethiopian" is a Greek amphobology which in Greek literally means "black faced" and was liberally applied as a generic term for all black people, irrespective of their nationality. The land of Cush, which is sometimes referred to as Lower Egypt, was also referred to as Nubia and Ethiopia by the Greeks.

During the times of the Old Testament, the kingdom of the Queen of Sheba was comprised of several countries known collectively as being Arabia. "South Arabia was, even in the ancient world, export country Number One for spices and it still is so today. Yet, it seemed to be shrouded in dark mystery. No man had ever seen it with his own eyes."[12] The author of this text was seemingly referring to the fact that no white man had ever seen Arabia. He continues, "A Frenchman, J. Halevy, and an Australian, Dr. Eduard Glaser, were the first white men actually to reach this ancient goal about a century ago. Since no foreigner, far less a European, was allowed to cross the frontier of the Yemen, and no permit could be obtained, Halevy and Glaser embarked on an enterprise which might have cost them their lives." [13] Keller continued on to describe how this group was actually able to obtain inscriptions as evidence of the existence of this kingdom. "Dedicatory inscriptions give us information about gods, tribes and cities of a million inhabitants. And the names of four countries 'The Spice Kingdoms' which are mentioned are: Minaea, Kataban, Hadhramaut and Sheba."[14] "The Israelites recognized their blood relationship with the Arabs. Most of these groups are linked with Abraham through his son Ishmael or through his second wife Keturah **(Genesis 25)**."[15]

The term "Ethiopia" is no longer applied to the area of lower Egypt, once known as the Cushite empire, but at the present time is recognized as being Nubia or Northern Sudan. The city of Axum which was the capitol and center of the kingdom of the Queen of Sheba, is now in the heart of the modern-day country of Ethiopia which is southeast of the Cushite empire or the Ethiopia of the Greeks. "Cush was the Ethiopia of the Greeks, corresponding to the modern Sudan."[16] To further cloud the issue of geography, the area of Arabia wherein modern-day Ethiopia is presently located was, in ancient times, referred to as Abyssinia. It is this modern country of Ethiopia that will be our focal point toward the end of this text.

Whether we call the land of Sheba Ethiopia, Abyssinia or Arabia, the reader is reminded at this time of God's promise to Abraham regarding his first son, Ishmael, whose mother was the Egyptian, Hagar. **Genesis (17:20)**:

> **"And as for Ishmael, I have heard thee: Behold I have blessed him, and will make him fruitful, and will multiply him exceedingly; twelve princes shall he beget, and I will make him a great nation."**

Ishmael took an Egyptian wife and is considered to be the father of the Arabians. The great peninsula southeast of Palestine **(II Chronicles 9:14; 17:11; Ezekiel 27:21)** and its people, traditionally descended from Ishmael **(II Chronicles 21:16; Nehemiah 2:19; Acts 2:11)**. The Ethiopians are, therefore, a Semitic people as they are a direct descendant of Abraham through Ishmael, all of whom are Hebrews, in that as previously discussed, the lineage of Abraham is traceable back to Heber, who in turn, descended from Shem (Sem). Additionally, the Davidic kingdom of David was established in Ethiopia through Menelik and even today, the star of David can be found in the ceiling of the ancient church of St. Mary in Lalibela, Ethiopia, although this is a Christian church. However, this makes perfect sense, since as we have previously described, the natural course for the religion of the Hebrews would have been Judao-Christian since during the Judaic period, the prophets foretold the coming of the Messiah with the birth of Jesus Christ then being the fulfillment of the scriptures. It was then the Magi, or Wisemen of the East, who arrived on camel-back in Jerusalem seeking Bethlehem which the prophets had foretold would be the birthplace of the Messiah.

**Matthew (2:1-6):**

> **"Now when Jesus was born in Bethlehem of Judae-a in the days of Herod the king, behold there came wisemen from the east to Jerusalem,**
>
> **Saying, where is he that is born king of the Jews? for we have seen his star in the east, and are come to worship him.**
>
> **When Herod the king had heard these things, he was troubled, and all Jerusalem with him.**
>
> **And when he had gathered all the chief priests and scribes of the people together, He demanded of them where Christ should be born.**
>
> **And they said unto him, In Bethlehem of Judae-e: for thus it is written by the prophet,**
>
> **And thou, Bethlehem, in the land of Juda, art not the least among the princes of Juda: for out of thee shall come a Governor, that shall rule my people Israel."**

It was the gifts of the Magi which provided the greatest clue to their identity as being out of Abyssinia or what is known today as Ethiopia. Both the resin myrrh and frankincense are resins obtained from the Balsam trees of Abyssinia (Arabia). When found outside of Arabia, it was almost always brought to these distant lands through trade. "Again, the most southerly country is Arabia; and Arabia is the only place that produces frankincense, myrrh, cassia, cinnamon, and the gum called ledanon."[17] It is the descendants of Ishmael who in those days were known as the Ish-mee-lites. **Genesis (37:25):**

> **"And they sat down to eat bread: and they lifted up their eyes and looked, and, behold, a company of Ish-mee-lites came from Gil-e-ad with their camels bearing spicery and balm and myrrh, going to carry it down to Egypt.**

Just as a note of interest, it was to the Ish-mee-lites that the sons of Jacob sold their younger brother, Joseph, and their caravan took him on to Egypt.

**Genesis 37:28):**

> **"Then, there passed by Midianites merchantmen; And they drew and lifted up Joseph out of the pit, and sold Joseph to the Ish-mee-lites for twenty pieces of silver: and they brought Joseph into Egypt."**

It is these Ish-mee-lites that came out of Abyssinia or modern-day Ethiopia upon whom we will focus our attention at a later point in this text.

Once again, returning to the subject of the Priesthood, as Josephus has pointed out, it appeared that the priesthood of the Hebrews continued up until the period of the Babylonian captivity during which time the Hebrews once again entered a period of servitude, this time lasting seventy years. Josadek, the high priest at that time, was also amongst the captives. It was this period of Babylonian captivity under Nebuchadnezzar which brought an end to the Hebrew nation as it had been known, and as Josephus describes, "and he took those Jews that were their captives, and led them away to Babylon; and such was the end of the nation of the Hebrews, as it hath been delivered down to us, it having twice gone beyond the Euphrates; for the people of the ten tribes were carried out 1of Samaria by the Assyrians in the day of King Hosea; after which the people of the two tribes that remained after Jerusalem was taken [were carried away] by Nebuchadnezzar, the king of Babylon and Chaldea."[18] And this would have occurred in approximately the year 587 B.C.

Following the seventy-year period of servitude, it was Jesus, the son of Josadek, who took the high priesthood once the captives returned home, and the priesthood of the Hebrews continued until the Hellenistic period of the ancient Greeks. The impact of Hellenism on the ancient Hebrews will be examined in some detail in the following chapter.

As we have already discussed in Chapter II, prior to the appointment of Aaron, the first of the Hebrew priests, there was Melchizedec who was priest and king of Salem (Jerusalem), but who unlike mortal men, was "without father, without mother, without descent, having neither beginning of days, nor end of life; but made unto the son of God; abideth a priest continually." **(Hebrews 7:3.)** Jesus, whose genealogy through Mary can be traced back to Judah, like Melchizedec, was also appointed to the priesthood forever. **Hebrews (5:5-6):**

> **"So also Christ glorified not himself to be made an high priest; but he that said unto him, THOU ART MY SON, TO DAY HAVE I BEGOTTEN THEE.**
>
> **As he saith also in another place, THOU ART A PRIEST FOR EVER AFTER THE ORDER OF MELCHISEDEC."**

The fact that Jesus was to arise after the order of Melchisedec and not be called after the order of the Levites and Aaron, is interesting and a point which is addressed in **Hebrews 7:11-12):**

> **"If therefore perfection were by the Levitical priesthood (for under it the people received the law,) what further need was there that another priest should rise after the order of Melchisedec, and not be called after the order of Aaron?**
>
> **For the priesthood being changed, there is**

**made of necessity a change also of the law."**

Hebrews continues (9:11-15):

> **"But Christ being come an high priest of good things to come, by a greater and more perfect tabernacle, not made with hands, that is to say, not of this building;**
>
> **Neither by the blood of goats, and calves, but by his own blood he entered in once into the holy place, having obtained eternal redemption for us.**
>
> **For if the blood of bulls and of goats and the ashes of an heifer sprinkling the unclean, sanctifieth to the purifying of the flesh:**
>
> **How much more shall the blood of Christ, who through the eternal Spirit offered himself without spot to God, purge your conscience from dead works to serve the living God?**
>
> **And for this cause he is the mediator of the new testament, that by means of death, for the redemption of the transgressions that were under the first testament, they which are called might receive the promise of eternal inheritance."**

Finally, it is of interest to note that the prophesied split in the kingdom of Israel out of necessity brought a division that went well beyond the area of Palestine, as was the case with the establishment of the Davidic kingdom in Abyssinia (Ethiopia). The conquest of the Middle East and Northern Africa, including Egypt, by Alexander "the Great" which marked the dawning of Hellenism, took a heavy toll on the God-appointed, Hebrew, Levitical priests.

---

## SEMITIC AND HAMITIC GENEOLOGIC LINKS OF THE PATRIARCHS

ABRAHAM + HAGAR (Egyptian)

ISHMAEL + (Egyptian Wife)
MOSES + (Ethiopian Wife)
JOSEPH + (Egyptian Wife)

ESAU + (Hamitic Wife)
JUDAH + (All Wives Hamitic)

## TABLE OF NATIONS

* see Josephus pg. 30, 31

### SONS OF HAM (Genesis & I Chronicles)

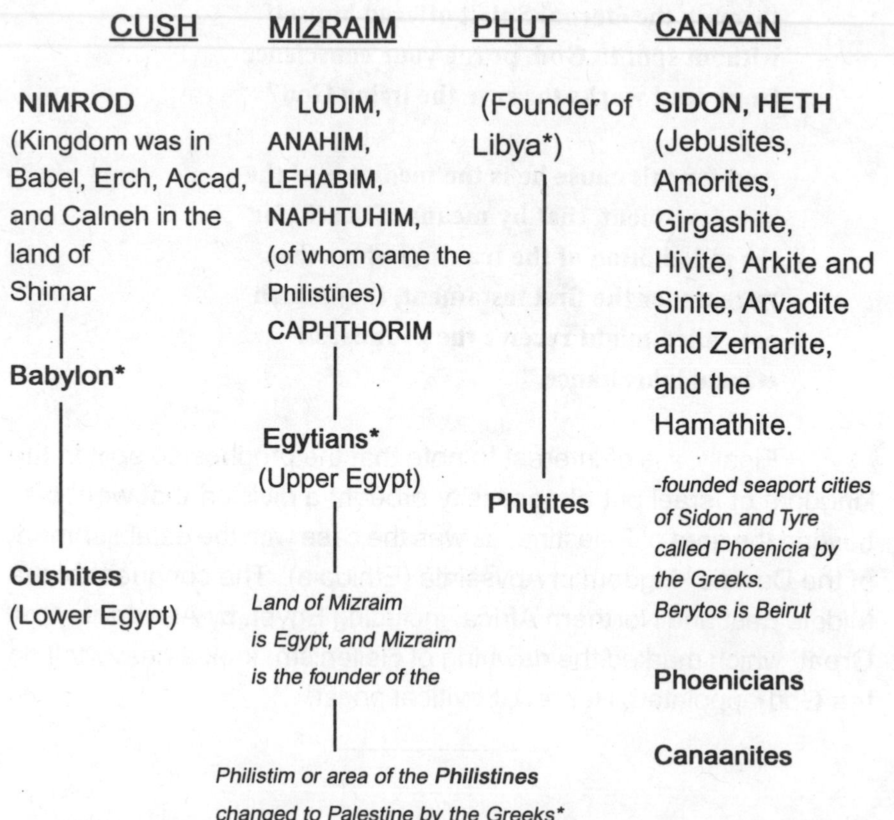

# SONS OF SHEM (SEM)

**Genesis (10:22):**

The children of Shem; Elam,
and Asshur, and Arphaxad,
and Lud, and Aram.

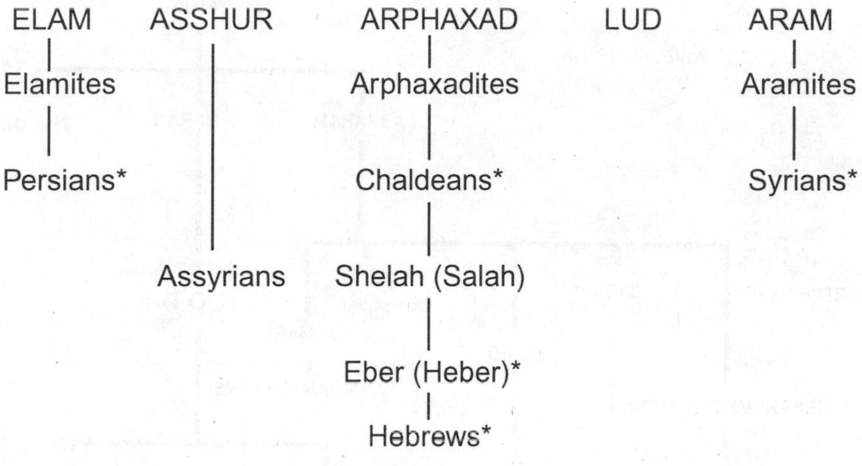


**(Chronicles 1:18)**
And Arphaxad begat Shelah,
and Shelah begat Eber.

In ancient times, the families settled in areas that were given the same name as the family grew into a tribe, then at times becoming a city or nation of people.

Family names which had become the names of geographical areas were changed by the Greeks.

* Complete Works of Josephus, pp. 31,32

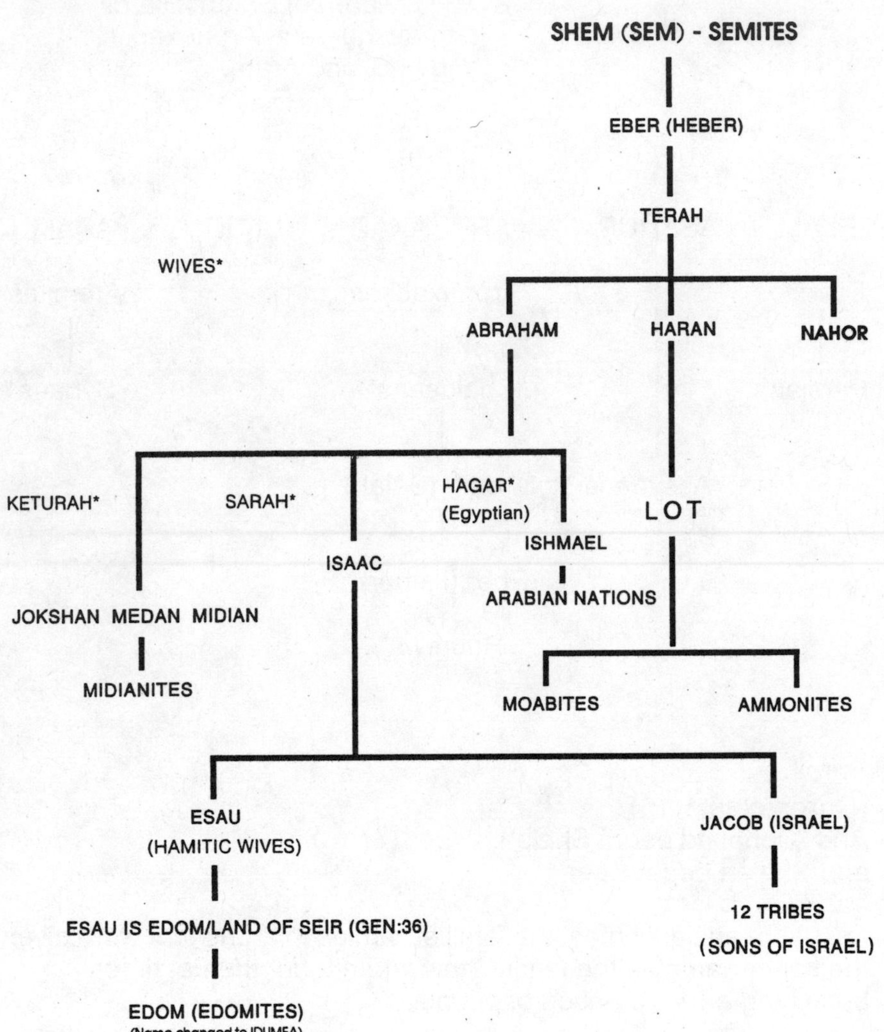
SHEM (SEM) - SEMITES
EBER (HEBER)
TERAH
WIVES*
ABRAHAM
HARAN
NAHOR
KETURAH*
SARAH*
HAGAR*
(Egyptian)
LOT
ISHMAEL
ISAAC
ARABIAN NATIONS
JOKSHAN MEDAN MIDIAN
MIDIANITES
MOABITES
AMMONITES
ESAU
(HAMITIC WIVES)
JACOB (ISRAEL)
12 TRIBES
(SONS OF ISRAEL)
ESAU IS EDOM/LAND OF SEIR (GEN:36)
EDOM (EDOMITES)
(Name changed to IDUMEA)

When Malachi, the last book of the Old Testament, was written in approximately 450 B.C., the city states of the Greeks had been recently formed, as Rome had not yet emerged as a formidable empire. To the contrary, the Phoenicians and Carthaginians continued to monopolize large areas of what was to become Southern Spain and Southerly portions of Italy including Cilicia, as they effectively contained the Romans until approximately 265 B.C. It has been argued that this ability to hold Rome at bay was recognized by Alexander, who made no attempt to invade this North African Empire that extended deep into Europe. It should be pointed out that beyond Greece and later Roman civilization, Europe as we know it today did not exist, and accordingly, the word appears nowhere in the scriptures. Outside of these areas the wandering Germanic tribes continued to do so , including the Anglo-Saxons which did not invade Britain successfully until after 600 A.D.

* Complete Works of Josephus, pp. 30,31

# ISLES OF THE GENTILES

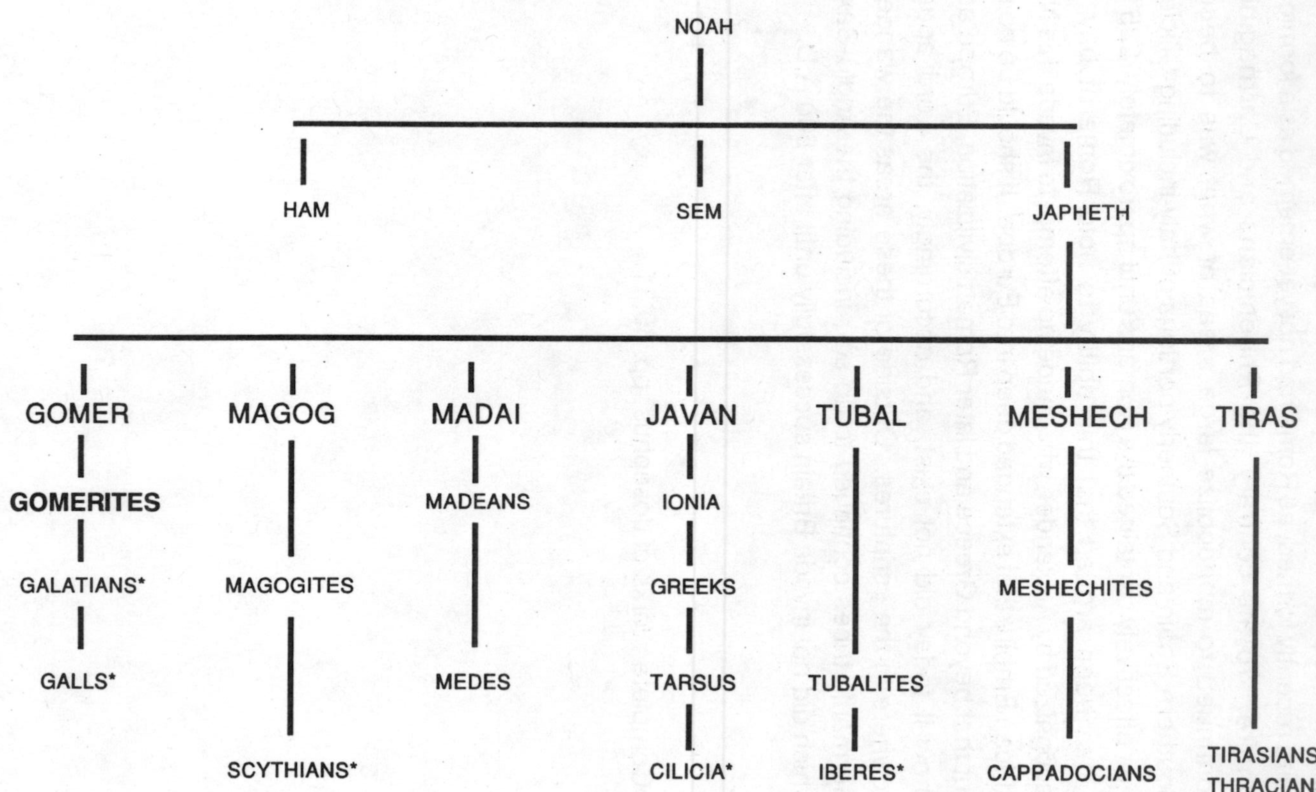

# PATRIARCHS MATRIARCHS AND LINEAGE TO THE PRIESTHOOD

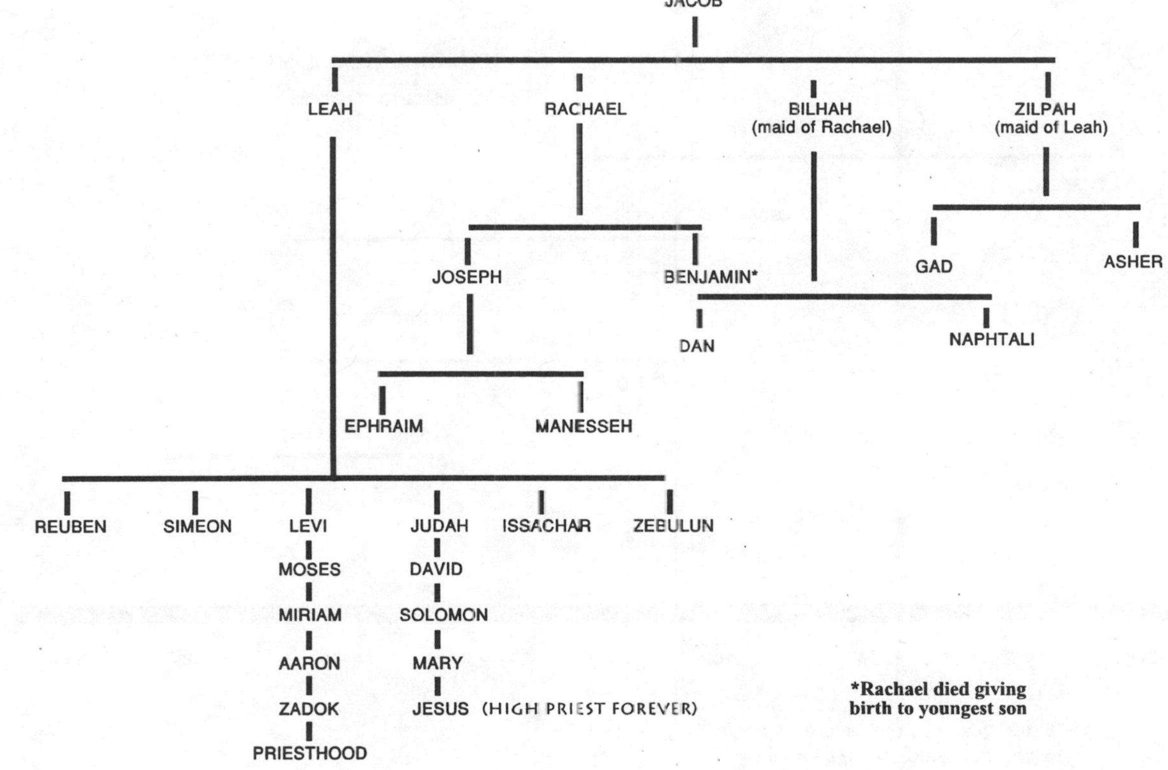

# BIRTH OF ABRAHAM TO THE DEATH OF JOSEPH (361 YEARS)

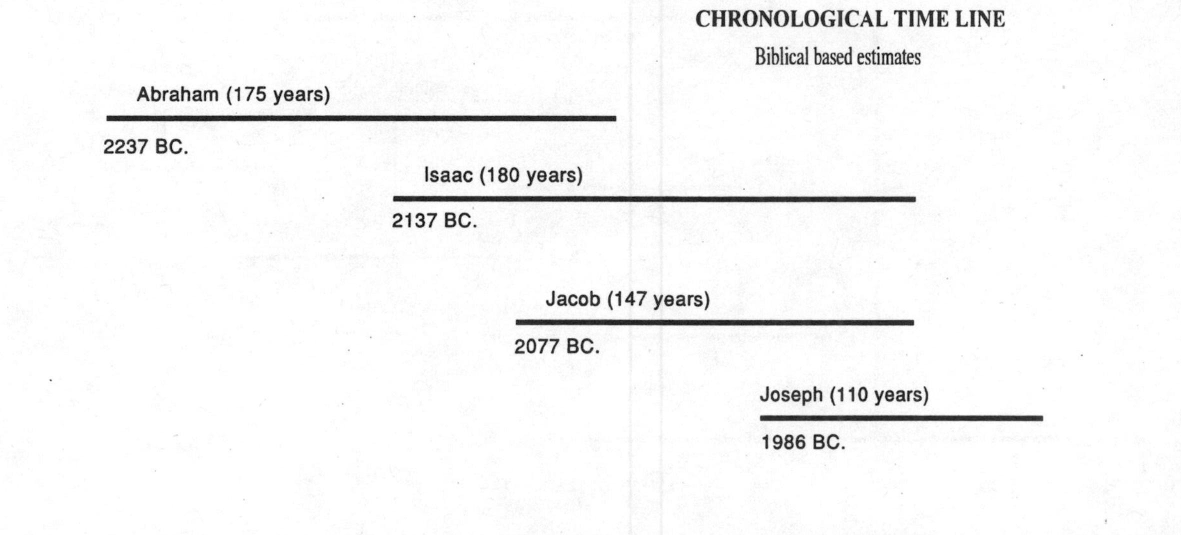


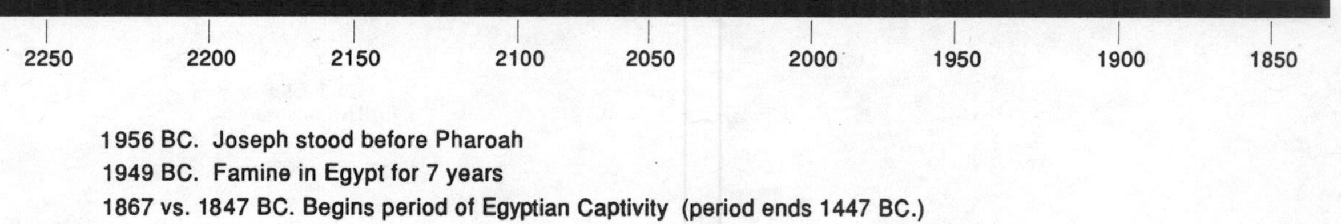


1956 BC. Joseph stood before Pharoah
1949 BC. Famine in Egypt for 7 years
1867 vs. 1847 BC. Begins period of Egyptian Captivity (period ends 1447 BC.)

As Ashur
At Athens
Az Axum
B Babylon
Ca Carthage
Cr Crete
Cy Cypress
E Elam
H Haran
J Jerusalem (Salem)
Je Jericho
K Kush
M Macedonia
Ma Mauretania
N Numidia
Ni Ninevah
P Phoenicia
Ph Philistim (Philistines)
R Rome
SC Scythia
SH Sheba
Th Thrace

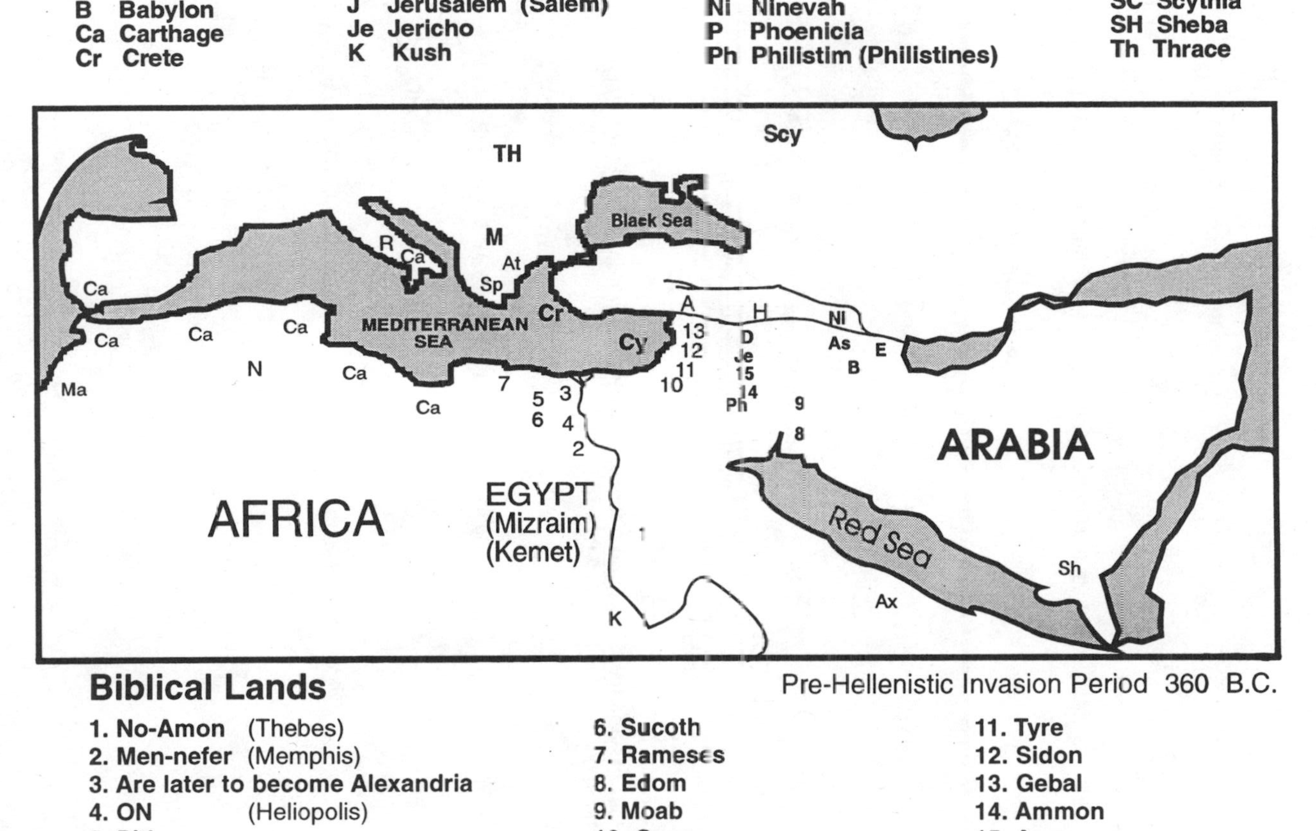


## Biblical Lands

Pre-Hellenistic Invasion Period 360 B.C.

1. No-Amon (Thebes)
2. Men-nefer (Memphis)
3. Are later to become Alexandria
4. ON (Heliopolis)
5. Pithom
6. Sucoth
7. Rameses
8. Edom
9. Moab
10. Gaza
11. Tyre
12. Sidon
13. Gebal
14. Ammon
15. Aram

* Ca Carthagian Empire was Phoenician controlled

## Part IV notes:

[1]A Salute to Historic African Kings and Queens, Vol 6, p 11

[2]Black Athena, Vol. II, p. 640

[3]The Old Testament Survey, p. 26

[4]Holman Bible Dictionary, p. 623

[5]A Salute to Historic African Kings and Queens, p. 11

[6]Ibid., p. 11.

[7]The Sign and the Seal, Graham Hancock, p. 4.

[8]The Complete Works of Josephus, p. 425

[9]The Complete Works of Josephus, Translated by William Whiston, p. 185.
[10]Ibid., p. 186.

[11]The Complete Works of Josephus, p. 186.

[12]The Bible as History, Werner Keller, p. 224

[13]Ibid.

[14]Ibid

[15]Holman Bible Dictionary, p. 80

[16]The Ancient Engineers, L. Sprague DeCamp, p.37

[17]Herodotus, p. 248.

[18]The Complete Works of Josephus, p. 222.

## PART V

## DISPERSION OF THE HEBREWS (DIASPORA)

As has been previously described, the nation of Israel was split between the son of Solomon, Rehoboam, whose following included the tribes of Judah and Benjamin; and Jeroboam, who served as a servant of Solomon, who went on to lead the remaining ten tribes as had been foretold by the prophet Ahijah in the days of Solomon. Thus the Northern Kingdom (Israel) was founded under Jeroboam, whereas the Southern Kingdom (Judah) was formed under Rehoboam, the latter of which retained control over the temple in Jerusalem. Meanwhile, the followers of Jeroboam eventually made Tirjah their capitol which continued until, once again, the followers of Jeroboam (Israel) further divided into two parts.

**I Kings (16:21-24):**

> **"Then the people of Israel divided into two parts: half of the people followed Tibni the son of Ginath to make him king; and half followed Omri.**
>
> **But the people that followed Omri prevailed against the people that followed Tibni the son of Ginath: so Tibni died and Omri reigned.**
>
> **In the thirty and first year of Asa king of Judah began Omri to reign over Israel, twelve years: six years reigned he in Tirzah.**
>
> **And he bought the hill Samaria of Shemer for two talents of silver and built on the hill, and called the name of the city which he built, after the name of Shemer, owner of the hill, Samaria."**

I Kings (16:25, 28-30):

> **"But Omri wrought evil in the eyes of the Lord, and did worse than all that were before him."**
>
> **"So Omri slept with his fathers, and was buried in Samaria: and Ahab his son reigned in his stead.**
>
> **And in the thirty and eighth year of Asa king of Judah began Ahab the son of Omri to reign over Israel: and Ahab the son of Omri reigned over israel in Samaria twenty and two years.**
>
> **And Ahab the son of Omri did evil in the sight of the Lord above all that were before him."**

Asa became the king of Judah during the twentieth year of reign of Jeroboam over Israel, and he continued to reign for forty-one years in Jerusalem. Asa was looked upon with favor. I Kings (15:11-14):

> **"And Asa did that which was right in the eyes of the Lord, as did David his father.**
>
> **And he took away the sodomites out of the land, and removed all the idols that his fathers had made.**
>
> **And also Maachah his mother, even her he removed from being queen, because she had made an idol in a grove; and Asa destroyed her idol, and burnt it by the brook Kidron.**
>
> **But the high places were not removed: nevertheless Asa's heart was perfect with the Lord all his days."**

On the other hand, the Northern Kingdom (Israel) continued

**ASSYRIAN KING SARGON II 722 - 705 B.C.**

NORTHERN KINGDOM OF ISRAEL PERIOD OF CAPTIVITY

the practice of idolatry and when Ahab, Omri's son, became king of Israel, he went on to marry Jezebel who in turn, convinced him to make the city the center of worship for Baal.

**I Kings (16:31-32):**

> **"And it came to pass, as if it had been a light thing for him to walk in the sins of Jeroboam, the son of Nebat, that he took to wife Jezebel the daughter of Ethbaal king of the Zidonians, and went and served Baal, and worshipped him.**
>
> **And he reared up an altar for Baal in the house of Baal, which he had built in Samaria."**

Ahab was killed in a battle with the Assyrians and subsequently was buried in Samaria. Meanwhile, Jehoshaphat, son of Asa, began to reign over Judah in the fourth year of Ahab's reign as the king of Israel. Jehoshaphat was thirty-five years old when he began his reign and he continued to reign for twenty-five years in Jerusalem. **I Kings (22:43-44):**

> **"And he walked in all the ways of Asa his father; he turned not aside from it, doing that which was right in the eyes of the Lord: nevertheless the high places were not taken away; for the people offered and burnt incense yet in the high places.**
>
> **And Jehoshaphat made peace with the king of Israel."**

In contrast, as compared to the king of Judah, the king of Israel who was now Ahaziah, the son of Ahab, continued idolatry and the worship of Baal. **I Kings (22:51-53):**

> **"Ahaziah the son of Ahab began to reign over Israel in Samaria the seventeenth year of Jehoshaphat king of Judah, and reigned two years over Israel.**

**And he did evil in the sight of the Lord, and walked in the way of his father, and in the way of his mother, and in the way of Jeroboam the son of Nebat who made Israel to sin:**

**"For he served Baal, and worshiped him, and provoked to anger the Lord God of Israel, according to all that his father had done."**

The Northern Kingdom fell to Assyria in approximately 721 B.C. **II Kings (17:5-7):**

**"Then the king of Assyria came up throughout all the land, and went up to Samaria, and besieged it three years.**

**In the ninth year of Hoshea the king of Assyria took Samaria, and carried Israel away into Assyria, and placed them in Halah and in Habor by the river of Gozan, and in the cities of Medes.**

**For so it was, that the children of Israel had sinned against the Lord their God, which had brought them up out of the land of Egypt, from under the hand of Pharaoh king of Egypt, and had feared other gods."**

The Diaspora refers to the dispersion of the Hebrews into other geographical areas with the first such dispersion occurring under Assyrian domination. **11 Kings (17:22-23):**

**"For the children of Israel walked in all the sins of Jeroboam which he did; they departed not from them;**

**Until the Lord removed Israel out of his sight, as he had said by all his servants the prophets. So was israel carried away**

**out of their own land to Assyria unto this day."**

In addition, it can be said that the king of Assyria was largely responsible for other groups then immigrating into the city of Samaria after their abandonment by the Israelites who had been taken into captivity by the Assyrians. **II Kings (17:24):**

**"And the king of Assyria brought men from Babylon, from Cuthah, and from Ava, and from Hamath, and from Sepharvaim, and placed them in the cities of Samaria instead of the children of Israel: and they possessed Samaria, and dwelt in the cities thereof."**

Thus the Northern Kingdom (Israel) of the Hebrews was completely disrupted. **II Kings (18:11-12):**

**"And the king of Assyria did carry away Israel unto Assyria, and put them in Halah and in Habor by the river of Gozan, and in the cites of the Medes:**

**Because they obeyed not the voice of the lord their God, but transgressed his covenant, and all that Moses the servant of the Lord commanded, and would not hear them, nor do them."**

Now only the Southern Kingdom (Judah) remained intact and it was Hezekiah, the son of Ahzaz, king of Judah, that reigned at that time. **II Kings (18:3-9):**

**"And he did that which was right in the sight of the Lord, according to all that David his father did.**

**He removed the high places, and brake the images, and cut down the groves, and brake in pieces the brasen serpent that Moses had made: for unto those days the children of Israel did burn incense to it: and he called**

**it Nehushtan.**

**He trusted in the Lord God of Israel; so that after him, none was like him among all the kings of Judah, nor any that were before him.**

**For he clave to the Lord, and departed not from following him, but kept his commandments, which the Lord commanded Moses.**

**And the Lord was with him; and he prospered whithersoever he went forth: and he rebelled against the king of Assyria, and served him not.**

**"He smote the Philistines, even unto Gaza, and the borders thereof, from the tower of the watchmen to the fenced city.**

**And it came to pass in the fourth year of the king Hezekiah, which was the seventh year of Hoshea son of Elah king of Israel, that Shalmaneser king of Assyria came up against Samaria, and besieged it."**

Ten years later, Sennacherib, king of Assyria prepared to take the fenced city of Judah. II Kings (19:15-16):

**"And Hezekiah prayed before the Lord, and said, O Lord God of Israel, which dwellest between the cherubims, thou art the God, even thou alone, of all the kingdoms of the earth; thou hast made heaven and earth.**

**Lord, bow down thine ear, and hear: open, Lord, thine eyes, and see: and hear the words of Sannacherib, which hath sent him to reproach the living God."**

II Kings (19:20):

> **"Then Isaiah the son of Amoz sent to Hezekiah, saying, Thus saith the Lord God of Israel, That which thou hast prayed to me against Sennacherib king of Assyria I have heard."**

II Kings (19:32-35):

> **"Therefore thus saith the Lord concerning the king of Assyria, He shall not come into this city, nor shoot an arrow there, nor come before it with shield, nor cast a bank against it.**
>
> **By the way that he came, by the same shall he return, and shall not come into this city, saith the Lord.**
>
> **For I will defend this city, to save it, for mine own sake, and for my servant David's sake.**
>
> **And it came to pass that night, that the angel of the Lord went out, and smote in the camp of the Assyrians an hundred fourscore and five thousand: and when they arose early in the morning, behold, they were all dead corpses."**

Concerning the king of Assyria, Sennacherib, through the prophet, Isaiah, it was foretold that he would die by the sword in his own land. II Kings (19:7):

> **"Behold, I will send a blast upon him, and he shall hear a rumour, and shall return to his own land; and I will cause him to fall by the sword in his own land."**

II Kings (19:36-37):

> **"So Sennacherib king of Assyria departed, and went and returned, and dwelt at Nineveh.**
>
> **And it came to pass, as he was worshipping**

**in the house of Nisroch his god, that Adrammelech and Sharezer his sons smote him with the sword: and they escaped into the land of Armenia. And Esarhaddon his son reigned in his stead."**

Nineveh is worthy of mention here, in that it is perhaps the oldest civilization on the face of the earth, being established by Nimrod **(Genesis 10:9-12).** It was the greatest of the capitols of the ancient Assyrian empire, located in the area of Mesopotamia which today is known as Iraq. The demise of Nineveh was foretold in the biblical book of Nahum. **Nahum (3:7):**

**"And it shall come to pass, that all they that look upon thee shall flee from thee, and say, Nineveh is laid waste: who will bemoan her? whence shall I seek comforters for thee?"**

Concerning the subject of Judah once again, that is, the Southern Kingdom, while it was spared the attack of the Assyrians through divine intervention, it was foretold by Isaiah the Prophet that the day would come when the kingdom of Judah would fall under the siege of a distant power, the Babylonians. **II King (20:16-18):**

**"And Isaiah said unto Hezekiah, Hear the word of the Lord.**

**Behold, the days come, that all that is in thine house, and that which thy fathers have laid up in store unto this day, shall be carried into Babylon: nothing shall be left, saith the Lord.**

**And of thy sons that shall issue from thee, which thou shalt beget, shall they take away; and they shall be eunuchs in the palace of the king of Babylon."**

**II Kings (20:20)** continues:

**"And the rest of the acts of Hezekiah, and**

**all his might, and how he made a pool and a conduit, and brought water into the city, are they not written in the book of the chronicles of the kings of Judah?"**

The water system that was created by Hezekiah can still be seen today in Jerusalem and in itself is somewhat of an amazing entity, in that it is a tunnel which was cut through stone beneath the earth by two teams of diggers working one at each end. It is still uncertain to this day how the two teams working, that is, digging independent of one another, were able to meet and have the tunnels interconnect at the mid point.

Manasseh, the son of Hezekiah, reigned for 55 years in Jerusalem. Unfortunately, Manasseh re-established idolatry and the worship of Baal and he made a grove just had been the case of the former king of Israel, Ahab, before its fall. Manasseh did the unthinkable, in that, he went on to place a graven image of the grove In the temple of the Lord which had been the former resting place of the Ark of the Covenant. **(II Kings 21:6-13)**:

**"And he made his son pass through the fire, and observed times, and used enchantments, and dealt with familiar spirits and wizards: he wrought much wickedness in the sight of the Lord, to provoke him to anger.**

**And he set a graven image of the grove that he had made in the house, of which the Lord said to David, and to Solomon his son, In this house, and in Jerusalem, which I have chosen out of all the tribes of Israel, will I put my name for ever:**

**Neither will I make the feet of Israel move any more out of the land which I gave their fathers; only if they will observe to do according to all that I have commanded them, and according to all the law that my servant**

**Moses commanded them.**

**But they hearkened not: and Manasseh seduced them to do more evil than did the nations whom the Lord destroyed before the children of Israel.**

**And the Lord spake by his servants the prophets, saying,**

**Because Manasseh king of Judah hath done these abominations, and hath done wickedly above all that the Amorites did, which were before him, and hath made Judah also to sin with his idols:**

**Therefore thus saith the Lord God of Israel, Behold, I am bringing such evil upon Jerusalem and Judah, that whosoever heareth of it, both his ears shall tingle.**

**And I will stretch over Jerusalem the line of Samaria, and the plummet of the house of Ahab: and I will wipe Jerusalem as a man wipeth a dish, wiping it, and turning it upside down."**

On the death of Manasseh, his son, Amon began his reign at the age of twenty-two; however, he reigned for only two years in Jerusalem since he, too, served the idols of his father and worshipped them. Amon was the victim of a conspiracy which was initiated by his own servants; however, following his death, the people rose up against those that had conspired against him and Josiah, the son of Amon, became the reigning king of Judah. It was during that time that Hilkiah, the high priest, found a long-lost book of the law in the temple which, indeed, revealed that the wrath of the Lord would fall upon Judah. **II Kings (22:16-17):**

**"Thus saith the Lord, Behold, I will bring evil upon this place, and upon the inhabitants thereof, even all the words of the book which**

**the king of Judah hath read:**

**Because they have forsaken me, and have burned incense unto other gods, that they might provoke me to anger with all the works of their hands; therefore my wrath shall be kindled against this place, and shall not be quenched."**

II Kings (23:1-7):

**"And the king sent, and they gathered unto him all the elders of Judah and of Jerusalem.**

**And the king went up into the house of the Lord, and all the men of Judah and all the inhabitants of Jerusalem with him, and the priests, and the prophets, and all the people, both small and great: and he read in their ears all the words of the book of the covenant which was found in the house of the Lord.**

**And the king stood by a pillar, and made a covenant before the Lord, to walk after the Lord, and to keep his commandments and his testimonies and his statutes with all their heart and all their soul, to perform the words of this covenant that were written in this book. And all the people stood to the covenant.**

**And the king commanded Hilkiah the high priest, and the priests of the second order, and the keepers of the door, to bring forth out of the temple of the Lord all the vessels that were made for Baal, and for the grove, and for all the host of heaven: and he burned them without**

**Jerusalem in the fields of Kidron, and carried the ashes of them unto Beth-el.**

**And he put down the idolatrous priests, whom the kings of Judah had ordained to burn incense in the high places in the cities of Judah, and in the places round about Jerusalem;**
**them also that burned incense unto Baal, to the sun, and to the moon, and to the planets and all the host of heaven.**

**And he brought out the grove from the house of the Lord, without Jerusalem, unto the brook Kidron, and burned it at the brook Kidron, and stamped it small to powder, and cast the powder thereof upon the graves of the children of the people.**

**And he brake down the houses of the sodomites that were by the house of the Lord, where the women wove hangings for the grove."**

Unfortunately, all of Judah was not in accord with Josiah, as described in II Kings (23:8-9):

**"And he brought all the priests out of the cities of Judah, and defiled the high places where the priests had burned incense, from Geba to Beer-sheba, and brake down the high places of the gates that were in the entering in of the gate of Joshua the governor of the city, which were on a man's left hand at the gate of the city.**

**Nevertheless the priests of the high places came not up to the altar of the Lord in Jerusalem, but they did eat of the unleavened bread among their brethren."**

In an attempt to alter the fate of Judah as it had been written in the book of the Old Testament which was found by the priests, Josiah continued in his attempt to purge the holy land of its idol worshippers, even leaving Jerusalem to go to the land of Samaria that had been inhabited by the Israelites prior to its being taken into captivity by the Assyrians. **II Kings (23:20,24):**

> **"And he slew all the priests of the high places that were there upon the altars, and burned men's bones upon them, and returned to Jerusalem.**
>
> **Moreover the workers with familiar spirits, and the wizards, and the images, and the idols, and all the abominations that were spied in the land of Judah and in Jerusalem, did Josiah put away, that he might perform the words of the law which were written in the book that Hilkiah the priest found in the house of the Lord."**

However, the scriptures were to be fulfilled as **II Kings (23:25-27)** continues:

> **"And like unto him was there no king before him, that turned to the Lord with all his heart, and with all his soul, and with all his might, according to all the law of Moses; neither after him arose there any like him.**
>
> **Notwithstanding the Lord turned not from the fierceness of his great wrath, wherewith his anger was kindled against Judah, because of all the provocations that Manasseh had provoked him withal.**
>
> **And the Lord said, I will remove Judah also out of my sight, as I have removed Israel, and will cast off this city Jerusalem which I have chosen, and the house of which I said, My name shall be there."**

King Josiah of Israel entered into a battle which was raging between the Egyptian Pharaoh Necho II (Wehemibre) and the Assyrians during which time he was killed. **II Kings (23:29-30):**

> **"In his days, Pharaoh-nechoh king of Egypt went up against the king of Assyria to the river Euphrates: and king Josiah went against him; and he slew him at Megiddo, when he had seen him.**
>
> **"And his servants carried him in a chariot dead from Megiddo, and brought him to Jerusalem, and buried him in his own sepulchre. And the people of the land took Jehoahaz the son of Josiah, and anointed him, and made him king in his father's stead."**

The reign of Jehoahaz, who was twenty-three years old at the time, was very brief, in that he reigned only three months in Jerusalem before being taken prisoner by Pharaoh, with Pharaoh-Necho II making Eliakim, also a son of Josiah, king in place of Josiah, his father. **(II Kings 23:31-37.)** It was Pharaoh Necho II that changed the name of Eliakim to Jehoiakim, and Jehoiakim paid a taxation to Egypt in silver and gold according to the commandment of Pharaoh.

In accordance with the scripture, the king of Babylon, Nebuchadnezzar made Jehoiakim, king of Judah, his servant for three years, at which time Jehoiakim rebelled against him and the scriptures were fulfilled. II **Kings (24:1-3):**

> **"In his days, Nebuchadnezzar king of Babylon came up, and Jehoiakim became his servant three years: then he turned and rebelled against him.**
>
> **And the Lord sent against him bands of the Chaldees, and bands of the Syrians, and bands of the Moabites, and bands of the children of Ammon, and sent them against Judah to destroy it, according to the word of the Lord, which he spake by his servants the prophets.**

**Surely at the commandment of the Lord came this upon Judah, to remove them out of his sight, for the sins of Manasseh, according to all that he did;"**

Jehoiakim died during the siege, and his son, Jehoiachin, surrendered the city to the Babylonians in 597 B.C. All of Jerusalem, including the men of valor were taken to Babylon where they were held in captivity for seventy years. Nebuchadnezzar, the king of Babylon, appointed Mattaniah, his father's brother king of Jerusalem and thereafter changed his name to Zedekiah.

**II Kings (24:18-20):**

**"Zedekiah was twenty and one years old when he began to reign, and he reigned eleven years in Jerusalem. And his mother's name was Hamutal, the daughter of Jeremiah of Libnah.**

**And he did that which was evil in the sight of the Lord, according to all that Jehoiakim had done.**

**For through the anger of the Lord it came to pass in Jerusalem and Judah, until he had cast them out from his presence, that Zedekiah rebelled against the king of Babylon."**

It was this invasion by Nebuchadnezzar of Jerusalem that led to the large destruction of the city, including the holy temple **(II Kings 21:1-22)**. The subsequent invasion of Babylon by king Nebuchadnezzar was foretold in the book of Jeremiah.

**Jeremiah (46:25-26):**

**"The Lord of hosts, God of Israel, saith; Behold, I will punish the multitude of No, and Pharaoh, and Egypt, with their gods, and their kings; even Pharaoh, and all them that trust in him:**

**And I will deliver them into the hand of**

**those that seek their lives, and into the hand of Nebuchadrezzar king of Babylon, and into the hand of his servants: and afterward it shall be inhabited, as in the days of old, saith the Lord."**

At this point, it appeared as though the nation of Israel had been completely disrupted, but the prophesy of Jeremiah, as it continued, made it clear that this was not, indeed, the end of Israel. **Jeremiah (46:27-28):**

**"But fear not thou, O my servant Jacob, and be not dismayed, O Israel: for, behold, I will save thee from afar off, and thy seed from the land of their captivity; and Jacob shall return and be in rest and at ease, and none shall make him afraid.**

**Fear thou not, O Jacob my servant, saith the Lord: for I am with thee; for I will make a full end of all the nations whither I have driven thee: but I will not make a full end of thee, but correct thee in measure; yet will I not leave thee wholly unpunished."**

We have now reached a critical point in the history of the Hebrew people in which both the Northern Kingdom and the Southern Kingdom ceased to exist, their inhabitants being taken as captives and the ten tribes of Samaria vanishing as a nation of people. The Assyrian conquest of the Northern Kingdom occurred as a result of the expansionist activities of its king, Sargon II. (See plate.) As has been previously discussed, those of the Southern Kingdom (Judah) who comprised the remaining two tribes, that is, of Judah and Benjamin, were taken into captivity by the Babylonians.

From a religio-philosophical perspective, it is interesting to note that the Babylonians, or more specifically, the Chaldeans were also Hebrews, as it will be recalled that Abraham himself was a Chaldean. These Semitic people were known as fierce fighters and were the driving force behind the establishment of the New Babylonian Empire. King Nabopolassar's reign in Babylon brought the Chaldeans to power. This Semitic people established a new Babylonian empire (626-539 B.C.). Nabopolassar's son, Nebuchadnezzar II (604-562) built the city of Babylon in splendor, creating the famed "hanging gardens.[1] It should be recalled that Abraham believed in one God and was separated from the Chaldeans who practiced polytheism. Thus, even though the Chaldeans were Hebrews through ancestry, that is, they were the descendants of Heber and a Semitic people (Heber was a descendant of Sem), they shared a different religious philosophy than did Abraham and later Moses. The idolatry of the Chaldean Hebrews included Bel and Merodach. By the time of the Babylonian captivity, many of the Hebrews of Judah had adopted polytheism which included the worship of Baal; however, under the yoke of Babylonian captivity, many reverted back to monotheism as they called upon God to release them and allow their return to Judah. Meanwhile, the Babylonians continued in idolatry worship and their fate, as well as that of the children of Israel was foretold in **Jeremiah (50:1-13):**

> **"The word that the Lord spake against Babylon and against the land of the Chaldeans by Jeremiah the prophet.**
>
> **Declare ye among the nations, and publish, and set up a standard; publish, and conceal not: say, Babylon is taken, Bel is confounded, Merodach is broken in pieces; her idols are confounded, her images are broken in pieces.**
>
> **For out of the north there cometh up a nation against her, which shall make her land desolate, and none shall dwell therein: they shall remove, they shall depart, both man and beast.**
>
> **In those days, and in that time, saith the Lord, the children of Israel shall come, they and the children of Judah together, going and weeping: they shall go, and seek**

**the Lord their God.**

**They shall ask the way to Zion with their faces thitherward, saying, Come, and let us join ourselves to the Lord in a perpetual covenant that shall not be forgotten.**

**My people hath been lost sheep: their shepherds have caused them to go astray, they have turned them away on the mountains: they have gone from mountain to hill, they have forgotten their resting-place.**

**All that found them have devoured them: and their adversaries said, We offend not, because they have sinned against the Lord, the habitation of justice, even the Lord, the hope of their fathers.**

**Remove out of the midst of Babylon, and go forth out of land of the Chaldeans, and be as the he goats before the flocks.**

**For, lo, I will raise and cause to come up against Babylon an assembly of great nations from the north country: and they shall set themselves in array against her; from thence she shall be taken: their arrows shall be as of a mighty expert man; none shall return in vain.**

**And Chaldea shall be a spoil: all that spoil her shall be satisfied, saith the Lord.**

**Because ye were glad, because ye rejoiced, O ye destroyers of mine heritage, because ye are grown fat as the heifer at grass, and bellow as bulls;**

**Your mother shall be sore confounded; she**

**that bare you shall be ashamed: behold, the hindermost of the nations shall be a wilderness, a dry land, and a desert.**

**Because of the wrath of the Lord it shall not be inhabited, but it shall be wholly desolate: every one that goeth by Babylon shall be astonished, and hiss at all her plagues."**

The prophesy continues, **Jeremiah (50:29, 38):**

**"Call together the archers against Babylon: all ye that bend the bow, camp against it round about; let none thereof escape: recompense her according to her work; according to all that she hath done, do unto her: for she hath been proud against the Lord, against the Holy One of Israel."**

**"A drought is upon her waters; and they shall be dried up: for it is the land of graven images, and they are mad upon their idols."**

The prophesy of Jeremiah continues, **Jeremiah (51:5-6, 11):**

**"For Israel hath not been forsaken, nor Judah of his God, of the Lord of hosts; though their land was filled with sin against the Holy Oneof Israel. Flee out of the midst of Babylon, and deliver every man his soul: be not cut off in her iniquity; for this is the time of the Lord's vengeance; he will render unto her a recompence."**

**"Make bright the arrows; gather the shields; the Lord hath raised up the spirit of the kings of the Medes: for his device is against Babylon, to destroy it; because it is the vengeance of the Lord, the vengeance of his temple."**

Prior to this prophesy by Jeremiah concerning the fall of Babylon, there was another interesting turn of events just prior which had followed the conquest of Jerusalem by the Babylonian king Nebuchadnezzar, as previously described in **II Kings (24:14):**

> **"And he carried away all Jerusalem, and all the princes, and all the mighty men of valour, even ten thousand captives, and all the craftsmen and smiths: none remained save the poorest sort of the people of the land."**

King Jehoiachin was also taken into captivity, and his father's brother, Mattaniah, was made the new king of Jerusalem by the king of Babylon who changed his name to Zedekiah.
**II Kings (24: 18-20):**

> **"Zedekiah was twenty and one years old when he began to reign, and he reigned eleven years in Jerusalem. And his mother's name was Hamutal, the daughter of Jeremiah of Libnah.**
>
> **And he did that which was evil in the sight of the Lord, according to all that Jehoiakim had done.**
>
> **For through the anger of the Lord it came to pass in Jerusalem and Judah, until he had cast them out of his presence, that Zedekiah rebelled against the king of Babylon."**

So now for an expanded account of what occurred between the time of Zedekiah's appointment and his ultimate revolt against Babylon, we turn to the ancient historian, Josephus:

"Now when Zedekiah had preserved the league of mutual assistance he had made with the holy Babylonians for eight years, he brake it, and revolted to the Egyptians, in hopes, by their assistance, of overcoming the Babylonians. When the king of Babylon knew this, he made war against him. He laid his country to waste, and took his fortified towns and came to the city of Jerusalem itself to besiege it: But when the king of Egypt heard what circumstances Zedekiah, his ally was in, he took a great army with him, and came into Judea, as if he would raise siege; upon which the king of Babylon departed from Jerusalem, and met the Egyptians, and joined battle with them, and beat them; and when he had put them to flight, he pursued them, and drove them out of all Syria." [2]

Then, the prophet Jeremiah offered advice to King Zedekiah, as taken from Josephus: "That he should deliver the city up to the Babylonians; and he said, that it was God who prophesied this by him, that [he must do so] if he would be preserved, and escape out of the danger he was in, and that then neither should the city fall to the ground, nor should the temple be burned; but that [if he disobeyed,] he would be the cause of these miseries coming upon the citizens, and of the calamity that would befall his whole house. The king heard this, he said that he would be willing to do what he persuaded him to, and what he declared would be to his advantage, but that he was afraid of those of his own country that had fallen away to the Babylonians, lest he should be accused by them to the king of Babylon, and be punished." [3]

Rather than delivering the city of Jerusalem to the Babylonian king, Zedekiah took his family and fled; however, he was caught and accused by Nebuchadnezzar, who had appointed him king, of being a traitor and was taken into captivity in Babylon. The high priest, Josedek was also carried away into captivity. **II Kings (25:7-12):**

**"And they slew the sons of Zedekiah before his eyes, and put out the eyes of Zedekiah, and bound him with fetters of brass, and carried him to Babylon.**

**And in the fifth month, on the seventh day of the month, which is the nineteenth year of king Nebuchadnezzar king of Babylon, came Nebuzaradan, captain of the guard, a servant of the king of Babylon, unto Jerusalem:**

**And he burnt the house of the Lord, and the king's house, and all the houses of Jerusalem, and every great man's house burnt he with fire.**

**And all the army of the Chaldees, that were with the captain of the guard, brake down the walls of Jerusalem round about.**

**Now the rest of the people that were left in the city, and the fugitives that fell away to the king of Babylon, with the remnant of the multitude, did Nebuzaradan the captain of the guard carry away.**

**But the captain of the guard left of the poor of the land to be vinedressers and husbandmen."**

So the temple burning under Nebuzaradan occurred in the year 586 B.C., eleven years after the period of the Babylon captivity of the Hebrews had begun under Nebuchadnezzar in the year 597 B.C.

In fulfillment of the scriptures which had predicted the fall of Babylon, it was the Persian, Cyrus the Great, that united the Medes and the Persians in what became known as the Achaemenid Empire in the year 549 B.C. following the overthrow of his father-in-law, king Astyages, who had been the king of Medes. The Achaemenid Empire under Cyrus continued to expand and in fulfill-ment of the prophesy, in 539 the Chaldean-dominated Babylonian empire fell.

In the following year, a new era for the Hebrews began as Cyrus issued a decree claiming their freedom to return to Jerusalem. Since Cyrus had allowed the Hebrews the freedom of worship and observing their customs, many chose to remain in Babylon. II **Chronicles (36:21-23):**

**"To fulfill the word of the Lord, by the mouth of Jeremiah, until the land had enjoyed her sabbaths: for as long as she lay desolate**

**she kept sabbath, to fulfill three-score and ten years.**

**Now in the first year of Cyrus king of Persia, that the word of the Lord spoken by the mouth of Jeremiah might be accomplished, the Lord stirred up the spirit of Cyrus king of Persia, that he made a proclamation throughout all his kingdom, and put it also in writing, saying,**

**Thus saith Cyrus king of Persia, All the kingdoms of the earth hath the Lord God of heaven given me; and he hath charged me to build him an house in Jerusalem, which is in Judah. Who is there among you of all his people? The Lord his God be with him, and let him go up."**

Ezra (1:5-8):

**"Then rose up the chief of the fathers of Judah and Benjamin, and the priests, and the**

**Levites, with all them whose spirit God had raised, to go up to build the house of the Lord which is in Jerusalem.**
**And all they that were about them strengthened their hands with vessels of silver, with gold, with goods, and with beasts, and with precious things, beside all that was willingly offered.**

**Also Cyrus the king brought forth the vessels of the house of the Lord, which Nebuchadnezzar had brought forth out of Jerusalem, and had put them in the house of his gods;**

**Even those did Cyrus king of Persia bring forth by the hand of Mithredath the treasurer, and numbered them unto Sheshbazzar, the prince**

**of Judah."**

The very fact that such a prince could exist is reflective of the freer reign of Cyrus, who actually allowed willful control by the inhabitants of his kingdom. However, for those who returned to Jerusalem and started building the temple, some of the adversaries of the Hebrews hired counselors to interfere and block the building of the temple throughout the remainder of the reign of Cyrus.
Ezra (4:1-5):

> **"Now when the adversaries of Judah and Benjamin heard that the children of the captivity builded the temple unto the Lord God of Israel;**
>
> **Then they came to Zerubbabel and to the chief of the fathers, and said unto them, Let us build with you: for we seek your God, as ye do; and we do sacrifice unto him since the days of Esarhaddon king of Assur, which brought us up hither.**
>
> **But Zerubbabel, and Jeshua, and the rest of the chief of the fathers of Israel, said unto them, Ye have nothing to do with us to build an house unto our God; but we ourselves together will build unto the Lord God of Israel, as king Cyrus the king of Persia hath commanded us.**
>
> **Then the people of the land weakened the hands of the people of Judah, and troubled them in building.**
>
> **And hired counsellors against them, to frustrate their purpose, all the days of Cyrus king of Persia, even until the reign of Darius king of Persia."**

The Persian empire continued to flourish under Darius, who also encouraged the rebuilding of the temple; however, upon completion of the temple, although many of the items which had been previously taken had been returned to the Hebrews to refurnish

**Darius the Great** issued a drecree for the rebuilding of the Hebrew temple built in **538 B.C.**

*Standing behind the Persian King Darius is his son Xerxus (ahasuerus ). The son of Xerxus was Artaxerxus to whom the prophet Nehemiah was cup bearer during his captivity. (Nehemiah 2:1)*

*Wall relief from palace at Persepolis*

**Stairway to the Persian palace of Darius the great**
548 - 486 B.C.

the temple, one object remained conspicuously missing, as had been prophesied by Jeremiah the prophet. **Jeremiah (3:16):**

> **"And it shall come to pass, when ye be multiplied
> and increased in the land, in those days,
> saith the Lord, they shall say no more,
> The ark of the covenant of the Lord: neither
> shall it come to mind: neither shall they
> remember it; neither shall they visit it;
> neither shall that be done any more."**

Josephus specifically identifies the enemies of the tribes of Judah and Benjamin as the Samaritans. Recalling now that two-hundred years earlier, the Northern Kingdom of Samaria was completely disrupted as its inhabitants were taken into captivity, with only the poor remaining, and according to Josephus, they had grown evil.

"But when the Samaritans, who were still enemies to the tribes of Judah and Benjamin, heard the sound of the trumpets, they came running together and desired to know what was the occasion of this tumult; and when they perceived that it was from the Jews who had been carried captive to Babylon, and were rebuilding their temple, they came to Zorobabeel and to Jeshua and to the heads of the families, and desired that they would give them leave to build the temple with them, and to be partners with them in building it; for they said, 'We worship their God, and especially pray to Him, and are desirous of their religious settlement, and this ever since Shalmaneser, the king of Assyria, transplanted us out of Cuthah and Medea to this place.'"[4]

So it was these people then, the transplanted plus the remnant of the poor that were left behind following the exile of the Hebrews into Babylon, that in the period which followed, became the Samaritans. For further insight in as to why the Samaritans were the enemies of the Hebrews, as previously described, we now turn to Josephus, page 230, wherein it is described how Darius came to the conclusion that the Hebrews should be released, as well as what led to their conflict with the Samaritans upon their return.

In what was seemingly an anniversary party after his first

year of reign, in which he hosted the rulers of the lands within his own empire, Josephus gives us this account:

"Now in the first year of the king's reign, Darius feasted those that were about him, and those born in his house, with the rulers of the Medes, and the princes of the Persians, and the toparchs of India and Ethiopia, and the generals of the armies of his hundred and twenty-seven provinces; but when they had eaten and drunken to satiety and abundantly, they everyone departed to go to bed at his own house, and Darius the king went to bed; but after he had rested a little part of the night, he awaked and not being able to sleep anymore, he fell into conversation with the three guards of his body, and promised that to him who should make an oration about points that he should inquire of, such as should be most agreeable to truth, and to the dictates of wisdom, he would grant it as a reward for his victory, to put on a purple garment, and to drink in cups of gold, and to sleep upon gold, and to have a chariot with bridles of gold, and a head-tire of fine linen, and a chain of gold about his neck, and to sit next to himself, on account of his wisdom: 'And, says he, he shall be called by cousin.'"[5]

Then it followed that after listening to the discourse of the first two, it was Zorobabell whose oration most pleased the king for its wisdom and truth, and as his reward, Zorobabell was granted his wish that he be allowed to return to Jerusalem with the Hebrews that were to be freed and given free rein to rebuild the temple, which had been pillaged and burned earlier. And the decree was written.

"He also sent letters to those rulers that were in Syria and in Phoenicia to cut down and carry cedar trees from Lebanon to Jerusalem, and to assist him in building the city. He also wrote to them, that all the captives who should go to Judea should be free; and he prohibited his deputies and governors to lay any king's taxes upon the Jews: He also permitted that they should have all the land which they could possess themselves of without tributes. He also enjoined the Idumeans and the Samaritans and the inhabitants of Coelesyria, to restore those villages which they had taken from the

Jews; and that, besides this, fifty talents should be given them for the building of the temple."[6]

Thus, because they had to give up the land which they had previously inherited when the Hebrews entered exile, especially when coupled by the decree that they not be taxed, it can be seen how the animosity of the Samaritans in the area could grow to such an extent that they could now be described as enemies.

In their attempt to block the rebuilding of the temple, the Samaritans wrote to King Darius that the temple that was being built by the Hebrews appeared to be more like a fort than a temple. However, it was about this time that some of the earlier records of King Cyrus had surfaced, amongst which was a book in which it was written as follows:

"Cyrus the king, in the first year of his reign, commanded that the temple should be built in Jerusalem; and the altar in the height three-score cubits, and its breadth of the same with three edifices of polished stone, and one edifice of stone of their own country; and he ordained that the expenses of it should be paid out of the king's revenue. He also commanded that the vessels which Nebuchadnezzar had pillaged [out of the temple] and had carried to Babylon, should be restored to the people of Jerusalem; and that the care of these things should belong to Sanabassar, the governor and president of Syria and Phoenicia, and his associates, that they may not meddle with that place, but may permit the servants of God, the Jews and their rulers, to build the temple."[7]

Upon finding this book, Darius directed the Samaritans and others in the area not to obstruct the Hebrews in their rebuilding of the temple, and he sent them a copy of the epistle from which King Cyrus' decree had been read and instructed them that they were to follow the instructions, as had been written. And indeed, the temple was finished in seven years. Thus the prophesies of Haggai, who was the first of the prophets who spoke to the exiles after they had returned to Palestine, were fulfilled.

The ministry of Haggai began in 520 B.C. and overlapped

that of Zechariah. It is felt that the final text of the Old Testament, that is, the book of Malachi, was written between 400 and 433 B.C.

It is important at this time to reiterate that the Old Testament was written in Hebrew or the literal "lip of Canaan" (Isaiah 19:18). As previously discussed, the word "Jew" is a Greek term which made its first appearance in the Old Testament at the time in which the scriptures were translated into Greek, almost two-hundred years after the final book of Malachi had been written. The Old Testament was not available in any European language until a portion of the Old Testament was paraphrased, known as the Targum, which in approximately 300 B.C. was translated into Greek. There was no complete translation of the Old Testament Scriptures until 200 B.C., which came to be known as the Septuagint. It was during the Greek translation that the terms "Jew" and "Hebrew" were used interchangeably, and this followed the European invasion of Mesopotamia and Northern Africa and what has been described as the "Dawn of Hellenism."

In the original transcription of the Hebrew text, there were seventy books. This is an important fact which is alluded to in the account of the crucifixion which was written by Nicodemus.

> **"And it is our custom annually to open this holy book for an assembly, and to search there for the counsel of God. And we found in the first of the seventy books, where Michael, the archangel is speaking to the third son of Adam the first man, an account that after five-thousand five-hundred years, Christ, the most beloved son of God was to come to earth."**[8]

Even though the Greek translation of the text came to eventually represent something less than seventy books, the name "Septuagint" which literally means "seventy" remained. When later asked why the book was called the Septuagint, the response was that it resulted from seventy scholars sitting down for seventy-two days, working independent, but miraculously transcribing the text of the Hebrews word for word into Greek without any variation amongst the seventy scholars.

The subsequent translation into Latin and other European languages was largely dependent upon the Greek translation of the original Hebrew text. This was necessary as the result of an unfortunate practice by the Greeks, in that following the translation of the Hebrew text, they frequently buried them or destroyed the original writings. "The difficulty of tracing the history of the Old Testament text is the scarcity of the manuscripts that go back beyond the 9th and 10th centuries. One reason for this scarcity is the practice by Jewish scribes of burying old manuscripts in a storehouse called a "genizah" and then destroying these manuscripts."[9]

---

## Part V notes:

[1]Biblical Times, Amanda O'Neill, p. 52.

[2]The Complete Works of Josephus, p. 218.

[3]Ibid, p. 219

[4]Ibid, p.232

[5]Ibid. p.230

[6]The Complete Works of Josephus, p. 230.

[7]Ibid. p.233.

[9]Lost Books of the Bible, Nicodemus 22:10-11.

[10]Holman Bible Dictionary, p. 184

## PART VI

## INVASION OF HELLENISM

The Hellenistic Age has been defined as "the period which began with the conquest of Alexander the Great and ended about three hundred years later: characterized by the spread of Greek language and culture throughout the Near East."[1] As previously alluded to, Alexander's campaign also extended into North Africa, and more specifically, Egypt. The Hellenistic Period impacted heavily upon the Hebrews and all people of the known world at that time, and had more to do with the adoption of other cultural traditions than with the spread of Greek civilization. Certainly, it can be said that spiritual wisdom was lacking on the part of the Greeks, in that it will be recalled that prior to the conquest of this region by Alexander, the Old Testament scriptures did not exist in Greek or any European language, and as a result, Greeks, Macedonians, Alexander included, as well as the Romans, were all pagan worshipers.

The Greek historian, Herodotus, wrote the classic, The Histories in approximately 450 B.C., that is more than one hundred years prior to the onset of the Hellenistic Period. Herodotus wrote that Greek culture was largely borrowed from Egyptian culture and that even the "Greek gods" came to Greece from Egypt. "The names of nearly all the gods came to Greece from Egypt."[2] "I was told that this Heracles was one of the twelve gods. Of the other Heracles, with whom the Greeks are familiar, I could get no information anywhere in Egypt. Nevertheless, it was not the Egyptians who took the name "Heracles" from the Greeks. The opposite is true: It was the Greeks who took it from the Egyptians-those Greeks, I mean, who gave the name to the son of Amphitryon. There is plenty of evidence to prove the truth of this, in particular the fact that both the parents of Heracles - Amphitryon and Alcmene - were of Egyptian origin."[3]

The modern day linguist, Martin Bernal, writes, "I believe that many of the Greek divine names, such as Apollo, Athena and so on, were in fact Egyptian and that when Herodotus said 'name' he usually meant just that, name."[4] Even the columnar style of architecture which became the hallmark of classical Greek temples was borrowed from Egyptian temple architecture which had already been in existence for centuries. "The familiar three orders of classical Greek temple columns - doric, ionic and corinthian - probably evolved from Egyptian temple columns with their lotus, papyrus and date palm capitals."[5]

We now know, due to the discovery of mathematical tablets found in Egypt, that knowledge of geometry, including what is now called Pythagoras' Theorem, existed thousands of years in Egypt prior to the birth of Pythagoras. Even the Greek historian, Herodotus, acknowledged that geometry was not invented in Greece. "Perhaps this was the way in which geometry was invented, and passed afterwards into Greece - for knowledge of the sundial and gnomon and the twelve divisions of the day came into Greece from Babylon."[6] "Although the professions of architect (architekton), engineer (technites), and machine maker (mechanopoios), were recognized as respectable, Greek technical achievements of the Golden Age were rather modest." "The streets of most Greek cities were muddy, filthy alleys, although a few were paved with slabs of fieldstone with a dressing of mortar. There was no attempt at drainage."[8]

The aforementioned statements seem to suggest that Hellenism was something other than the one way spread of Greek culture. A truer reflection of what took place can probably be found in the following account which offers, "Alexander and the successors founded scores of new cities in the conquered lands. They encouraged thousands of Greeks and Macedonians to settle in these cites side by side with Persians, Syrians, Egyptians, and other native people. Hellenes swarmed out of barren Greece to serve in the armies and bureaucracies of the successors, forming a ruling class in the new kingdoms. The interloping Greeks soon mingled with the native upper classes. Greek culture influenced the Orientals, while Oriental ideas affected the Greeks. The brilliant Graeco-Oriental civilization that resulted is called the Hellenistic."[9]

It should be pointed out at this time to the reader that Northeast Africa, that is, Egypt and the area extending into and including Mesopotamia was often referred to as Oriental civilization.

Many of the Greek practices were considered to be unclean. "This is the reason why no Egyptian, man or woman, will kiss a Greek or use a Greek knife, spit, or cauldron or even eat the flesh of a bull known to be clean, if it has been cut with a Greek knife."[10]

Herodotus is considered to be amongst the greatest of the Greek historians whose work survives to this day. Not unlike many of the other scholars of his time, Herodotus spent a considerable amount of time in Egypt, which was considered to be the educational and cultural center of the ancient world. He was certainly in a good position to contrast the two cultures. Accordingly, he wrote, "I will never admit that the similar ceremonies performed in Greece and Egypt are the result of mere coincidence - had that been so, our rites would have been more Greek in character and less recent in origin. Nor will I allow that the Egyptians ever took over from Greece either this custom or any other."[11]

It can now be seen that the assertions of the ancient historians such as Herodotus would seem to suggest that in his zeal to conquer other distant lands, Alexander, the Macedonian, was motivated by forces other than a zeal to spread "culture." If a psychological profile were to be drawn from the historical accounts of major events which occurred in his life, out of necessity it would reflect that he was driven largely by mythical fantasies, dreams and a self-perception of grandiosity which placed him in the realm of the gods. In fairness to Alexander, even prior to his becoming the king of Macedonia at the young age of 21, there were forces present which paved the way for destiny and his ultimate fate which was that he was to die in battle at the age of 32 with the dubious distinction of having killed more people than any other person in history up until that point in time.

The fledgling Greek city-states were never considered to be a threat by Egypt or the Persian empire which later included all of

Mesopotamia and North Africa, including Egypt. If for no other reason than for their sheer numbers, the military force of the Persian empire was considered to be unsurmountable, and part of its strength came from mercenary forces from various countries, including Greece. Certainly, Macedonia, which was the least of the Greek city-states, was an unlikely threat to the Persian empire, that is, until the discovery of gold, which occurred just prior to the reign of Philip II, king of Macedon, which began in 359 B.C.

"In the opening years of his reign, Philip II, king of Macedon (359-336 B.C.), transformed the levee of his backwoods state into the largest and most efficient force in Greece."[12] Philip used gold to exert influence, as well as to build the strongest military force in Greece. Then, using the latter, he was able to annex Thessaly in 352 B.C. The desire of Philip II for power and control over the Greek city-states continued, and in 338 B.C., "The combined Theban-Athenian army was crushed at the battle of Chaeronea and the states of Greece forcibly enrolled into a pan-Hellenic league that took its orders from Philip. One of Philip's first announcements to the league proclaimed a crusade against Persia."[13] Two years later, Philip II was assassinated, thus his desire to conquer the Persian empire was not accomplished in his lifetime.

Meanwhile, Philip had assembled a huge army which had to be paid by his successor, Alexander, at a time in which the treasury was nearly bankrupt. If Alexander was to realize the dream of his father, that is, the conquest of Persian-dominated Asia, he would have to move swiftly, before the cost of the army would bankrupt his country. His plan was simple, that is, simply to begin the march toward Asia immediately, but to sack smaller countries along the way, and in confiscating their treasuries, he was able to not only sustain his military, but to build upon it, oftentimes hiring as mercenaries the remnants of defeated troops, rather than taking them as prisoners of war or killing them en masse. It was this tactic which caught Darius III, who was then king of the Persian empire, completely off guard, even though he was warned of the approaching army of Alexander.

Alexander's first encounter with Persian forces occurred near the Granicus River. Darius III had not yet joined his army at that time. Amongst the Persian forces there were 15,000 Greek mercenaries, but the Macedonian forces were better equipped for hand-to- hand combat. Accordingly, the scrimmage went badly for the Persian forces which ultimately retreated. "The Persians fell into confusion, then into flight. Alexander let them go; he concentrated his assault upon the Greek mercenaries, whom he regarded as traitors to Greece."[14]

"He also gave rites of burial to the Persian commanders and the Greek mercenaries who fell fighting in the enemy's ranks; the Greek prisoners he sent in chains to hard labor in Macedonia, as punishment for contravening the resolution of the League of Corinth by fighting in a foreign army against their own countrymen."[15] Following this initial route of Persian forces, the Greek coastal cities of Sardas and Ephesus, which were under Persian domination, were immediately surrendered to Alexander upon his arrival, as they had already heard of the defeat of the Persian forces and the city of Ephesus had already inspired the local people to kill their leaders which had supported Persian rule. "During the same period, representatives came from the towns of Magnesia and Tralles to offer their submission; he accordingly dispatched Parmenio with a force consisting of 2500 allied foot, 2500 Macedonians, and about 200 companion cavalry, giving instructions for a similar force under Alcimachus, son of Agathocles to proceed to the Aeolian towns and all the Ionian ones still subject to Persia."[16]

Alexander marched on to Milletus where once again a small Persian garrison which exerted control over the town, went down in defeat. Alexander continued his march towards Asia where city after city fell until he reached the Pinarus River where, for the first time, he was to meet Darius III in what proved to be a decisive battle in the quest for the Persian empire. By this point in time, the mercenary forces which had been added to the military of Alexander as he marched on toward Asia had grown both in terms of numbers and diversity. At the time of this meeting, it has been estimated that the Persian forces under Darius III were six-hundred thousand; thirty thousand of which were Greek mercenaries who now faced the Greek forces of Alexander, the Macedonian, whose Macedonian forces were thought to be a lesser number. Modern historians have contended that the estimates of the size of both the Persian force, as well as that of Alexander, had been greatly exaggerated. Such historians have placed the number of Greek mercenaries under Darius as being closer to twelve thousand, while the Macedonian segment of the troops under Alexander have been placed at five thousand. In any case, Darius faced a somewhat different army than he had anticipated in a carnival-like atmosphere, which included Darius III's own family members watching from the sidelines began to rapidly dissipate as Alexander's forces approached the battlefield.

The Persian army under Darius III's command was largely made up of mercenaries, as was the case of Alexander's. He took position on one side of the stream, with Alexander's forces lining up on the opposite side of the stream. Although clearly out- numbered, Alexander's forces prepared for the charge, which would involve not only crossing the stream, but negotiating a fairly steep grade on the other side which was thought to be still another advantage for the forces of Darius III which waited along the bank. From this point on, the nature and order of events which took place in what came to be known as "The Battle of Issus" varies somewhat from one historical text to the next, but the net effect was the same, in that Alexander's forces prevailed, forcing Darius III to flee into the desert, leaving behind his family. "Darius' headquarters were stormed and captured; his mother was taken, together with his wife (who was also his sister) and his infant son; in addition to these, two of his daughters fell into Alexander's hands with a few noble Persian ladies who were in attendance upon them."[17] Darius III escaped into the night and by the following day, approximately four thousand of his soldiers and mercenaries had reassembled.

Meanwhile, the Phoenicians who had been long-time trading partners with Greece remained neutral in their walled city of Tyre. Within the walls of Tyre was the most ancient temple of Heracles that was known to man at that time. As previously mentioned, the Egyptians also worshipped a Heracles, who according to Herodotus, was different from the Heracles of Greece. In any case, upon reaching the city, Alexander expressed a desire to offer a sacrifice; however, the Tyrians refused to admit any Persian or Macedonian within the walls of the city. This denial reportedly angered Alexander who was concerned that if he chose to march on to Egypt, having uncommitted Phoenicia at his back, along with the forces of Darius III, those forces could conceivably coalesce behind him or worse yet, focus an attack on Greece. Therefore, Alexander decided to take Tyre by force which would thereby enable him to enlist its powerful fleet of ships and militia under his command.

"Alexander had no difficulty in persuading his officers that the attempt upon Tyre must be made. He himself had further encouragement by a sign from heaven, for that very night, he dreamed that as he was approaching the walls of the town, Heracles greeted him and invited him to enter."[18] Despite this dream, this turned out to be perhaps the most difficult battle that Alexander had faced up until this time. In addition to the high walls of the city, it was actually situated on an island, in that, it was separated from the shore by a body of water. In addition, "Stone throwing catapults, first mentioned in connection with Alexander's siege of Tyre (minus 332) may have been invented in Phoenicia."[19] Of necessity, the battle plan against Tyre had to include engineers for the building of ramps and bridges which would be needed to scale the high walls of this island city.

Meanwhile the city of Jerusalem and the Hebrews who had rebuilt the temple were not very far away. However, his encounter with the holy city is not discussed in the majority of the texts which otherwise give a full accounting of the various events which occurred during his conquest of Asia, including Mesopotamia. For such an accounting, it is once again necessary for us to turn to Josephus who tells us that during the siege of Tyre, Alexander had sent to Jerusalem asking for provision for his troops, "But the high priest answered the messengers, that he had given his oath to Darius not to bear arms against him; and he said that he would not transgress this while Darius III was in the land of the living. Upon hearing this answer, Alexander was very angry; and though he determined not to leave Tyre, which was just ready to be taken, yet, as soon as he had taken it, he threatened that he would make an expedition against the Jewish high priest, and through him teach all men to whom they must keep their oaths. The siege of Tyre lasted for seven months before the city fell, then Alexander marched on to Gaza and a war which took still another two months. Following the conquest of Gaza, Alexander returned to Jerusalem."[20]

"Now Alexander, when he had taken Gaza, made haste to go up to Jerusalem; and Jaddua, the high priest, when he heard that, was in agony, and under terror, as not knowing how he should meet the Macedonians, since the king was displeased at his foregoing dis- obedience. The priest declared that he had arrived at the decision to welcome the Macedonian king, along with all the citizens of Jerusalem in a procession in which they were to be fully dressed. It was revealed to him in a dream that if he adhered to the plan which was to come to him from God, the Hebrews would not suffer any ill consequences from the Macedonian king."[21]

"...and when the Phoenicians and Chaldeans that followed him, thought that they should have liberty to plunder the city, and torment the high priest to death, which the king's displeasure fairly promised them, the very reverse of it happened; for Alexander, when he saw the multitude at a distance, in white garments, while the priests stood clothed with fine linen, and the high priest in purple and scarlet clothing, with his miter on his head, having the golden plate whereon the name of God was engraved, he approached by himself, and adored that name, and first saluted the high priest."[22]

Josephus continues, "However, Parmenio alone went up to him, and asked him how it came to pass, that when all others adored him, that he should adore the high priest of the Jews? To whom he replied, "I did not adore him, but that God who hath honored him with his high priesthood; for I saw this very person in a dream, in this very habit, when I was at Dios in Macedonia, who when I was considering with myself how I might obtain a dominion of Asia, exhorted me to make no delay, but boldly to pass over the sea thither, for that he would conduct my army and would give me the dominion over the Persians; whence it is, that having seen no other in that habit, and now seeing this person in it, and remembering that vision and the exhortation which I had in my dream, I believe that I bring this army under divine conduct, and shall therewith conquer Darius and destroy the power of the Persians, and that all things will succeed according to what is in my own mind."[23]

According to Josephus, "The book of Daniel was shewed him wherein Daniel declared that one of the Greeks should destroy the empire of the Persians, he supposed that himself was the person intended; and as he was then glad, he dismissed the multitude for the present, but the next day he called them to him, and bade them ask what favors they pleased of him; whereupon the high priest desired that they might enjoy the laws of their forefathers, and might pay no tribute on the seventh year. He granted all they desired; and when they entreated him that he would permit the Jews in Babylon and Media to enjoy their own laws also, he willingly promised to do hereafter what they desired: and when he said to the multitude, that if any of them would enlist themselves in his army on this condition, that they should continue under the laws of their forefathers, and live according to them, he was willing to take them with him, many were ready to accompany him in his wars."[24]

Alexander did, indeed, march on to Egypt and he found that the Persian forces under Darius III were very small and he took the cities without a battle. While Egypt contained great wealth in its treasuries, perhaps the greatest treasure was to be found in the books of the temples which contained an accumulation of knowledge dating back nearly five thousand years. It was with these same texts, largely, that Alexander went on to found the library and city of Alexandria which was to become the new center for higher education, not only in Egypt, but for the world. It should be pointed out that Alexander was no stranger to books in that Aristotle, who himself had studied in Egypt, became Alexander's teacher at the age of thirteen. That relationship continued and grew over a several-year period. Following the translation of the various texts which were collected at Alexandria, some of the students of Aristotle were later credited as being the authors of those books. Many of the texts in the library at Alexandria were written by the Egyptian high priest, Manetho.

"In the introduction of the statute of Serapis to Alexandria, as described by Plutarch (Manetho, FR. 80), Manetho the Egyptian was associated with the Greek Timotheus as a priestly advisor of King Ptolemy Soter. It is natural to suppose that the cult of Serapis itself, which is a conflation of Egyptian and Greek ideas intended to be acceptable to both nationalities, had already been organized with the help of the two priests and the magnificent temple in Rhakotis, the Egyptian quarter in the west of Alexandria, had doubtless been built."[25]

"Among Egyptians who wrote in Greek, Manetho, the priest, holds a unique place because of his comparatively early date (3rd century B.C.) and the interest of his subject matter - the history and religion of ancient Egypt."[26]

Alexander never saw the city of Alexandria or its great library since shortly after laying out its plans, he continued his war campaign, this time heading for deeper inside Asia Minor to, more specifically, the Arabian countries. He died en route without ever reaching the Arabian countries. However, the exact means of his death are unknown, just as the exact motivating factors behind his need to conquer people in distant lands have also remained a mystery. The entire epic is even more puzzling when one considers the fact that he never bothered to even seriously govern any of the lands which he had conquered, and as a result, following his death, the empire was divided amongst his generals and others who were in high command, with the biggest prize of Egypt going to first his son, and eventually to the Greek family of Ptolemy.

"The Greeks borrowed ideas from the Egyptians, the Babylonians, and the Phoenicians, much as these people in their time had borrowed ideas from each other. The remarkable thing about the Greeks of the Golden Age is that they made so much of their borrowings so quickly."[27]

While it has been previously mentioned that the tribes of Benjamin and Judah, which comprised the Southern Kingdom in Jerusalem, were carried off to Babylon during the period of the

Babylonian captivity which lasted for seventy years, it is a lesser known fact that the Chaldean-led Persian empire which was to follow, once again took captives from Jerusalem, but this time into Egypt as slaves. According to Josephus, "When Alexander had reigned twelve years, and after him Ptolemy Soter forty years, Philadelphius then took the kingdom of Egypt and held it for forty years within one. He procured the law to be interpreted, and set free those that were come from Jerusalem into Egypt, and were in slavery there, who were a hundred and twenty thousand."[28]

The reign of Philadelphius (Ptolemy II) was 285-246 B.C. While freeing a hundred and twenty thousand Hebrews was certainly a significant event in the reign of Ptolemy II (Philadelphius), the hallmark event which was to leave an indelible imprint on that period of time, was the fact that it was during this reign that the Old Testament was transcribed into Greek in its entirety for the first time. As has been previously mentioned, only the Targums, which paraphrased certain aspects of the Old Testament and had been transcribed less than one hundred years earlier, remained the sole access that the Greeks had to the Old Testament.

The king had endeavored to collect all the books of the earth into his private library at Alexandria. Demetrius Phalerius was in charge of making such acquisitions at any cost. The collection of books had already exceeded two hundred thousand when Demetrius brought it to Ptolemy's attention that the Hebrews had many books of the laws of their God which were written in Hebrew and would require a considerable effort to transcribe these volumes into Greek, but that it was an undertaking that might be worthwhile, as the Hebrews had believed that the texts were inspired by God. It was therefore suggested by Aristeus, who was a close friend of the king, that to assist them in getting the laws, not only copied, but transcribed into Greek, something of significance should be offered and he suggested that the king issue a decree in which the Hebrews, who were then captives in Egypt, should be freed. The king agreed and the decree was issued, the king himself paying each slave holder from the royal treasury, an amount which exceeded four hundred and sixty talents of gold.

An epistle was then drawn up in which the high priest at Jerusalem was notified of the release of the Hebrews and the request for the scriptures. The request for the law and its translation was accompanied by a hundred talents in money which was to be sent to the temple as a sacrifice and for other uses, along with an assortment of gold basins and vessels. The name of the Hebrew high priest who received the correspondence from the king was Eleazar. A portion of the correspondence read as follows: "I have determined to procure an interpretation of your law, and to have it translated out of Hebrew into Greek and to be deposited in my library. Thou wilt therefore do well to choose out and send me men of good character, who are now elders in age, and six in number out of each tribe. These, by their age, must be skillful in the laws, and of abilities to make an accurate interpretation of them; and when this shall be finished, I shall think that I have done a work glorious to myself."[29]

The high priest, Eleazar accepted the request of the king and sent forth seventy elders to the city of Alexandria from Jerusalem. "And when they were to come to Alexandria, and Ptolemy heard that they were come, and that the seventy elders were come also, he presently sent for Andreas and Aristeus, his ambassadors, who came to him, and delivered him the epistle which they brought him from the high priest, and made answer to all the questions he put to them by word of mouth. He then made haste to meet the elders that came from Jerusalem for the interpretations of the law; and he gave command, that everybody who came on other occasions should be sent away, which was a thing surprising, and what he did not used to do;"[30]

"But when he had sent those away, he waited for these that were sent by Eleazar; but as the old men came in with the presents, which the high priest had given them to bring to the king, and with the membranes, upon which they had their laws written in gold letters, he put questions to them concerning those books; and when they had taken off the covers wherein they were wrapt up, they shewed him the membranes. So the king stood admiring the thinness of those membranes, and the exactness of the junctures, which could not be perceived, (so exactly were they connected one with another);

and this he did for a considerable time."[31]

Following their arrival, the king entertained the elders for several days as he marveled at their responses to various philosophical questions which he had asked them. The elders were taken across a bridge onto an island which had housing accommodations and was thought to be perfect for their purpose in that it was quiet and offered few distractions, as they now had begun to undertake this monumental task.

"Now when the law was transcribed, and the labour of interpretation was over, which came to its conclusion in seventy-two days, Demetrius gathered all the Jews together to the place where the laws were translated, and where the interpreters were, and read them over."[32]

The glory and honor which was heaped upon the Hebrews in Egypt by Ptolemy was not an isolated event, in that such honors were also given them by the kings of Asia. "The Jews also obtained honors from the kings of Asia, when they became their auxiliaries; for Seleucus Nicator made them citizens of those cities which he built in Asia, and in the lower Syria, and in the metropolis itself, Antioch; and gave them privileges equal to those of the Macedonians and Greeks, who were the inhabitants insomuch that those privileges continue to this very day;"[33]

"Judah's attachment to the kingdom of the Ptolemys lasted for more than one hundred years. The Seleucids of Antioch forced their way southward, an expansion for which they had long been striving. After a victorious battle against Ptolemy V at the sources of the Jordan, Antiochus III, called The Great, took over Palestine in 195 B.C., and Judah thereby once more came under a new sovereignty."[34] Just as the Hebrews had willingly surrendered their city to the conquering Alexander of Macedonia, the same was to be the case upon the arrival of the army of Antiochus III. Prior to the arrival of Antiochus' army, General Scopas of Ptolemy's army had overthrown the nation of the Jews in Jerusalem as he set up garrisons which were manned by Egyptian forces.

King Antiochus then in an epistle written to the conquered King Ptolemy, wrote "Since the Jews, upon our first entrance on their country, demonstrated their friendship towards us; and when we came to their city, Jerusalem, received us in a splendid manner, and came to meet us with their senate, and gave abundance of provisions to our soldiers, and to the elephants, and joined with us in ejecting the garrison of the Egyptians that were in the citadel, we have thought fit to reward them, and to retrieve the condition of their city, which has been greatly depopulated by such accidents as have befallen its inhabitants, and to bring those that have been scattered abroad back to the city;" The epistle continued, "I would also have the work about the temple finished, and the cloister, and if there be anything else that ought to be rebuilt; and for the materials of wood, that it be brought them out of Judea itself, and out of the other countries and out of Libanus, tax-free; and the same I would have observed as to those other materials which will be necessary, in order to render the temple more glorious; and let all that nation live according to the laws of their own country; and let the senate and the priests, and the scribes of the temple, and the sacred singers, be discharged from pole-money and the crown tax, and other taxes also.."[35]

King Antiochus went on to develop a friendship with the conquered Ptolemy, eventually even yielding his daughter, Cleopatra to be the wife of Ptolemy, and as part of the dowry he gave Coele-Syria, Samaria, Phoenicia and Judea as the kings agreed to share in the collection of taxes.

It is noteworthy and should be pointed out at this time that following the conquest of Alexander and the influx of the Greeks and Macedonians into Asia Minor and Egypt, a caste system based on race was introduced for the first time. As has been discussed, as an inducement for the Hebrews to provide Ptolemy II (Philadelphus) with a copy of the Old Testament which was to be translated from Hebrew into Greek, the Hebrews were granted equal status with the Greeks and Macedonians while those in captivity were freed from slavery. Up until this point in time, the Macedonians and Greeks alone, except for rare exceptions, enjoyed the privileges of their citizenship. As might be expected, the decree from King Ptolemy caused a protest among the privileged class which was well described by Josephus. However, before reviewing the account of Josephus, it is important to recall that the Hebrews were Chaldeans in that they were descendants from Abraham who was from Chaldea and genealogically linked to Shem (Sem). On the other hand, the gentiles were from the line of Japheth. **Genesis (10:2-5):**

> **"The sons of Japheth; Gomer, and Magog, and Madai, and Gavan, and Tubal, and Meshech, and Tiras.**
>
> **And the sons of Gomer; Ashkenaz, and Riphath, and Togarmah.**
>
> **And the sons of Javan: Elishah, and Tarshish, Kittim, and Dodanim.**
>
> **By these were the isles of the Gentiles divided in their lands; every one after his tongue, after their families, in their nations.:**

Josephus records the following: "Now as to Javan and Madai, the sons of Japheth; from Madai came the Madeas, who were called the Medes by the Greeks, but from Javan, Ionia and all the Grecians are derived."[36]

As we have previously discussed, in addition to equal rights being granted to the Hebrews by Ptolemy II, this was also true from the kings of Asia. "The Jews also obtained honors from the kings of Asia, when they became their auxiliaries; for Seleucus Nicator made them citizens of those cities which he built in Asia, and in the lower Syria, and in the metropolis itself, Antioch, and gave them privileges equal to those of the Macedonians and Greeks, who were the inhabitants, insomuch that those privileges continue to this very day";[37] It should be kept in mind that to this very day that Josephus alludes to was the period shortly following the death of Christ. Prior to that time, however, the Greeks were overcome by the Romans, as we will discuss in the following chapter, but Josephus continues:

"In which behavior anyone may discern the equity and generosity of the Romans, especially of Vespasian and Titus, who, although they had been at a great deal of pains in the war against the Jews, and were exasperated against them, because they did not deliver up their weapons to them, but continued the war to the very last, yet did not they take away any of their aforementioned privileges belonging to them as citizens, but restrained their anger.."[38]

Josephus continues concerning the Herod, Marcus Agrippa: "We also know that Marcus Agrippa was of the like deposition toward the Jews: for when the people of Ionia were very angry at them, and besought Agrippa, that they, and they only, might have those privileges of citizens which Antiochus, the grandson of Seleucus (who by the Greeks was called 'the god'), had bestowed on them; and desired that, if the Jews were to be joint partakers with them, they might be obliged to worship the gods they themselves worshiped: But when these matters were brought to trial, the Jews prevailed, and obtained leave to make use of their own customs, and this under the patronage of Nicolaus of Damascus; for Agrippa gave sentence that he could not innovate."[39]

Gentiles are defined as people who are not part of God's chosen family at birth and thus can be considered "pagans." Though not synonymous in English, "Gentiles," "nations," "pagans," "heathens," are variants chosen by translators to render "Goyim" in Hebrew and "ethnoi" in Greek. ("Gentile" and "nation" suggest race or territory, while "pagans" and "heathen" suggest religion.)

Following the consolidation of the Roman empire, which was to eventually absorb all of the formerly held Greek empire, those with Roman citizenship were placed at the highest level of class distinction, while the Greeks followed, along with the Hebrews, and finally most natives of the conquered lands were collectively referred to as "Ethiopians" or "Egyptians." It was of great significance that the Hebrews were granted equal status with the Greeks, since if they had been included in the lower caste system of the "Ethiopians," it is likely that Jesus himself may not have had the kind of access to the temple that he enjoyed under the separate classification of

"Hebrew."

"If you were an inhabitant of Egypt but not a Roman, a citizen of one of the four poleis, or a Jew, then to the Roman government you were an Egyptian. No matter that you were descended from six or seven generations of military reservists, that class of hereditary privilege settled on the land under the Ptolemys. That privilege status was now gone, and with it those ethnic designations by which you used probably to proclaim your family's origin in the Greek or Macedonian homeland - Coan, Cretean, Thessalian, and so forth. In the government records you were all now Egyptians, nothing more."[40]

From an ancient papyrus at the Berlin Egyptian Museums - Greek Urkunden, an excerpt of BGU 1210 reveals, No. 39: "If a Roman man or woman is joined in marriage with an urban Greek or an Egyptian, their children follow the inferior status...

No. 45: If an urban Greek marries an Egyptian woman and dies childless, the fisc appropriates his possessions; if he has children, it confiscates two-thirds. But if he has begotten children of an urban Greek woman and has three or more children,
his possessions go to them; if two children, a fourth or a fifth [to each], if one child, a half.

No. 49: Freed men of Alexandrians may not marry Egyptian women.

No. 51: The son of a Syrian man and an urban Greek woman married an Egyptian woman and was sentenced to a stated fine.

No. 53: Egyptians who, when married to discharged soldiers, styled themselves Romans are subject to the provision on violation of status."[41]

To present a comprehensive scope of world history is not the intent of this text which largely, instead, has focused upon those issues ultimately affecting the Hebrews. For instance, it was not the intent of this text to at all infer that following the conquest of Tyre by the army of Alexander that the seafaring activities of the Phoenicians had come to its final chapter. To the contrary, as early as the 8th century B.C., the Phoenicians had colonized the city of Carthage. At the time of the march of Alexander on Tyre in 332 B.C., Carthage had grown into an empire itself, extending along the northern coast of Africa from Egypt all the way to what is now known as Morocco, as well as a portion of Europe which included southern Spain and Sicily. Following the conquest of Egypt, it is not clear why Alexander did not march on to Carthage which was adjacent to Egypt. It is likely that he gave consideration to the fact that the Carthaginians and their formidable fleet were largely responsible for the earlier containment of the rising Roman power. Following the fall of Tyre to Alexander, the Phoenicians at Carthage were to continue maintaining their empire for still another hundred years.

Roman expansionism, a concern of Alexander who had left his home country of Macedonia, was effectively contained until the first Punic War (264-241 B.C.) "'Punic,' a contracted form of Phoenician, is used as a synonym for Carthaginian. It was the General Hannibal out of Carthage, that even today is held by many as the world's greatest wartime strategist, who came very close to an all out attack on Italy by crossing the Alps."[42] "...in the battle of Cannae, his masterpiece, Hannibal annihilated them. For the next decade, the Romans refused his offers of battle and restricted themselves to harassing him from the cities that, for lack of a siege train, he could not take. As the years passed, his position gradually deteriorated and the Romans gained the strategic initiative when they conquered Spain (210-206 B.C.). In 204 B.C., a Roman army landed on Carthaginian homeground. Hannibal, blockaded into ineffectuality in the Italian toe, was recalled to Africa, and finally met defeat at the battle of Zama (202); Carthage surrendered the next year."[43]

While given the circumstances, the Hebrews fared reasonably well during the periods of occupation by foreign invaders. At one point, the decree was reversed by Antiochus IV (reigned 175-164 B.C.). "In 169, he made a savage attack on Jerusalem, butchering many citizens and plundering the temple, and then set out to crush Judaism entirely. He desecrated the Jews' holy places, banned

Sabbath observation and circumcision, and ordered Jews to worship Zeus."[44]

These actions sparked what came to be known as the Maccabite rebellion which was lead by Judas Maccabeus. Following intense fighting, the Hebrews were able to re-enter Jerusalem in the year 165 B.C. "Judas was killed in the battle of Eleasa, and the contest for independence was successfully continued by his brothers, Jonathan and Simon until B.C. 135. Independence was granted in 142 B.C. "Reaction was swift, led by the Hasmonean (Maccabeus) family, 'The Maccabees,' and for eighty years the Jews had 'Independence' under Hasmonean rule (142-63 B.C.), until Pompey (106-48 B.C.) claimed Palestine for Rome. A nominal Jewish kingdom was permitted by the Romans under Herod the Great (37-4 B.C.), and to a greatly limited extent under other Herodian rulers."[45]

"The Romans were, as a rule, not harsh masters in their conquered provinces. Especially in the East, they were always willing to allow considerable religious and national liberty. But, unfortunately, the dynasty to which they confided the government of Palestine, the Herodian, was not of pure Hebrew descent: It came from Idumea. The Idumean rulers sometimes bearing the title of king, sometimes other titles, tried to pass themselves off as Jews among the Jews, but they were in their hearts no more nor less than Greek-Roman pagans of the then prevailing type of religious indifference and in their policy was always to weaken and subdue the national feeling of the Hebrews by the introduction of Greek and Roman elements of civilization."[46]

We have previously mentioned that the Targums were Aramaic paraphrases of the Old Testament. While they were not complete translations of the Hebrew text, they did allow Gentile exposure to the religion of the children of Israel. "They originated because the Jews in the synagogues in the Middle East could not understand the Hebrew scripture. Someone stood alongside the reader of the text (read in Hebrew) and recited Aramaic paraphrases, which in time became stereotyped."[47]

The various Jewish sects began shortly before the time of

Christ. The Sadducees and the Pharisees were to become the Jewish sects which were most vocal and adverse to the teachings of Christ. The Hebrew religion spread for it was known that a small contingency of Hebrews had even built a temple of Yahweh on the island of Elephantine in Egypt and as early as 200 B.C., the first century Egypt and other areas well outside of traditional Jerusalem had come to embrace the religion of the Hebrews. "In the first decades of the first century A.D., Philo, a wealthy Jew of Alexandria steeped in Greek philosophy, produced voluminous works in Greek, works that we still read today, in which he explains the books of his Bible to non-Jewish readers in terms and concepts belonging to the Hellenic tradition. In one of his writings, Philo states that in his time, a million Jews lived in Alexandria."[48] While the figure cited by Philo is thought to be an exaggeration, it is still useful in that it reflects that not only was the Hebrew religion being adopted by large numbers of people, but it was also undergoing somewhat of a change as Hellenic traditions, which later Christ referred to as "rituals," were being introduced to this ancient religion.

The comment of Philo, who had been living in Alexandria, Egypt, in describing great populations of "Jews" living there in the early portion of the first century, did not seem to fit the ancient definition of the word, and undoubtedly many of them had never set foot in Judea. Thus it is clear that by this point in time, that is, the early decades of the first century and probably earlier, the word "Jew" had evolved to mean something other than one from the land of Judea, and by the accounting offered by Philo, it would seem that the word "Jew" was now applicable to a religion that was distinctly different from the traditional Judaism of the Hebrews.

Even in the ancient times of Josephus, who lived shortly after the time of Christ, there were those who believed that the Hebrews were, indeed, Egyptians; however, Josephus points out that they originally came from "Mesopotamia." "I think it necessary to mention those names, that I may disprove such as believed that we came not originally from Mesopotamia, but are Egyptians."[49] He went on to name all of the seventy that came into Egypt originally at the time in which Joseph was governor over all the land, second only to Pharaoh.

As previously mentioned, the Hebrews built a temple on Elephantine Island, but they were everywhere, as Josephus describes, particularly in Alexandria since out of necessity the Egyptian priests served as professors, since most of the texts were written in their language.

"Now these Jews are already gotten into all cities; and it is hard to find a place in the habitable earth that hath not admitted this tribe of men, and is not possessed by them; and it hath come to pass that Egypt and Cyrne, as having the same governors, and a great number of other nations, imitate their way of living, and maintain great bodies of these Jews in a particular manner, and grow up to greater prosperity with them, and make use of the same laws with that nation also. Accordingly, the Jews have places assigned them in Egypt, wherein they inhabit, besides what is particularly allotted to this nation at Alexandria, which is a large part of that city."[50]

Josephus seemingly identifies the ancient geographer, Strabo, as being among those who misstated that the Hebrews were originally Egyptian. "In Egypt, therefore, this nation is powerful because the Jews were originally Egyptians, and because the land wherein they inhabit, since they went thence, is near Egypt. They also removed into Cyrne, because this land adjoined to the government of Egypt, as well as does Judea or rather formally under the same government. And this is what Strabos says."[51]

In any case, the natives of the land of Egypt and Mesopotamia bore a similar physical appearance. As previously discussed, those in Mesopotamia spoke the same language which was considered to be West Semitic, but different dialects. Some scholars believe that Hebrew was the original language of all mankind, but this concept is not embraced by all. "Many of the 19th century scholars, reacting against the biblical picture of Hebrew as the language of Adam and the speech of all mankind until the fall of the Tower of Babel, fiercely denied that it was perfect or original."[52] In any case, Hebrew has been defined as a "Canaanite dialect spoken in the kingdoms of Israel, Judah and Moab between 1500 and 500 B.C. For religious reasons, it is often treated as a distinct language."[55]

One of the objectives of the Hebrew uprising which came to be known as the Maccabean Revolt was to be the restoration of traditional Judaism. They felt that their religion had become tainted by Hellenistic traditions. Aside from pressure by foreigners who were getting more and more involved in their religion, there were problems with their own high priest yielding to such pressures. In their "zeal to restore the law," the name "zealot" was first applied to Maccabeus and his followers who in their attempt to shake off the yoke of Roman rule did not hesitate to use force against force. For that reason today, the word "zealot" is oftentimes accompanied by the word "fanatic." "'Zealot' a member of a fanatical Jewish party (A.D. 6-70) in almost continual revolt against the Romans."[54] Some of the twelve disciples in the ministry of Jesus were known zealots such as Simon Niger, referred to as Simon "the Canaanite" (Matthew 10:4) or "the zealot" **(Luke 6:15).**

**Luke (6:13-16):**

> **"And when it was day, he called unto him his disciples: and of them he chose twelve, whom also he named apostles;**
>
> **Simon, (whom he also named Peter,) and Andrew his brother, James and John, Philip and Bartholomew,**
>
> **Matthew and Thomas, James the son of Alphaeus, and Simon called Zelotes,**
>
> **And Judas the brother of James, and Judas Iscariot, which also was the traitor.**

"Simon" is the Hellenized name for "Simeon" and it is unlikely that the person who has been described as "Simon the Zealot" would use the Greek form of his name. And so more accurately, "Simon" should be "Simeon." Simeon was named after the second son of Jacob by Leah (Genesis 29:33). The name was sometimes used to denote the ancestors of the tribe of Simeon. "Simeon" the second son of Jacob, by Leah **(Genesis 29:33)**; ancestor of the tribe of Simeon." A unique feature of Hebrew personal names is that they literally meant something and therefore, the Hellenization of the Hebrew text is a matter that is not to be taken lightly since meanings and identities could be forever lost, which was seemingly the objective in most cases.

Additionally, changing the names of places is a matter not to be taken lightly since, for instance, most biblical scholars of today will tell you that Jerusalem was founded as a holy city by the Hebrews. However, when armed with knowledge that Jerusalem is, indeed, a name created by the Greeks for Salem which in Hebrew means "peace," it will be recalled that Melchizedek was the king and high priest of Salem to whom even Abraham paid tithes long before the days of Moses. Furthermore, when given the biblical account of Melchizedek which follows, it can be clearly seen that Jerusalem (Salem) was established first as a holy city by God himself. **Hebrews (7:1-6):**

> **"For this Melchisedec, king of Salem, priest of the most high God, who met Abraham returning from the slaughter of the kings, and blessed him;**
>
> **To whom also Abraham gave a tenth part of all; first being by interpretation King of righteousness, and after that also King of Salem, which is, King of peace;**
>
> **Without father, without mother, without descent, having neither beginning of days, nor end of life; but made like unto the Son of God; abideth a priest continually.**
>
> **Now consider how great this man was unto whom even the patriarch Abraham gave the tenth of the spoils.**
>
> **And verily they that are of the sons of Levi, who receive the office of the priesthood, have a commandment to take tithes of the people according to the law, that is, of their brethren, though they come out of the loins of Abraham.**

**But he whose descent is not counted from them received tithes of Abraham, and blessed him that had the promises."**

Hebrews (7:11-14):

**"If therefore perfection were by the Levitical priesthood (for under it the people received the law,) what further need was there that another priest should rise after the order of Melchisedec, and not be called after the order of Aaron?**

**For the priesthood being changed, there is made of necessity a change also of the law.**

**For he of whom these things are spoken pertaineth to another tribe, of which no man gave attendance at the altar.**

**For it is evident that our Lord sprang out of Juda; of which tribe Moses spake nothing concerning the priesthood."**

By virtue of the fact that Melchisedec was the king and high priest of Salem (Jerusalem) in the days when the surrounding area was known as the land of Canaan and prior to the arrival of Abraham, it is clear that neither Moses nor Abraham was the first to introduce the concept of monotheism. The same God that the Hebrews claimed as their own, as the God of the children of Israel, was the same God that had already been introduced to the Canaanites. The Canaanites apparently fell into disfavor after failing to follow the teachings of Melchisedec. Hebrew, Canaanite, Phoenician, Moabite and Ugarite are all considered to be separate dialects of the same language. As we discussed earlier, the land of Kemet which literally meant "black land" was renamed "Egypt," the natives being labeled "Egyptians" and lowest of the castes. The southern Cushite empire came to be known as Ethiopia and the term "Ethiopians" was applied to all people of the northern aspect of Asia Minor and were considered to be the lowest in the castes.The term "Ethiopian" meant"burnt face" in Greek and even the Hebrews were "burnt faced" in the likeness of Jesus who was described as burnished bronze or "feet like unto fine brass, as if burned in a furnace." **(Revelation 1 :15.)**

The word "Ethiopian" like the word "Jew" is an amphobology, that is, a word having more than one meaning. On the one hand, Ethiopian referred to the lowest category in the caste system, while at the same time serving as a generic term for all the natives of the newly conquered lands of the Greek empire. Such an example can be found in the account given in which Moses fled Egypt shortly after killing an overseer of the Hebrew slaves. He was described as fleeing into Midian which was the settlement of the Midianites who, as previously described, were the descendants of the of the union between Abraham and Keturah. Moses went on to marry the daughter of the Midianite priest of On, but for the purpose of the Greek translation of the text, rather than simply referring to her as a Midianite, as her father was a Midianite, she instead was referred to as an Ethiopian. That is, in the generic sense of the word that was applied to all native people since Midian clearly lies outside of the borders of the Cushite empire, which had been renamed Ethiopia by the Greeks.

It is noted that this term was also applied to the Ishmaelites who, as previously discussed, descended from the union between Abraham and the Egyptian handmaiden, Hagar. It will be recalled that it was Ishmael that was known as the father of the Arabians and they are called Ethiopians even until this day. Through Abraham then, the Ethiopians of today are both a Semitic and Hebrew people. The Davidic line of Judaism was introduced through the Queen of Sheba. These points have been reiterated just make the point, the term "burnt faced" was applied to all the native people of the land, stretching throughout all of the Middle East and even encompassing Arabia.

The Edomites were Hebrews, in that they were descendants of Esau, the brother of Jacob. However, since they were not descendants of Jacob, they were not considered to be members of the tribe of Israel, even though they were clearly related, as both descended from Isaac. Edomites occupied the "land of Seir," which came to be known as the country of Edom. **Genesis (32:3):**

> **"And Jacob sent messengers before him to Esau, his brother unto the land of Seir, the country of Edom."**

However, with the invasion of the Greeks, the native Edomites were categorized as Ethiopians and the name of the country was changed to Idumea. The Moabites and Ammonites descended from Lot, the nephew of Abraham, and accordingly were Hebrews, although they were not the seed of Abraham and thusly, were treated as such, but they were truly blessed by God.

During the period of the exodus from slavery in which Moses led the Hebrews through the wilderness, Moses was given this directive. **Deuteronomy (2:3-9):**

> **"And the Lord spake unto me saying, Ye have compassed this mountain long enough: turn you northward.**
>
> **And command thou the people, saying, Ye are to pass through the coast of your brethren the children of Esau, which dwell in Seir; and they shall be afraid of you: take ye good heed unto yourselves therefore:**
>
> **Meddle not with them; for I will not give you of their land, no, not so much as foot breadth; because I have given mount Seir unto Esau for a possession.**
>
> **Ye shall buy meat of them for money, that ye may eat; and ye shall also buy water of them for money That ye may drink.**
>
> **For the Lord thy God hath blessed thee in all the works or thy hand: he knoweth thy walking**

**through this great wilderness: these forty years the Lord thy God hath been with thee; thou hast lacked nothing.**

**And when we passed by from our brethren the children of Esau, which dwelt in Seir, through the way of the plain from Elath, and from Ezion-gaber, we turned and passed by the way of the wilderness of Moab.**

**And the Lord said unto me, Distress not the Moabites, neither contend with them in battle: for I will not give thee of their land for a possession; because I have given Ur unto the children of Lot for a possession."**

As discussed, during the Greco-Roman period, the Hebrews had spread throughout the biblical land, including Egypt, as a result of the Diaspora.

As Josephus tells us, the concept of monotheism, that is of one true God, was present in Egypt at the time of Abraham. "Now, after this, when a famine had invaded the land of Canaan, and Abram had discovered that the Egyptians were in a flourishing condition, he was disposed to go down to them, both to partake of the plenty they enjoyed, and to become an auditor of their priest, and to know what they said concerning the gods; designing either to follow them, if they had better notions than he, or to convert them to a better way, if his own notions prove the truest." [55]

As has been previously mentioned, the Hamitic line of the Canaanites had knowledge of monotheism prior to the arrival of Abraham, as even Abraham himself paid tithes to Melchisedec, the high priest of Jerusalem. The genealogic branches of the Semites and Hamites continued to intertwine as evidenced by the fact that the zealot Hebrew, Simeon ("the Canaanite") or Simon Niger as he was sometimes called, was an apostle of Christ.

The Hebrews, by decree, were given equal status with the Greeks. This was very important because following the appointment of Herod approximately 40 B.C., he appointed those loyal to him to the priesthood, thus disrupting the Zadokite line of priests which had been reportedly reinstalled during the reign of the Maccabees. As discussed, the Edomites had always been considered the long-time cousins of the Hebrews, in that they were the descendants of Esau. Edom was Hellenized by the Greeks who changed the name to Idumea. The Herods were from Idumea, and the Herodians were a political party which supported Herod whose ambition was to establish an Idumean dynasty in Judea. Concerning the family of Herod, "All its members were very zealous in professing the Mosaic law, though they did not keep it; very desirous to give no offense to Jewish prejudices, though they despised them; and very painstaking in flattering Jewish vanity, when thereby they could further their own plans. But as they could never hope to realize their great ambition to establish an Idumean dynasty in Judea without the support of the Romans, many of the Herod family were educated in Rome or had lived there for a long time. Thus they became sort of middlemen between the Greek-Roman civilization, Greek-Roman paganism and Judaism, to the great injury of the Jews. The first Roman emperor Augustus Caesar, appointed Herod the Great,'as the king of Judea, the latter of which gained the distinction of being one of the cruelest rulers that ever lived, being credited with rebuilding the temple at the same time, 'He also adorned Jerusalem with other splendid buildings, but they were theaters and amphitheaters, and were intended to aid the introduction of pagan games and festivals among the Jews."[56] The first Herod, king of Judea, was the same Herod who reigned at the time of the birth of Christ.

By decree from first the Greeks and then the emperor of Rome, the Hebrews that could trace their lineage back to the twelve tribes had easy access to the temple, as did the Edomites, their close cousins. However, with their more distant cousins, the Moabites and Ammonites, access to the temple decreased, as the genealogic lines with the tribes of Israel became more blurred.. Herodian and Roman supporters which were to become the Sadducees were appointed by the Idumean Greek, Herod. The Pharisees, another of the "Jewish sects" had formed shortly prior to the coming of the Messiah, and was comprised of Greeks that opposed Roman rule, as well as some Hebrews. It is said that the Hebrew Apostle Paul himself was a Pharisee. However, the most vocal were those who had least access to the temple, who yearned unceasingly for the return to traditional Judaism, that is, the restoration of the Zadokite line of priests and the coming of the Messiah. Amongst those who suffered the most, the view of the Messiah was a king that would come and defeat the Roman and Greek intruders which had become their oppressors.

Perhaps the most rigorous toward the restoration of tradition were the Nazarites, sometimes spelled "Nazirite," who were characterized by having periods of time of devotion in which they consecrated themselves to the Lord, living a life of purity and abstaining from certain things such as alcoholic beverages. John the Baptist, and for a period of time Paul, the disciple of Jesus, were counted amongst their numbers.

The most militant amongst the Hebrews were the zealots as they were considered to be a direct threat to Roman rule and had an established track record of a guerrilla style of warfare that was very effective against the Romans and the Greeks before them. Needless to say, at times, they could be armed, as the servant of the Jewish sect high priest found as they attempted to arrest Jesus Christ; he lost his ear. **Luke (22:50-51):**

> **"And one of them smote the servant of the high priest, and cut off his right ear.**
>
> **And Jesus answered and said, Suffer ye thus far. And he touched his ear, and healed him."**

**John (18:10-11):**

> **"Then Simon Peter, having a sword, drew it, and smote the high priest's servant, and cut off his right ear. The servant's name was Malchus.**

**Then said Jesus unto Peter, Put up thy sword into the sheath: the cup which my Father hath given me, shall I not drink it?"**

It was both the downtrodden, as well as the highly spirited Hebrews who looked to the coming of the Messiah as their king and Saviour from the Romans, since the scriptures foretold that he would be of the royal lineage of King David.

Meanwhile it was Caesar's appointment of Herod as the governor of Judea that ultimately sealed the fate of the Hebrews, as these political appointees of Herod became the new temple leaders. The Herodians, who had supported the Herod family and Roman rule, became the greatest benefactors of such appointments, as they went on to become the Sadducees, the wealthiest of the newly formed Jewish sects. The Greek-inspired Jewish sect known as the Pharisees opposed Roman rule, but in spite of this fact, along with the Sadducees, they were the most powerful of the Jewish sects at the time of Christ.

The disruption of the Zadokite line of the priesthood, and the long-held Hebrew authority over the temple was to ultimately lead to the loss of the identity of the Hebrews, as the Pharisees and Sadducees interjected their own rituals into temple worship services, and traditional practices took a back seat.

In the period of Moses and for a substantial time that followed, the priests could not own property, and instead, were dependent upon the tithes of the tribes to sustain them and the temple, with all objects of value remaining the property of the temple. At various times throughout history, the temple housed and controlled great wealth, as was the case shortly prior to the time of Christ when the newly appointed Sadducees largely gained control over the temple. It was these newly formed Jewish sects which, prior to the coming of the Messiah, adopted many of the religious ceremonies of the Hebrews, while at the same time, other rituals were interjected; and of the seventy books of the Hebrew text, only the first five, which were known as the Pentateuch, also known as the "Samaritan Pentateuch," were adopted by the Jewish sects.

It will be recalled that the Samaritan Community of the Hebrews, which comprised the Northern Kingdom or ten tribes, was taken into captivity in approximately the 7th century, B.C., which would have been prior to the time in which many of the subsequent books of the Hebrew text were written. Along with their diminishing control of the temple, came a diminution of the traditional way of life for the Hebrews and as might be expected, there was an associated loss of identity which increased with the passage of time. In addition, following the Greek translations of the Old Testament in 200 B.C., or the "Septuagint" as it came to be known, the original Hebrew texts of the scriptures grew scarce, until they had become nearly extinct with many of the original scripts being deliberately destroyed.

Prior to the time of Christ and for hundreds of years thereafter, the religious texts existed in scroll form, and were handwritten, usually on papyrus, a type of paper derived from a reed plant native to Egypt, or sometimes they were written on animal membranes, leather or other materials. Due to the fact that each scroll of some of the books of the Bible could be up to 20 feet or more in length, and involved a labor-intensive effort by the scribes that copied them, they were quite expensive. They were so expensive that outside of the direct access through the temple or library, personal ownership of a copy of the scriptures was oftentimes limited to the very wealthy. It was the confiscation of the Hebrew texts and the lack of concern for those books beyond the Pentateuch which contributed to ignorance of those prophesies which related to the coming of the Messiah. As Christ had knowledge of all of the scriptures, his doctrine seemed foreign to many of those who were in control of the temple during his time. It was the confiscation and destruction of these books which directly contributed to the lack of knowledge of the scriptural prophesies which told of the coming of the Messiah. However, it can be said that the greatest crime of the Hellenistic period was not so much the confiscation of the texts, but the failure to read them. Ultimately, it was the ignorance of the scriptural law, along with the combination of greed, arrogance, politics and hypocrisy which led to what was to become man's greatest crime against man and God... the crucifixion of God's only begotten Son.

We will examine the politics of the time in the next chapter which, as might be expected, found the temple leaders to be at odds with many of the traditional Hebrews which was ultimately to give rise to radical Hebrew groups known as "the zealots" and the assassins or "sicarii," which in Latin literally meant "dagger men," both of which violently opposed Greco-Roman rule. The appointment of political appointees over the temple greatly diminished hope for any future restoration of the Godly-appointed priesthood of the Levites. Along with the loss of their association with the ministry of the temple and the priesthood came the loss of their identity, as the Grecian temple appointees of Herod absorbed nearly all aspects of their culture, even their means of dress, including the priestly robes and phylacteries, which were leather strips traditionally worn by the Hebrews on their heads and their arms. The issue of such hypocrisy was addressed by Christ Himself, who in one case offered a clue which has since led to what is seemingly incontrovertible evidence as to the physical appearance of the Hebrews. This account can be found in **Matthew (23:1-8):**

> **"Then spake Jesus to the multitude, and to his disciples,**
>
> **Saying, The scribes and the Pharisees sit in Moses' seat:**
>
> **All therefore whatsoever they bid you observe, that observe and do; but do not ye after their works: for they say, and do not.**
>
> **For they bind heavy burdens and grievous to be borne, and lay them on men's shoulders; but they themselves will not move them with one of their fingers.**
> **But all their works they do for to be seen of men: they make broad their phylacteries, and enlarge the borders of their garments,**

**"HEADS OF PRISONERS"** - CAPTIVES IN EGYPT
MIDDLE KINGDOM, 1863 B.C.
COURTESY OF THE LOS ANGELES COUNTY MUSEUM OF ART
WILLIAM RANDOLPH HEARST COLLECTION

**And love the uppermost rooms at feasts, and the chief seats in the synagogues,**

**And greetings in the markets, and to be called of men Rabbi, Rabbi.**

**But be not ye called Rabbi: for one is your Master, even Christ; and all ye are brethren."**

Regarding phylacteries, it should be pointed out at this time that two types were worn by the Hebrews, with one leather strip being worn on the forehead, called a frontlet (which means to see); and the other worn on the arm. This band of leather was sometimes attached to a case-like object, which contained within, writing on a small roll of parchment. **Exodus (13:9,16):**

**"And it shall be for a sign unto thee upon thine hand, and for a memorial between thine eyes, that the Lord's law may be in thy mouth: for with a strong hand hath the Lord brought thee out of Egypt."**

**"And it shall be for a token upon thine hand, and for frontlets between thine eyes: for by strength of hand the lord brought us forth out of Egypt."**

**Deuteronomy (11:18):**

**"Therefore shall ye lay up these my words in your heart and in your soul, and bind them for a sign upon your hand, that they may be as frontlets between your eyes."**

While some modern biblical archeologists have written that there has been almost no mention amongst the ancient Egyptian writings alluding to the Hebrew captivity, as is now dear that there was, indeed, one traditional marker which distinguished the ancient

Hebrews from other native people, in that they wore phylacteries (frontlets). The ancient Egyptians were quite meticulous in keeping historical records. Accordingly, even the fine detail of these phylacteries can be seen in many ancient inscriptions. Ironically, it is the phylactery or frontlet, which literally means "to see," which has allowed us to peer into the past and to unmistakably be able to identify the Hebrews from all other people of their time.

One remarkable example of such phylacteries worn in ancient times can be seen in the bust of "foreign slaves" in Egypt dating back to 1863 B.C., entitled "Heads of Prisoners," which is on display at the Los Angeles County Museum. The accounts of the captivity period in Egypt ranged from 400 to 420 years (1847-1447 B.C.), or as previously discussed, the date of the exodus, 1447 B.C. plus 420 years, or (1867-1447 B.C.), if the latter figure is to be employed. The figures on display at the L.A. County Museum represent only a small portion of a larger composition which was dated 1863 B.C. or four years following the onset of Hebrew captivity. This also represents an excellent example of how the phylacteries, mentioned by Christ in the Bible and which were the identifying markers of the Hebrews nearly four thousand years ago, are still useful in identifying them from other native people of the ancient times.

Remarkably, in spite of the impact of Hellenism and the obliteration of the natives in the biblical lands over two thousand years ago, it was the Bible that lighted the way in showing us the physical appearance of the people who by some accounts were declared to be extinct and with no known remaining evidence of their existence, except for the language. (See photo.)

---

# Part VI notes:

[1] Funk and Wagnalls - New Comprehensive International Dictionary- 1973, p. 586.

[2]The Histories, Herodotus, p. 149.

[3]Ibid., p. 146.

[4]Black Athena, Vol. II, Martin Bernal, p. 109.

[5]The Ancient Engineers, L. Sprague DeCamp, p. 46.

[6]The Histories, Herodotus, p.169.

[7]The Ancient Engineers, L. Sprague DeCamp, p. 98.

[8]Ibid., p. 98.

[9]The Ancient Engineers, L. Sprague DeCamp, p. 115.

[10]The Histories, Herodotus, p. 145.

[11]Ibid., p. 149.

[12]The Penguin Atlas of Ancient History, Collin McEvedy, p. 58.

[13]Ibid., p. 58.

[14]The Nature of Alexander, Mary Renault, p. 92.

[15]The Campaigns of Alexander, Arrian (Flavius Arrianus Xenophon), p. 76.

[16]Ibid. p. 78.

[17]The Campaigns of Alexander, Arrian (Flavius Arrianus), p. 121.

[18]The Campaign of Alexander, Arrian, Translated by Aubrey De Selincourt, p. 132.

[19]The Ancient Engineers, L. Sprague DeCamp, p. 106.

[20]The Complete Works of Josephus, p. 243.

[21]Ibid., p. 244.

[22]Ibid., p. 244.

[23]Ibid. p. 244.

[24]Ibid., p. 244.

[25]Manetho, translated by W. G. Waddell, p. xii.

[26]Ibid., p. vii.

[27]The Ancient Engineers, L. Sprague DeCamp, p. 87.

[28]The Complete Works of Josephus, p. 245.

[29]The Complete Works of Josephus, p. 247

[30]Ibid., p. 249.

[31]Ibid., p. 249.

[32]Ibid., p. 250.

[33]The Complete Works of Josephus, p. 251.

[34]The Bible as History, Warner Keller, p. 344.

[35]The Complete Works of Josephus, p. 252.

[36]Ibid., p. 31.

[37]The Complete Works of Josephus, p. 251.

[38]Ibid., p. 51.

[39]The Complete Works of Josephus, p. 251.

[40]Life in Egypt Under Roman Rule, Naphtali Lewis, p. 31.

[41]Ibid., p. 33.

[42]The Penguin Atlas of Ancient History, Collin McEvedy, p. 65.

[43]Ibid., p. 66.

[44]Biblical Times, Amanda O'Neal.

[45]Old Testament Survey, p. 487.

[46]Bible Dictionary and Concordance, p. 912. - 1943 John A. Dixon Publishing Co.

[47]The Holman Bible Dictionary, p. 184.

[48]Life in Egypt Under Roman Rule, p. 229.

[49]The Complete Works of Josephus, p. 54.

[50]The Complete Works of Josephus, p. 295.

[51]Ibid., p. 295.

[52]Black Athena, Vol. I, Martin Bernal, p. 344.

[53]Black Athena, Vol. II, Martin Bernal, p. 640.

[54]Funk and Wagnall's New Comprehensive International Dictionary, p. 1462.

[55]The Complete Works of Josephus, p. 33.

[56]Bible Dictionary and Concordance, p. 914

## PART VII

## MESSIANIC PROPHESIES

"'Messiah' is a Hebrew term meaning 'anointed one,' 'one sent by God to save others.' In Hebrew belief, the coming savior of the Jewish people; in Christianity, Jesus."[1]

"Israel came to see each succeeding king as God's anointed one, the Messiah, who would deliver them from their enemies and establish the nation as God's presence on earth."[2] It has the same meaning in Hebrew as the Greek translation "Christos" with "Messias" also being a Greek form of the word "Messiah." There are over 120 verses concerning the Messiah for which references can be found in the Old Testament with fulfillment to be found in the New Testament. One example of such can be found in **Isaiah (7:14)**:

> **"Therefore the Lord himself so give you a sign;**
> **Behold, a virgin shall conceive, and bear a son,**
> **and shall call his name Im-man'-u-el."**

Then in turning to the New Testament, **Matthew (1:23)**:

> **"Behold, a virgin shall be with child, and shall bring forth a son, and they shall call his name Em-man'-u-el, which being interpreted is, God with us."**

The name by which the Messiah was called during the period of his own lifetime largely depended upon the relationship that he had with those that addressed him. For instance, "Jesus" is the Greek form for the Hebrew personal name of "Jehoshua" which is more often seen in its contracted form of "Joshua," with "Jesus," which means "saviour," being used exclusively in the New Testament. As was prophesied in the book of Isaiah and later confirmed in the New Testament text of Matthew, the Messiah was to be called "Immanuel," a Hebrew name which means "God with us." As we have previously discussed, the book of Psalms reveals that the Lord was to be of the order of the king and high priest of Salem Melchizedek through whom the holy city that came to be later known as Jerusalem first came to be known as a holy city. The word "Salem" itself literally means "peace." Just as Melchizedek was the high priest and king of Salem or the king of peace, the prophet Isaiah told us that the child to be born was to be known as the "Prince of Peace."

**Isaiah (9:6):**

> **"For unto us a child is born, unto us a child is given: and the government shall be upon his shoulder: and his name shall be called Wonderful, Counsellor, The Mighty God, The everlasting Father, The Prince of Peace."**

As was prophesied, the government was, indeed, upon his shoulders to such an extent that although during his ministry on earth he performed miraculous wonders, which could only be achieved through God himself, the Messiah chose to conceal his true identity out of necessity since the biblical world had now fallen under the rule of the Roman government, and for anyone to identify himself as being a king would be tantamount to sedition, a crime which was punishable by death. The prophets had foretold that the Messiah would come out of the small town of Bethlehem and that he, indeed, would be a ruler. **Micah (5:2):**

> **"But thou, Beth'-lehem Eph'ratah, though thou be little among the thousands of Judah, yet out of thee shall he come forth unto me that is to be ruler in Israel; whose goings forth have been from of old, from everlasting."**

Whether he was referred to as the ruler of Israel, the king of the Hebrews, Christos which is the Greek form of the anointed one, Jesus, which means saviour, or the Hebrew form which is Joshua the contracted form of Jehoshua, he was sought after even prior to the time of his birth. He was sought after by the Hebrews who had envisioned the Messiah to be a warrior type and king, as he was supposed to come out of the house of David, that would free their nation from the Roman oppression and restore their previous status and control of the temple.

Yet, there was still a more ominous figure that was also waiting for the Messiah, but for a different reason. That, of course, was the Idumean who was appointed king of Judea by the first Roman emperor, Augustus Caesar. King Herod, who came to be known by some as Herod the Great, ruled Judea for nearly 40 years. It was this same Herod who sought out the wise men as he desperately attempted to identify the time and place of the birth of the "king of the Hebrews." **Matthew (2:1-5):**

> **"Now when Jesus was born in Bethlehem of Judaea in the days of Herod the kin, behold, there came wise men from the east to Jerusalem,**
>
> **"Saying, Where is he that is born King of the Jews? for we have seen his star in the east, and are come to worship him.**
>
> **When Herod the king had heard these things, he was troubled, and all Jerusalem with him.**
>
> **And when he had gathered all the chief priests and scribes of the people together, he demanded of them where Christ should be born.**
>
> **And they said unto him, In Bethlehem of Judaea; for thus it is written by the prophet," ...**

I should point out at this time, for the benefit of any reader that has not read the first six chapters, that the word "Jew" is a Greek term which is not synonymous with the word "Hebrew." When the verses are viewed from the author's perspective, that is of Matthew, who was a disciple of Christ and himself a Hebrew, it is highly likely that the word "Jew" was inserted as a result of the Greek translation.

King Herod went on to advise the wise men that once they reached Bethlehem and located the child, to be sure to bring him word of such since he was interested in worshipping the newborn king. Matthew (2:7-11):

> **"Then Herod, when he had privily called the wise men, enquired of them diligently what time the star appeared.**
>
> **And he sent them to Bethlehem, and said, Go and search diligently for the young child; and when ye have found him, bring me word again, that I may come and worship him also.**
>
> **When they had heard the king, they departed; and, lo, the star, which they saw in the east, went**
>
> **before them, till it came and stood over where the young child was.**
>
> **"When they saw the star, they rejoiced with exceeding great joy.**
>
> **And when they were come into the house, they saw the young child with Mary his mother, and fell down, and worshipped him: and when they opened their treasures, they presented unto him gifts; gold, and frankincense, and myrrh."**

Herod was very much despised by the native Hebrews who saw him as a foreigner even though he claimed to be Idumean, he was clearly not a native Edomite, which were considered to be the cousins of the Hebrews. It will be recalled that the Greeks changed the name of Edom to Idumea. It was only the threat of the Roman army which supported Herod that kept him in power, and even under those circumstances there were several attempts on his life. In one case, the assassins, a dagger-bearing radical group amongst the Hebrews plotted to kill him, but unknowingly, their group had been infiltrated by an informer who, in turn, advised Herod of the plot against his life. Those that were involved were rounded up and tortured to death. According to the account offered by Josephus, the informer was also later killed by the Hebrews as he was torn apart, limb by limb and was fed to the dogs.

It was probably the appointment of the Herodians, the political party that supported Herod that contributed most to the dissolution of the Hebrew tradition and religion as they introduced new customs into the temple and these new temple leaders became known as the Sadducees. Of the three major Jewish sects, all of which formed shortly before the time of Christ, that is, the Pharisees, the Sadducees and the Essenes, it is only the latter that were genetically linked to the Hebrews. Although they represented only a small splinter group, they were considered to be the most staunchly traditional amongst the Hebrews and chose to live in isolation.

"For there are three philosophical sects among the Jews. The followers of the first of whom are the Pharisees; of the second, the Sadducees; and the third sect, who pretends to a severer discipline, are called Essens. These last are Jews by birth, and seem to have a greater affection for one another than the other sects have. These Essens reject pleasures as an evil, but esteem continence, and the conquest over our passions, to be virtue."[3]

The Sadducees were amongst the wealthiest of the Greeks, it was the Pharisees that were thought to be more the intellectuals when it came to the law, oftentimes to an excess as they interjected their own traditions and laws, which were extremely burdensome and not always based on the scripture. While the Essenes are not mentioned in the Old Testament or New Testament, the recently found Dead Sea Scrolls were found in an area that is believed to have been inhabited by the Essenes. The Pharisees and Sadducees are not mentioned in the Old Testament since the last book of the Old Testament was written, nearly four hundred years before the appearance of these latter two groups.

The political power of the time was concentrated in the hands of the politically oriented Sadducees that supported Roman rule, and to a lesser extent, by the Pharisees, although they held high ranking temple positions. The Essenes, on the other hand, as mentioned, chose to live alone and were largely apolitical and therefore, found favor with Herod, but it was the masses of the Hebrew people that were left with only token representation on the temple council. Thus, they were rendered impotent and thereby could offer no resistance or little resistance as they saw their nearly 1500-year-old religion being disassembled before their very eyes. At one point, Herod reduced their tax burden by a third, as he tried to change his image among the Hebrews; however, his attempt failed, as Josephus describes:

"For they were uneasy at him, because of the innovations he had introduced into their practices of the dissolution of their religion, and of the disuse of their own customs, and the people everywhere talked against him, like those that were still more provoked and disturbed at his procedure; against which discontent he greatly guarded himself, and took away the opportunities they might have to disturb him, and enjoined them to be always at work; nor did he permit the citizens either to meet together, or to walk, or eat together, but watched everything they did and when any were caught, they were severely punished; in many there who were brought to the citadel Hyrcania, both openly and secretly, and were there put to death; and there were spies set everywhere, both in the city and in the roads, who watched those who met together." [4]

During Herod's reign, he completed several great public works projects, including the rebuilding of the temple and the creating of an amphitheater and other remarkable buildings for the time, and as he grew older, towards the end of his 37-year reign, he grew more cruel and suspicious as he had many of his own family members put to death. Herod, from the beginning, had envisioned a family dynasty and while he had many successes during his reign, there were many tragedies in his life. Perhaps the worst that he is known for is the wholesale massacre of Hebrew children after the wise men failed to return and advise him of the birthplace of Christ. The holy infant escaped harm, as his family fled to Egypt where they lived until the death of Herod, which ended his 37-year reign in the year 4 B.C. **Matthew (2:10-16):**

**"When they saw the star, they rejoiced with**

**exceeding great joy.**

**And when they were come into the house, they saw the young child with Mary, his mother, and fell down, and worshipped him: and when they had opened their treasures, they presented unto him gifts; gold, and frankincense, and myrrh.**

**And being warned of God in a dream that they should not return to Herod, they departed into their own country another way.**

**And when they were departed, behold, the angel of the Lord appeareth to Joseph in a dream, saying, Arise, and take the young child and his mother, and flee into Egypt, and be thou there "until I bring thee word: for Herod will seek the young child to destroy him.**

**When he arose, he took the young child and his mother by night, and departed into Egypt.**

**And was there until the death of Herod: that it might be fulfilled which was spoken of the Lord by the prophet, saying, Out of Egypt have I called my son.**

**Then Herod, when he saw that he was mocked of the wise men, was exceeding wroth, and sent forth, and slew all the children that were in Bethlehem, and in all the coasts thereof, from two years old and under, according to the time which he had diligently enquired of the wise men."**

Many involved in biblical research have concluded that Christ was born in approximately the year 7 B.C. and, indeed, a search has revealed that an astronomical event did occur in the year 7 B.C. which some have concluded may have been associated with the star of Bethlehem. "Finally, in 1925, the German scholar, P. Schnabel, deciphered the 'papers' in neo-Babylonian cuneiform of a famous professional institute in the ancient world, the School of Astrology at Sippar in Babylonia. Among endless series of prosaic dates of observations, he came across a note about the position of the planets in the constellation of Pisces. Juniper and Saturn are carefully marked in over a period of five months. Reckoned in our calendar the year was 7 B.C.!"[5]

"The position of the stars can be calculated backwards with equal precision. In the year 7 B.C., Juniper and Saturn did, in fact, meet in Pisces and, as Kepler had already discovered, they met three times. Mathematical calculations establish further that this three-fold conjunction of the planets was particularly clearly visible in the Mediterranean area."[6]

As has been previously stated, the lineage of the Virgin Mary can be traced to King David and the tribe of Judah. You will recall that the Hebrew, David, married the wife of Urias, a Hittite, following the death of Urias and it was through this union that the youngest of his sons, Solomon, was born. **Matthew (1:6-7):**

> **"And Jesse begat David the king; and David the king begat Solomon of her that had been the wife of Urias;**
>
> **And Solomon begat Roboam; and Roboam begat Abia; and Abia begat Asa..."**

While the Zadokite lineage to the priesthood was disrupted by the Ptolemy's appointment, this disruption continued right down to the time of Christ with Annas and Caiaphas being the high priest appointees during the ministry of Jesus. While the high priesthood had become a political appointment, occasionally, Hebrew priests were able to attain such a position, one such priest being Zacharias of the lineage of Abia. The lineage of Zacharias to Abia is traced back to Solomon and David of the tribe of Judah. Zacharias was married to Elisabeth who was of the lineage of Aaron of the tribe of Levi. Both Zacharias and Elisabeth were elderly when Zacharias was informed by an angel that Elisabeth was to have a son who was to be called John, which in Hebrew is "Johanan" meaning "whom Jehovah loves." Elisabeth, in turn, was a cousin of Mary and was six-months pregnant with John when Mary was informed of the impending birth of the baby Jesus. Luke (1:5,6):

> **"There was in the days of Herod, the king of Judaea, a certain priest named Zacharias of the course of Abia: and his wife was of the daughters of Aaron, and her name was Elisabeth.**
>
> **And they were both righteous before God, walking in all the commandments and ordinances of the Lord blameless."**

Luke (1:13-16):

> **"But the angel said unto him, Fear not, Zacharias: for thy prayer is heard; and thy wife Elisabeth shall bear thee a son, and thou shalt call his name John.**
>
> **And thou shalt have joy and gladness; and many shall rejoice at his birth.**
>
> **For he shall be great in the sight of the Lord, and shall drink neither wine nor strong drink; and he shall be filled with the Holy Ghost, even from his mother's womb.**
>
> **And many of the children of Israel shall he turn to the Lord their God."**

The Protevangelion is an historical account of the birth of the Jesus and the Virgin Mary, and while considered to be canonical in some Eastern churches it was not included in the Bibles of the protestant and catholic churches. The Protevangelion describes how Mary's parents, Anna and Joachim, left Mary at the age of three, with the temple priest to be educated there, at which time, Zacharias, who was later to become the father of John the Baptist, was the high priest. Just prior to the birth of Jesus, a decree was issued from Emperor Augustus that all Hebrews were to be taxed and accordingly, they were to return to their cities of origin for such purpose. Thus, Joseph set out for Bethlehem, the place of his birth. The Virgin Mary, having been informed that she was to bring forth the Messiah, the only begotten son of God, according to the account of the Protevangelion, she became distressed with pain just outside the city of Bethlehem and Joseph found a cave.

It should be pointed out that by some ancient accounts, the birth of Christ actually took place in a cave in Bethlehem, although he later rested in a manger in Bethlehem, when there were no hotel accommodations available, due to the influx of people that had come to the city of Bethlehem by decree. The following is the account offered in the Protevangelion, chapter XIV, verses 9-13:

> **"And the midwife went to along with him, and stood in the cave. Then a bright cloud overshadowed the cave, and the midwife said, This day my soul is magnified, for mine eyes have seen surprising things, and salvation is brought forth to Israel. But on a sudden the cloud became a great light in the cave, so that their eyes could not bear it. But the light gradually decreased, until the infant appeared, and sucked the breast of his mother Mary.**
>
> **Then, the midwife cried out, and said, How glorious a day is this, wherein mine eyes have seen this extraordinary sight!"**

It is believed that the site of the cave has been identified and is the location of The First Church of the Nativity.

> **At the close of the 3rd century, Eusebius, Bishop of Caesarea, writes: "The inhabitants of the place bear witness of the story that has come down to them from their fathers, and they**

**confirm the truth of it and point out the cave in which the virgin brought forth and laid the child."[7]**

The author continues:

> **"The First Church of the Nativity was built over this cave on the initiative of the Empress Helena, mother of the Emperor Constantin, in 325."[8]**

It should be pointed out that some biblical scholars have written that it is contradictory, in that at times, the Bible refers to Christ as a Nazarene which would suggest that he was from Nazareth, while at other times clearly stating that he was born in Bethlehem. In actuality, there is no such contradiction. This matter is very well addressed in the Gospel of Matthew which clearly describes that after the death of Herod, Joseph was advised that he could leave Egypt and was to go to Israel. He, instead of returning to Bethlehem, turned aside and went to parts of Galilee, more specifically, Nazareth, a city located in the lower portion of Galilee, 65 miles north of the city of Jerusalem. Therefore, while he was born in Bethlehem, his stay there was very brief and shortly therafter, he and his family moved to Egypt to escape Herod. However, thereafter, he spent his childhood and much of his life until his ministry began in the city of Nazareth, and therefore, he was called a Nazarene.

**Matthew (2:19-23):**

> **"But when Herod was dead, behold, an angel of the Lord appeareth in a dream to Joseph in Egypt, Saying, Arise, and take the young child and his mother, and go into the land of Israel: for they are dead which sought the young child's life.**
>
> **And he arose and took the young child and his mother, and came into the land of Israel.**
>
> **But when he heard that Achelaus did reign in Judaea in the room of his father Herod, he was afraid to go thither: notwithstanding, being warned of God in a dream, he turned aside into**

**the parts of Galilee:**

**And he came and dwelt in a city called Nazareth; that it might be fulfilled which was spoken by the prophets, He shall be called a Nazarene."**

Some scholars have raised a concern that there is no mention of Nazareth in the Old Testament. To our readers, this should not come as any surprise since we presently have only 39 of the original 70 texts of the Hebrews which comprise the Old Testament. Many, if not most of the scholarly concerns originate from this very fact, that is, some of the original books have been taken away from us throughout the ages, this in turn, has understandably created holes in our knowledge of events which took place In the pre-Christian era.
On the other hand, modern day archeologists and historians, when been truthful, have helped us to fill in and gaps that were created by the missing texts.

One such example is the case of King Herod who died in 4 B.C. , leaving the territories over which he had control to his three sons. The Roman government failed to recognize the will, at least in its entirety, and accordingly denied the heirs of Herod the designation of King, but rather indicated that they were to be called "Tetrarchs," which In itself would seem to imply that each of the sons was to reign over one fourth of the area which had been controlled by Herod. The only problem here is the fact that Herod did not have four sons, he only had three. One author writes, "Antipas and Philip were both called 'Tetrarchs' (ruler of a fourth part of a province) which would have made literal sense if Herod's kingdom had been divided among four sons rather than three. However, it might be reason that Archelaus as the fourth, received a double share and ruled two fourths of the kingdom, while Antipas and Philip ruled one-fourth" [9]

I would propose to another perhaps more likely possibility based upon a papyrus roll which can be found in East Berlin's Egyptian Museum which has been alluded to earlier in this text. In spite of Herod's claim that he was an Idumean, because of his loyalty to Caesar and the fact that he had been appointed as king by Caesar because of his display of loyalty to Rome, it would be very unusual for Caesar to have denied Herod the ultimate, which was considered to be a Roman citizenship. To those born outside of Rome, Roman citizenship was only granted under certain conditions which in many cases involved an unusual display of loyalty to Rome. Soldiers not born in Rome who served in its military spent as long as twenty years in the course of their service, but afterwards, they were granted a Roman citizenship and the special privileges that accompanied such an appointment.

Then, as now, there was a tax on dying. The ancient papyrus reveals, "If Egyptians, after a father's death record their father as a Roman, a fourth is confiscated. [10]

The same source reveals that, "Soldiers who style themselves Romans without having received a legal discharge are fined a fourth of their property." Accordingly, while the Herod family considered themselves Idumeans, it would seem as though the same rule would apply if they were not deemed to be Roman citizens. Thus, this is perhaps the most likely explanation as to why the sons were referred to as tetrarchs, each of the sons ruling over a quarter of the region ruled by their father, while the fourth part was confiscated by Rome as taxation following the death of Herod.

Following the decree by Herod that all the children under the age of two were to be killed that were in the city of Bethlehem, the following account is offered in the Protevangelion. I should point out at this time that the Protevangelion is thought by many to have been written by James and has been referred to as the Gospel of **James. Chapter XVI, verses 1-16:**

> **"Then Herod, perceiving that he was mocked by the wise men, and being very angry, commanded certain men to go and kill all the children that were in Bethlehem, from two years old and under. But Mary hearing that the children were to be killed, being under much fear, took the**

**child, and wrapped him up in swaddling clothes, and laid him in an ox manger, because there was no room for them in the inn.**

**Elisabeth also, hearing that her son John was about to be searched for, took him and went up unto the mountains, and looked around for a place to hide; And there was no secret place to be found. Then, she groaned within herself, and said, O mountain of the lord, receive the mother with the child. For Elisabeth could not climb up. And instantly, the mountain was divided and received them. And there appeared to them an angel of the Lord, to preserve them.**

**But Herod made search after John, and sent servants to Zacharias, when he was at the altar, and said unto him, Where hast thou hid thy son? He replied to them, I am a minister of God, and a servant at the altar; how should I know where my son is?**

**So the servants went back, and told Herod the whole; at which he was incensed, and said, Is not this son of his like to be king in Israel? He sent therefore again his servants to Zacharias saying, Tell us the truth, where is thy son, for you know that your life is in my hand. So, the servants went up and told him all this:**

**But Zacharias replied to them I am a martyr for God, and if he shed my blood, the Lord will receive my soul.**

**Besides know that ye shed innocent blood. However Zacharias was murdered in the entrance of the temple and altar and about the partition;"**

As Mary and Joseph fled to Egypt with the infant to escape Herod, it has been written in ancient accounts that the mere presence of the holy infant caused idols to fall down and to be destroyed and Mary at times would use the infants bath water as holy water and cured many that had afflictions.

There is little knowledge of the life of Christ between the time of his youth and the age of 30 when his ministry began after being baptized in the Jordan River by John the Baptist.

**Matthew (3:13-17):**

> **"Then cometh Jesus from Galilee to Jordan unto John, to be baptized of him.**
> **But John forbade him, saying, I have need to be baptized of thee, and comest thou to me?**
>
> **And Jesus answering said unto him, Suffer it to be so now: for thus it becometh us to fulfil all righteousness. Then he suffered him.**
>
> **And Jesus, when he was baptized, went up straightway out of the water: and lo, the heavens were opened unto him, and he saw the spirit of God descending like a dove, and lighting upon him:**
>
> **And lo a voice from heaven, saying, This is my beloved Son, in whom I am well pleased."**

While Jesus preached to all, it seemed as if the Hebrews were an area of special focus as he even selected most, if not all of his disciples from the Hebrews. As it will be recalled, it was the Hebrews that looked to the coming of the Messiah as they attempted to endorse him again and again as the king of the Hebrews a title which he did not readily accept, and to have done so would have constituted sedition against Caesar and Rome, which would have been punishable by death.

Before we progress further, it should be pointed out that the first complete English translation of the Bible was not available until 1382 A.D. This was accomplished by John Wycliffe and his colleagues. A paraphrased version of the Bible was first translated into Anglo-Saxon after 670 A.D. Interestingly enough, prior to 400 A.D., the Bible was available in Latin, Syriac, Coptic, Ethiopic, Armenian, and Georgian. Coptic is the last derivative of the ancient Egyptian language. The Vulgate version of the Bible, which was to be adapted by the Roman Catholic church in 1200 A.D. was based on translations which came from both Hebrew and Greek manuscripts. Just as Jesus himself was a Hebrew and most, if not all of the disciples were Hebrews, as might be expected, many of the texts of the Old Testament were written in Hebrew. **Matthew (4:18-19)** marks the beginning of the selection of the disciples by Christ, and it should be pointed out that he chose them , they did not choose him.

> **"And Jesus, walking by the sea of Galilee, saw two brethren, Simon called Peter, and Andrew his brother, casting a net into the sea: for they were fishers.**
>
> **And he saith unto them, 'Follow me, and I will make you fishers of men."**

As previously discussed, "Simon" is the Hellenized or Greek form of "Simeon," which in Hebrew means "a hearing." Also as we have previously discussed, Simeon was one of the sons of Jacob or Israel, and accordingly, his descendants were said to be of the tribe of Simeon or Simeonites. Simeon, the fisherman who later became the disciple of Jesus, was also later to be known as Peter, the name given to him by Christ, meaning "the rock." It should be pointed out that the Anglo-Saxons were a wandering Germanic tribe that went on to conquer Britain 500 years later in the 5th and 6th centuries A.D.. They, of course, are known as the English or British of today. As previously discussed, there was no complete version of the Bible in their own language until the contribution of John Wycliffe which did not occur until 1382 A.D. However, even the Anglo-Saxons could not resist the temptation of interjecting themselves into the Bible. Christ continued to recruit his disciples, **Matthew (4:21-22):**

> **"And going on from thence, he saw other two brethren, James the son of Zebedee, and John**

**his brother, in a ship with Zebedce their father, mending their nets; and he called them.**

**And they immediately left the ship and their father, and followed him."**

"James (English form of Jacob from the Heb, 'heel-catcher or supplanter')."[12] Meanwhile, "John" is the Greek form of the Hebrew name "Jo-ha-nan," meaning "to whom Jehovah is merciful."[13] It goes without saying that by supplantation of the Hebrew names with Greek and English names, there can be no better way to conceal their identity as having been Hebrew. The scriptures continue, **Matthew (4:23,24):**

**"And Jesus went about all Galilee, teaching in their synagogues, and preaching the gospel**

**of the kingdom, and healing all manner of sickness and all manner of disease among the people.**

**And his fame went throughout all Syria: and they brought unto him all sick people that were taken with divers diseases and torments, and those which were possessed with devils, and those which were lunatick, and those that had the palsy; and he healed them."**

It is very important to note that synagogues were a Greek innovation. From the time of Moses until the building of the temple by King Solomon, which did not begin until the year 967 B.C., worship took place in a tabernacle or tent which also housed the Ark of the Covenant. Later, the temple was built in Jerusalem by Solomon which was the implementation of a project that had been envisioned by David, largely for the purpose of finding a permanent resting place for the Ark of the Covenant. Therefore, in the Old Testament, there is no reference to synagogues since the temple was the center place of worship for the Hebrews. By the time of Christ, however, synagogues were quite common and spread throughout the land and were considered to be local places of worship.

There was a brief period of time in which two temples existed in Jerusalem, however, as we have alluded to this fact in the past. Prior to or shortly following the invasion of the Greeks, a temple was built in Elephantine in Egypt, which served their growing Hebrew population. It is believed by some that this site served as a temporary resting place for the Ark of the Covenant after its removal from Jerusalem. Returning now to the recruitment of the disciples, **Matthew (9:9):**

> **"And as Jesus passed forth from thence, he saw a man, named Matthew, sitting at the receipt of custom: and he saith unto him, 'Follow me.' And he arose, and followed him."**

**Matthew (10:1-4):**

> **"And when he had called unto him his twelve disciples, he gave them power against unclean spirits, to cast them out, and to heal all manner of sickness and all manner of disease.**
>
> **Now the names of the twelve apostles are these; The first , Simon, who is called Peter, and Andrew his brother; James the son of Zebedee, and John his brother.**
>
> **Philip and Bartholomew; Thomas and Matthew the publican; James the son of Alphaeus, and Lebbaeus, whose surname was Thaddaeus;**
>
> **Simon the Canaanite, and Judas Iscariot, who also betrayed him."**

Mark was the surname of John, the disciple of Jesus. Marcus is the Latin form of Mark which was used in **Colossians 4:10** describes Marcus as being related to Barnabas. Barnabas was a Levite whose name was Joses until such time when he later joined the apostles and they called him Barnabas. Therefore, John Mark or Johannan was clearly a Hebrew. Later in this text we will demonstrate that perhaps all of the original twelve disciples were Hebrews. While the legion of disciples around Christ grew with his ministry, only the twelve that we have listed as such were called apostles by Christ. It should be pointed out that Lebbaeus was also known as Judas to the disciples, brother of James. Judas, the brother of James, is not to be confused with Judas Iscariot, a second disciple with the same name, who has the distinction of being the betrayer of Christ.

Syriac, Aramaic and Hebrew are all very similar languages, and in actuality Syriac and Aramaic are probably one and the same, based upon the fact that Syria is "the Greek name for the country which the Hebrews call Aram, or 'the region of Tyre.'"[14] Aram was the son of Shem and grandson of Noah. **(Genesis 10:22-23.)** Aramians then were considered to be the descendants of Aram and the Aramian geographical area "consisted of the loose confederation of towns and settlements spread over what is now called Syria, as well as in **some parts of Babylon from which Jacob and Abraham came. (Deuteronomy 26:5)**[15] Actually, **Deuteronomy (26:5-9)** describes the elderly Jacob that is father of the twelve tribes of Israel who in joining his son, Joseph, in Egypt was described as a Syrian.

> **"And thou shalt speak and say before the Lord thy God, A Syrian ready to perish was my father, and he went down into Egypt, and sojourned there with a few, and became there a nation, great, mighty, and populous:**
>
> **And the Egyptians evil entreated us and afflicted us, and laid upon us hard bondage:**
>
> **And when we cried unto the Lord God of our fathers, the Lord heard our voice, and looked upon our affliction, and our labour, and our oppression:**
>
> **And the Lord brought us forth out of Egypt with a mighty hand, and with an outstretched arm, and with great terribleness, and with signs and**

**with wonders:**

**And he hath brought us into this place and hath given us this land, even a land that floweth with milk and honey."**

The Aramaic language widely spread and was used throughout the biblical land from Persia to Egypt. The 5th century papyri found in Egypt at Elephantine where the ancient Hebrews had built a temple were also found to be largely written in Aramaic. As previously mentioned, the Vulgate version of the Bible was based upon Hebrew and Greek manuscripts. It was this form of the Bible, that is, the Vulgate form, which was to become the official version of the Roman Catholic church. The book of Malachi was the last book of the Old Testament and was written in the 4th century B.C. with the writings of the New Testament not taking place until the 1st century A.D. It would seem as though there was a gap of 400 years in which the Hebrews had stopped recording their history. However, the fact of the matter is that the Hebrews continued to record their history during this period, which is known as the Inter-testamental Period, and many of the works of this period, including Maccabees, were included in the Vulgate edition of the Bible and can be found, therefore, in today's Roman Catholic version of the Bible, but such were deleted from the King James version. As a result of such deletion, the Catholic Bible contains 49 books in the Old Testament as compared to the King James version which only contains 39 books.

**I Maccabees (2:7-14)** reveals:

**"Mattathias said, 'Alas, why was I born to see the destruction of my people, the ruin of the holy city, and to stand by when it is in the hands of the enemy? The holy places are controlled by foreigners, and the temple is desecrated. The vessels that were its glory have been carried away. Old men are murdered in the streets, and young men have been killed by the enemy's sword. Is there a nation that has not claimed its royal privilege? All its ornaments have been plundered. Freedom is**

**given way to slavery. Look at our sanctuary, how our beauty and our glory are laid waste, profaned by the Gentiles. What have we left for which to live?' Mattathias and his sons tore their garments, covered themselves with sackcloth, and were very sad."[16]**

This would have been in the year approximately 175 B.C. under the reign of King Antiochus during the 137th year of the reign of the Greeks. I **Maccabees** continues **(chapter 2, verses 23-26):**

**"Now as he finished speaking, a certain Jew came forward to offer sacrifice to the idols in the city of Modein, according to the king's regulations. When Mattathias saw this, he was not only saddened, but his hands trembled and his anger was fired because of his love of the law. He threw himself at the man and killed him on the altar. Moreover, at the same time, he killed the agent whom King Antiochus had sent to enforce the pagan sacrifices, and he pulled down the altar. In his zeal for the law, he showed the spirit Phinehas showed against Zimri the son of Salu."[17]**

Regarding the reference to Phinehas, this is a Hebrew personal name, meaning **"dark skin or mouth of brass."** Grandson of Aaron and high priest who, on several occasions aided Moses and Joshua."[18]

**I Maccabees (2:27-37):**

**"Mattathias went through the city shouting loudly, 'Everyone who has zeal for the law and wishes to keep it, follow me.' Then, he and his sons escaped into the mountains, leaving behind all their possessions. Because of the afflictions which had been heaped upon them, many who sought after judgment and justice retreated into the desert and lived there, with their children and wives and cattle.**

**Word reached the king in Jerusalem that his command had been broken by Israelites and in turn, after they refused to go before the king, they were killed in the desert."**

1 Maccabees (2:38-40):

**"The foreigners attacked them on the sabbath and they were killed, together with their wives, children and cattle, to a total of a thousand persons. When Mattathias and his friends learned of this news, they were very sad. Each man said to his neighbor, 'If we all do as our brothers have done, and not fight for our lives and beliefs against the pagans, they will now quickly cause us to disappear from the earth.'"**

The Zealot movement had just been formed. Their numbers grew as they were joined by more and more of the Hebrews.

I Maccabees 2:(42-50):

**"Some Hasideans, strong fighters of Israel, who had great respect for the law, along with others who fled the prosecution, joined them, giving added support. All of these formed an army which in its anger killed sinners and renegades. The subservient Jews fled to the pagans for safety. Mattathias and his friends went everywhere and tore down the idolatrous altars, and circumcised Israeli children who had not been circumcised. They pursued the turncoats and were successful in their fight. They wrestled the law out of the hands of the pagans and of the kings, and they did not allow the strength of Antiochus to abolish the law and religion of God.**

**"As the time of Mattathias' death came near, he said to his sons, 'Pride and violence are**

**on the increase. It is a time of violence and fury. Therefore, o my sons be zealous for the law, and give your lives to the covenant of your ancestors."**

The Hebrews successfully defeated the Greeks and Jerusalem remained autonomous until the time of the Romans, who appointed King Herod and temple worship once again became infiltrated by the pagans. As previously mentioned, the Herodians were appointed the chief priest positions and they came to be known as the Sadducees.

So as we can see, the Zealot movement was nearly 150 years old at the time of Christ with factions still active at that time, including one or more of the disciples, as we have previously discussed, specifically Simon Zelotes.

"Zeal for the law also brings the Zealots into alignment with the so-called "early church" whose adherence to the same zeal is repeatedly ascribed. The first figures cited in the Gospels as Simon Zelotes or Simon the Zealot, attests to at least one Zealot in Jesus' immediate entourage; and Judas Iscariot, whose name may well derive from the Sicarii, might be another. The most revealing of all, however, is Eisman's discovery - the original Greek term used to denote members of the early church. They are called, quite explicitly, 'Zelotai of the law' that is, 'Zealots.'[19] The author of Dead Sea Scrolls Deception continues, "To recapitulate, then, their merge, from the confusing welter of sobriquets and nomenclature, the figurations of a broad movement in which the Essenes, Zadokites, Nazoreans, Zealots and other such supposed factions effectively fused."[20] There will be a further discussion of the contribution of the Dead Sea Scrolls to our understanding of the times of Christ later on in this text. Earlier in this chapter as we discussed the various names for Christ, it was intended to be more than just an exercise in futility. It is important for our discussion of the "Messianic Secret."

It was written in the book of Daniel in the 6th century B.C.

that the Messiah would be referred to as the "Son of Man." Daniel (7:13-14):

**"I saw in the night visions, and, behold, one like the Son of man came with the clouds of heaven, and came to the Ancient of days, and they brought him near before him.**

**And there was given him dominion, and glory, and a kingdom, that all people, nations, and languages, should serve him: his dominion is an everlasting dominion, which shall not pass away, and his kingdom that which shall not be destroyed."**

Especially early in his ministry, Christ concealed the fact that he was Christ or the Saviour, as pointed out in Matthew (16:13-20):

**"When Jesus came into the coasts of Caesarea Philippi, he asked his disciples, saying, 'Whom do men say that I the Son of man am?'**

**And they said, Some say that thou art John the Baptist: some, Elias; and others, Jeremias, or one of the prophets.**

**He saith unto them, 'But whom say ye that I am?'**

**And Simon Peter answered and said, Thou art the Christ, the Son of the living God.**

**And Jesus answered and said unto him, 'Blessed art thou, Simon Bar-jona: for flesh and blood hath not revealed it unto thee, but my Father which is in heaven.**

**And I say unto thee, That thou art Peter, and upon this rock I will build my church; and the gates of hell shall not prevail against it. And I will give unto thee the keys of the**

**kingdom of heaven: and whatsoever thou shalt bind on earth shall be bound in heaven: and whatsoever thou shalt loose on earth shall be loosed in heaven.'**

**Then charged he his disciples that they should tell no man that he was Jesus the Christ."**

As per our earlier discussion, "Jesus" literally means "Saviour"; "Christ" means "anointed" and was the Greek equivalent to the word "Messiah." As was foretold in the scriptures, Christ referred to himself as "The Son of Man," but an interesting question is that given the fact that he told those that were closest to him, the disciples, not to call him Jesus Christ, what did they call him? Perhaps Emmanuel, the name first foretold in the Old Testament, with Mary being so advised just prior to the birth of the Holy Child.

While out of necessity, Christ had to conceal that he was, indeed, the one that Herod had attempted to kill during childhood, having been born king of the Hebrews, he would have been an easy target for those who were trying to bring him up on charges of sedition against Rome. For one to proclaim himself as being king in the Roman empire would be sedition, a charge punishable by death, by the means reserved for political prisoners, that is, dying on a cross. It was later that the Lord, indeed, revealed the fact that he, without question was the Lord and Saviour to Peter, James and John, but once again, this had to be kept a secret from those who were trying to do him harm. **Matthew (17:1-7):**

**"And after six days Jesus taketh Peter, James, and John his brother, and bringeth them up into an high mountain apart,**

**And was transfigured before them: and his face did shine as the sun, and his raiment was white as the light.**

**And, behold, there appeared unto them Moses and Elias talking with him.**

**Then answered Peter, and said unto Jesus, Lord, it is good for us to be here: if thou wilt, let us make here three tabernacles; one for thee, one for Moses, and one for Elias.**

**While he yet spake, behold, a bright cloud overshadowed them: and behold a voice out of the cloud, which said, This is my beloved Son, in whom I am well pleased; hear ye him.**

**And when the disciples heard it, they fell on their face, and were sore afraid.**

**And Jesus came and touched them, and said, 'Arise, and be not afraid.'"**

It was shortly thereafter that Christ was to for the first time verbally identify himself as the Messiah. Matthew (17:9-13):

**"And as they came down from the mountain, Jesus charged them, saying, 'Tell the vision to no man, until the Son of man be risen again from the dead.'**

**And his disciples asked him, saying, Why then say the scribes that Elias must first come?**

**And Jesus answered and said unto them, 'Elias truly shall first come, and restore all things.**

**But I say unto you, That Elias is come already, and they knew him not, but have done unto him whatsoever they listed. Likewise shall also the Son of man suffer of them.'**

**Then the disciples understood that he spake unto them of John the Baptist."**

In spite of his attempts before the throngs of people that

always followed him to minimize his birthright as the king of the Hebrews, through his teachings and miracles, it was clear to them that he was the long awaited Saviour and would free them from the yoke of foreign oppression. **Matthew (21:9-13):**

> **"And the multitudes that went before him, and that followed, cried, saying, Hosanna to the son of David: Blessed is he that cometh in the name of the Lord; Hosanna in the highest.**
>
> **And when he was come into Jerusalem, all the city was moved, saying, Who is this?**
>
> **And the multitude said, This is Jesus the prophet of Nazareth of Galilee.**
>
> **And Jesus went into the temple of God, and cast out all them that sold and bought in the temple, and overthrew the tables of the money changers, and the seats of them that sold doves.**
>
> **And said unto them, 'It is written, My house shall be called the house of prayer; but ye have made it a den of thieves."**

The scriptures continue in fulfillment of the Old Testament prophesy that he would be worshipped by children. **Matthew (21:14-16):**

> **"And the blind and the lame came to him in the temple; and he healed them.**
>
> **And when the chief priests and scribes saw the wonderful things that he did, and the children crying in the temple, and saying, Hosanna to the son of David; they were sore displeased,**
>
> **And said unto him, Hearest thou what these say? And Jesus saith unto them, 'Yea; have ye never read, Out of the mouth of babes and sucklings**

**thou has perfected praise?'"**

The word "lawyer" when used in the Bible usually referred to one who interpreted the law. It was the lawyers, along with the Sadducees and Pharisees that sustained the brunt of criticism by Jesus, as they were charged again and again with ignorance and misapplication of the law of God. **Matthew (22:29):**

> **"Jesus answered and said unto them, 'Ye do err, not knowing the scriptures, nor the power of God.'"**

**Luke (11:52-54):**

> **"Woe unto you, lawyers! for ye have taken away the key of knowledge: ye entered not in yourselves, and them that were entering in ye hindered.**
>
> **And as he said these things unto them, the scribes and Pharisees began to urge him vehemently, and to provoke him to speak of many things:**
>
> **Lay wait for him, and seeking to catch something out of his mouth, that they might accuse him."**

However, while complete freedom of speech did not exist, there was some leeway as long as the issues were well within the realm of religion, and could not be construed as being seditious, that is, comments against the emperor or Rome.

As pagans, the Romans did not understand or particularly concern themselves with what they perceived as trivial matters of religious philosophy, amongst the various factions within the temple. The responses of Jesus to the temple leaders was oftentimes direct, blunt and, indeed, such rebukes were at times almost scathing.

**Matthew (23:27-28):**

> **"Woe unto you, scribes and Pharisees,**

**hypocrites! for ye are like unto whited sepulchres, which indeed appear beautiful outward, but are within full of dead men's bones, and of all uncleanness.**

**Even so ye also outwardly appear righteous unto men, but within ye are full of hyprocrisy and iniquity."**

While undoubtedly the temple leaders found such comments infuriating, they had no recourse, as long as such comments were not directed against Ceasar or Rome.

The ministry of Christ was quite broad and diverse and in contrast to the ministries of the wealthy Sadducees that catered to the wealthy, that of Christ included many of the poor and disinfranchised for which, at times he was criticized; however, he held out this response. **Luke (7:33-35):**

**"For John the Baptist came neither eating bread nor drinking wine; and ye say, He hath a devil.**

**The Son of man is come eating and drinking; and ye say, Behold a gluttonous man, and a winebibber, a friend of publicans and sinners!"**

**But wisdom is justified of all her children."**

While the ministry of Christ focused upon the spread of such wisdom amongst all people, irrespective of socio-economic status, there were evil forces at work to counter such truth in an attempt to maintain the status quo of the temple whose leadership was now being suddenly threatened, as the following of the "Son of man" spread knowledge of his wisdom and works throughout the biblical lands.

**Luke (12:1-3):**

**"In the meantime, when they were gathered**

**together an innumerable multitude of people, insomuch that they trode one upon another, he began to say unto his disciples first of all, 'Beware ye of the leaven of the Pharisees, which is hypocrisy.**

**For there is nothing covered, that shall not be revealed; neither hid, that shall not be known.**

**Therefore whatsoever ye have spoken in darkness shall be heard in the light; and that which ye have spoken in the ear in closets shall be proclaimed upon the housetops.'"**

While the Bible is clearly the book of knowledge, we have een again and again how the key to such has been taken away ırough language and its manipulation. Therefore, if the key is to be und, once again, it will be through language and the elucidation of ıch will make possible a clear view into the past, as was one of the ırposes of the text. Fortunately, the Bible can be used for such a rpose as to yield a bold and clear picture of the biblical times and people.

For instance, when we think of Paul who was born in Rome l accordingly, a Roman citizen, who later became a disciple and ıstle to the Gentiles, we have one picture in mind until we are r told that Paul's first name was Saul and that he was of the tribe enjamin. There is an interesting account in Acts where Paul or l is actually being attacked by the other Hebrews.
; (21:28-40):

**"Crying out, Men of Israel, help: This is the man, that teacheth all men everywhere against the people, and the law, and this place: and further brought Greeks also into the temple, and hath polluted this holy place.**
**(For they had seen before with him in the city**

**Trophimus an Ephesian, whom they supposed that Paul had brought into the temple.)**

**And all the city was moved, and the people ran together: and they took Paul, and threw him out of the temple: and forthwith the doors were shut.**

**And as they went about to kill him, tidings came unto the chief captain of the band, that all Jerusalem was in an uproar.**

**Who immediately took soldiers and centurions, and ran down unto them: and when they saw the chief captain and the soldiers, they left beating of Paul.**

**Then the chief captain came near, and took him, and commanded him to be bound with two chains; and demanded who he was, and what he had done.**

**And some cried one thing, some another, among the multitude: and when he could not know the certainty for the tumult, he commanded him to be carried into the castle.**

**And when he came upon the stairs, so it was, that he was borne of the soldiers for the violence of the people.**

**For the multitude of the people followed after, crying, Away with him.**

**And as Paul was to be led into the castle, he said unto the chief captain, May I speak unto thee? Who said, Canst thou speak Greek?"**

**The chief captain, at that point began to inquire of Paul: "Art not thou that Egyptian, which before**

**these days madest an uproar, and leddest out into the wilderness four thousand men that were murderers?**

**But Paul said, I am a man which am a Jew of Tarsus, a city in Cilicia, a citizen of no mean city: and I beseech thee, suffer me to speak unto the people.**

**And when he had given him license, Paul stood on the stairs, and beckoned with the hand unto the people. And when there was made a great silence, he spake unto them in the Hebrew tongue, saying..."**

As the scriptures continue, Paul goes on to describe to the Hebrew crowd that had attacked him that he too had been a Zealot.
Acts (22:1-3):

**"Men, brethren and fathers, hear ye my defence which I make now unto you.**

**(And when they heard that he spake in the Hebrew tongue to them, they kept the more silence: and he saith,)**

**I am verily a man which am a Jew, born in Tarsus, a city in Cilicia, yet brought up in this city at the feet of Gamaliel, and taught according to the perfect manner of the law of the fathers, and was zealous toward God, as ye all are this day."**

Paul was a disciple who did not know Christ at the time of his ministry, but by some accounts was present during the reappearance of Christ following his death and resurrection. As the scriptures continue, Paul refers to the Greek-appointed high priest Ananias as a whitened wall, after being struck in the mouth.
Acts (23:2-3):

**"And the high priest Ananias commanded them that stood by him to smite him on the mouth.**

**Then said Paul unto him, God shall smite thee, thou whited wall: for sittest thou to judge me after the law, and commandest me to be smitten contrary to the law?"**

It will be recalled that Paul, before the Hebrew crowd, announced that he was a Zealot, but now being dragged before the Sadducees and Pharisees, indicates that he is a Pharisee.

**Acts (23:6):**

**"But when Paul perceived that one part were Sadducees and the other Pharisees, he cried out in the council, Men and brethren, I am a Pharisee, the son of a Pharisee: of the hope and resurrection of the dead I am called in question."**

We will later return to Paul, but once again, this was an exercise just to demonstrate the power of the scriptures in bringing biblical characters into full focus. Once again, it should be pointed out that the Intertestamental Writings which were part of the Hebrew Bible were largely destroyed by the Greeks and later Constantine in his attempt to "standardize the Bible" also ordered that certain of the Hebrew texts were to be seized and destroyed. The Intertestamental Texts focus largely upon the actions of the Greeks and the Romans and their attempts over a several hundred-year period to subjugate the Hebrews and pervert their religion and this is the reason that they have been largely not accessible to the general population for centuries. Certain of the texts once believed to have been destroyed, instead have been concealed, even perhaps until the present time, some may exist within the archives of the Vatican.

As Josephus has told us, when the Greeks came to power, they made every attempt to claim all of antiquity as their own. However, **Luke (8:17)** holds true today, just as it was true in the time of Christ, who told the disciples:

**"For nothing is secret, that shall not be made manifest; neither anything hid, that shall not be known and come abroad."**

The words of Christ ring true whether it be the actions of the Greeks who buried thousands of sculpted busts of the ancient Pharaohs and their families in huge pits, only now have many, if not all, been located, or the surfacing of the true identity of the Hebrews which is supported by the "new breed of scholars of the Dead Sea Scrolls" which have refused to follow the "orthodox tradition" of concealment of the contents of those scriptures.
Even though the Dead Sea Scrolls were largely discovered in the 1940s after having been hidden away for nearly two-thousand years, following what was seemingly an attempt to conceal these scriptural texts from the Romans with whom they were engaged in battle on an increasing scale. Christ foretold that such wars would continue; however, these events would not mark the end of the world.
**Ruth (21:9)**:

**"But when ye shall hear of wars and commotions, be not terrified: for these things must first come to pass; but the end is not by and by."**

It was earlier in the same conversation that Christ had foretold the destruction of the temple to some of those accompanying him who had made comments regarding the beauty of the stones.
Luke 21:5-6:

**"And as some spake of the temple, how it was adorned with goodly stones and gifts, he said, 'As for these things which ye behold, the days will come, in the which there shall not be left one stone upon another, that shall not be thrown down.'"**

Christ also foretold the destruction of the Hebrew nation as they would be ultimately surrounded by the Romans and many would die of the sword while many of those remaining would be carried off into slavery into various parts of the world. Such was foretold with pinpoint accuracy, as many of these same events, following their

occurrence, were recorded in the Dead Sea Scrolls.
Luke (21:20-24):

> **"And when ye shall see Jerusalem compassed with armies, then know that the desolation thereof is nigh.**
>
> **Then let them which are in Judaea flee to the mountains; and let them which are in the midst of it depart out; and let not them that are in the countries enter thereinto.**
>
> **For these are the days of vengeance, that all things which are written may be fulfilled.**
>
> **But woe unto them that are with child, and to them that give suck, in those days! for there shall be great distress in the land, and wrath upon this people.**
>
> **And they shall fall by the edge of the sword, and shall be led away captive into all nations: and Jerusalem shall be trodden down of the Gentiles, until the times of the Gentiles be fulfilled."**

Christ also foretold of the persecution of the disciples.
Luke (21:12-16):

> **"But before all these, they shall lay their hands on you, and persecute you, delivering you up to the synagogues, and into prisons, being brought before kings and rulers for my name's sake.**
>
> **And it shall turn to you for a testimony.**
>
> **Settle it therefore in your hearts, not to meditate before what ye shall answer:**

**For I will give you a mouth and wisdom, which all your adversaries shall not be able to gainsay nor resist.**

**And ye shall be betrayed both by parents, and brethren, and kinsfolks, and friends; and some of you shall they cause to be put to death."**

Christ prophesied that following his resurrection, many would claim to be the Messiah, but they were not to be followed. **Luke (21:8)**:

**"And he said, 'Take heed that ye be not deceived: for many shall come in my name, saying, I am Christ; and the time draweth near: go ye not therefore after them.'"**

The salvation of man, the premise upon which Christianity is based, is largely explained in three simple verses that can be found in **John (3:15-17)**:

**"That whosoever believeth in him should not perish, but have eternal life.**

**For God so loved the world, that he gave his only begotten Son, that whosoever believeth in him should not perish, but have everlasting lift.**

**For God sent not his Son into the world to condemn the world; but that the world through him might be saved."**

Accordingly, Christ was not found to be the sword-wielding messiah that the Hebrews had anticipated, that would free them from the yoke of Roman oppression; however these verses point to the fact that the coming of Christ was for a broader or deeper cause, that is, the salvation or saving of men's souls.

Nicodemus, a Pharisee and leader amongst the Jews, came to know Christ in those final days. **John (3:1-3)**:

**"There was a man of the Pharisees, named Nicodemus, a ruler of the Jews:**

**The same came to Jesus by night and said unto him, Rabbi, we know that thou art a teacher come from God: for no man can do these miracles that thou doest, except God be with him.**

**Jesus answered and said unto him, 'Verily, verily, I say unto thee, Except a man be born again, he cannot see the kingdom of God.'"**

Christ goes on to explain that salvation, or this rebirth, is dependent upon faith and trust in God and the acceptance of him as a personal saviour. John 3:9-15:

**"Nicodemus answered and said unto him, How can these things be?**

**Jesus answered and said unto him, 'Art thou a master of Israel, and knowest not these things?**

**Verily, verily, I say unto thee, We speak that we do know, and testify that we have seen; and ye receive not our witness.**

**If I have told you earthly things and ye believe not, how shall ye believe, if I tell you of heavenly things?**

**And no man hath ascended up to heaven, but he that came down from heaven, even the Son of man which is in heaven.**

**And as Moses lifted up the serpent in the wilderness, even so must the Son of man be lifted up:**

**That whosoever believeth in him should not**

**perish, but have eternal life.'"**

One of the most remarkable events that took place during the ministry of Christ was the lifting up or resurrection of Lazarus, the brother of Mary and Martha, who were of the town of Bethany. Lazarus had already been dead and buried in a cave for four days when he was called from his grave by Christ. This account can be found in John, chapter 11. News swept throughout the city and surrounding areas, and several days later, Jesus was greeted by a multitude of people during the Passover feast. The Pharisees at this point, feeling that they would lose all, were successful in their quest to get Jesus tried on charges of sedition, which ultimately led to the crucifixion, followed three days later by the resurrection.

The ancient accounts of what transpired immediately following the death of Jesus on the cross usually contained some, if not all of the following elements: The sun, which had shone brightly overhead, suddenly darkened as the sky became black through what has been described by some as an eclipse, at which time the moon and stars were visible. A blood red veil seemed to come down over the moon, as though the moon were crying bloody tears. The earth shook and crevices opened within the earth, which seemed to devour some of those who had been the perpetrators, while others emerged from their graves. As the earth started to shake, the curtain in the temple tore, as several of the synagogues sustained severe damage.

The biblical accounts, however, tend to be less graphic, as we find in **Luke (23:44-45)**:

> **"And it was about the sixth hour, and there was a darkness over all the earth until the ninth hour.**
>
> **And the sun was darkened, and the veil of the temple was rent in the midst."**

**Mark (15:37-38)**:

> **"And Jesus cried with a loud voice, and gave up the ghost.**

**And the veil of the temple was rent in twain from the top to the bottom."**

**The book of Nicodemus,** a non-canonical text, records in **chapter 8, verses 1-4:**

> **"And it was about the sixth hour and darkness was upon the face of the whole earth until the ninth hour.**
>
> **And while the sun was eclipsed, behold the veil of the temple was rent from top to bottom; and the rocks also were rent, and the graves opened, and many bodies of the saints which slept arose.**
>
> **And about the ninth hour, Jesus cried out with a loud voice saying, 'Eloi, Eloi, lama zabacthani?' which being interpreted, is, 'My God, my God, why hast thou forsaken me?'**
>
> **And after these things, Jesus said, "Father, into thy hands I commend my spirit; and having said this, he gave up the ghost."**

Following the resurrection that Sunday morning, Jesus first made his appearance to Mary Magdalene who had also been present during the crucifixion, and he later made his appearance to the disciples on numerous occasions, as well as crowds of others which at times exceeded five-hundred people. **John (21:25):**

> **"And there are also many other things which Jesus did, the which, if they should be written every one, I suppose that even the world itself could not contain the books that should be written. Amen."**

**Luke (24:44-53):**

> **"And he said unto them, 'These are the words which I spake unto you, while I was yet with you, that all things must be fulfilled, which were written in the law of Moses, and in the**

**prophets, and in the psalms, concerning me.'**

**Then opened he their understanding, that they might understand the scriptures,**

**And said unto them, 'Thus it is written, and thus it behoved Christ to suffer, and to rise from the dead the third day:**

**And that repentance and remission of sins should be preached in his name among all nations, beginning at Jerusalem.**

**And ye are witnesses of these things.**

**And behold, I send the promise of my Father upon you: but tarry ye in the city of Jerusalem, until ye be endued with power from on high.'**

**And he led them out as far as Bethany, and he lifted up his hands, and blessed them.**

**And it came to pass, while he blessed them, he was parted from them, and carried up into heaven.**

**And they worshipped him, and returned to Jerusalem with great joy:**

**And were continually in the temple, praising and blessing God. Amen."**

Mark (16:15-20):

**"And he said unto them, 'Go ye into all the world, and preach the gospel to every creature.**

**He that believeth and is baptized shall be**

**saved; but he that believeth not shall be damned.**

**And these signs shall follow them that believe; In my name shall they cast out devils; they shall speak with new tongues;**

**They shall take up serpents; and if they drink any deadly thing, it shall not hurt them; they shall lay hands on the sick, and they shall recover.'**

**So then after the Lord had spoken unto them, he was received up into heaven, and sat on the right hand of God.**

**And they went forth, and preached every where, the Lord working with them, and confirming the word with signs following. Amen."**

Matthew (28:16-20):

**"Then the eleven disciples went away into Galilee, into a mountain where Jesus had appointed them.**

**And when they saw him, they worshipped him: but some doubted.**

**And Jesus came and spake unto them, saying, 'All power is given unto me in heaven and in earth.**

**Go ye therefore, and teach all nations, baptizing them in the name of the Father, and of the Son, and of the Holy Ghost:**

**Teaching them to observe all things whatsoever I have commanded you: and lo, I am with you**

**alway, even unto the end of the world. Amen.'"**

While following the resurrection, the message from Christ was clear that the disciples were to go out to all nations and preach the gospel, earlier, that is, during the time of his ministry, as we have mentioned in the past, the focus seemed to be on the "lost sheep of Israel." Therefore, it seems that during the ministry, the disciples believed that Christ was, indeed, the Son of God, while even the possibility of salvation for the Gentiles, that is, the Greek and Roman oppressors, was seemingly inconceivable at that time. While the possibility of salvation for the Gentiles remained a continuing question for the disciples, there was one before and one after who saw through Jesus Christ that Gentiles would, indeed, be enlightened. There was one who came before, whose name was Simeon. **Luke (2:25-32):**

**"And, behold, there was a man in Jerusalem,
whose name was Simeon; and the same man was
just and devout, waiting for the consolation
of Israel: and the Holy Ghost was upon him.**

**And it was revealed unto him by the Holy Ghost,
that he should not see death, before he had
seen the Lord's Christ.**

**And he came by the Spirit into the temple: and
when the parents brought in the child Jesus, to
do for him after the custom of the law,**

**Then took he him up in his arms, and blessed
God, and said,**

**Lord, now lettest thou thy servant depart in
peace, according to thy word:**

**For mine eyes have seen thy salvation,
Which thou hast prepared before the face of
all people;**

**A light to lighten the Gentiles, and the glory**

**of thy people, Israel."**

It followed that Saul, otherwise known as Paul, a Hebrew by genealogy, a Roman citizen by birth, and a Pharisee by choice, had a vision of Christ that was to forever change his life. Prior to this experience, Paul was feared as an enforcer of the Pharisees who persecuted and imprisoned many for their belief in Christ. The account of Paul's conversion can be found in the book of **Acts, Chapter 9, verses 13-15**:

**"Then Ananias answered, Lord, I have heard by many of this man, how much evil he hath done to thy saints at Jerusalem:**

**And here he hath authority from the chief priests to bind all that call on thy name.**

**But the lord said unto him, 'Go thy way: for he is a chosen vessel unto me, to bear my name before the Gentiles, and kings, and the children of Israel:"**

As the book of Acts continues, it goes on to describe how Paul became one of the biggest advocates of Christ as he spoke in synagogues throughout the land. Needless to say, those who knew him prior to his conversion were confused and suspicious, as was true of the disciples, who did not trust him. Meanwhile, the Pharisees from whom he had defected had already plotted to kill him. The book of **Acts** continues, **chapter 9, verses 26-30**:

**"And when Saul was come to Jerusalem, he assayed to join himself to the disciples: but they were afraid of him, and believed not that he was a disciple.**

**But Barnabas took him, and brought him to the apostles, and declared unto them how he had seen the Lord in the way, and that he had spoken to him, and how he had preached boldly at Damascus in the name of Jesus.**

**And he was with them coming in and going out at Jerusalem.**

**And he spake boldly in the name of the Lord Jesus, and disputed against the Grecians: but they went about to slay him.**

**Which when the brethren knew, they brought him down to Caesarea, and sent him forth to Tarsus."**

Paul was perhaps the most suited to address what was to largely become a Greco-Roman Gentile audience because of the fact of his Roman citizenship. The caste system, as previously discussed, was firmly in place with the natives of the biblical lands being the lowest in ranking, that is, with the exception of the Hebrews, who generally speaking, at this time were ranked only second to the Romans, a status that they enjoyed for the most part, along with the Greeks. At times, there was friction between these two groups, as depicted in the book of Acts, chapter 6, in which the Greeks are complaining that the Hebrew widows were receiving preferential treatment as they were given a greater food allotment than the Greek widows. Acts (6:1-4):

**"And in those days, when the number of the disciples were multiplied, there arose a murmuring of the Grecians against the Hebrews, because t heir widows were neglected in the daily ministration.**

**Then the twelve called the multitude of the disciples unto them, and said, It is not reason that we should leave the word of God, and serve tables.**

**Wherefore, brethren, look ye out among you seven men of honest report, full of the Holy Ghost and wisdom, whom we may appoint over this business.**

**But we will give ourselves continually to prayer,**

**and to the ministry of the word."**

There were many benefits to being a Roman citizen, one of the greatest of which was the fact that local municipalities had limited control over Roman citizens and if it was suspected that a law was broken, a Roman citizen was entitled to a trial in Rome. This is alluded to in **Acts (16:35-38)**:

> **"And when it was day, the magistrates sent the serjeants, saying, Let those men go.**
>
> **And the keeper of the prison told this saying to Paul, The magistrates have sent to let you go: now therefore depart, and go in peace.**
>
> **But Paul said unto them, They have beaten us openly uncondemned, being Romans, and have cast us into prison; and now do they trust us out privily? nay verily; but let them come themselves and fetch us out.**
>
> **And the serjeants told these words unto the magistrates: and they feared, when they heard that they were Romans."**

The terms "Ethiopian" and "Egyptian" were used interchangeably for the native people whose title carried a stigma which denoted those of the lowest ranking in the cast. Thus, this system was the forefather of racism. When he was referred to as an Egyptian, Paul was quick to announce that he was a Hebrew and Roman citizen. **Acts (21:38-39)**:

> **"Art thou that Egyptian, which before these days madest an uproar and leddest out into the wilderness four thousand men that were murderers?**
>
> **But Paul said, I am a man which am a Jew of Tarsus, a city in Cilicia, a citizen of no mean city: and I beseech thee, suffer me to speak unto the people."**

Paul was to rely on his Roman citizenship again and again as can be found throughout the book of Acts as he spread the word of God to the Gentiles. In addition to being a missionary of tireless energy, Paul was also a prolific writer with much of his work being deemed canonical and finding its way into the New Testament, including the epistles, Romans through Philemon. The book of Acts, which is largely about the conversion and missionary experiences of Paul, although the author of Acts, by most scholars, is thought to be Luke. In actuality, when one examines the fine biographical detail concerning the life of Paul, it would be hard to deny that he would seemingly deserve credit as a contributing author.

Luke has been traditionally described as a Greek physician however, only the latter is substantiated by fact. As far as his Greek identity is concerned, that is based purely upon conjecture which has been extrapolated upon to reach the conclusion that Luke was Greek. "One conjecture holds that Theophilus was unsaved and that Luke wrote the letter to persuade his belief in Christ."[21]
A review of the various explanations reveals that "unsaved" has been interpreted by some to mean that he was a "Gentile." This was eventually carried a step further by some to say that he was Greek. "Luke was a physician and traveling companion of the Apostle Paul. He wrote his gospel for a cultured Greek named **Theophilus (1:3)** in order to show the true humanity of Jesus and his place in history."[22]

Now turning to the quoted source in The Catholic Living Bible, not only looking at 1:3, but a wider expanse, extending from
1:1 to 5:

> **"Dear friend who loves God. [a]Several biographies of Christ have already been written using as their source material the reports, circulating among us from the early disciples and other eyewitnesses. However, it occurred to me that it would be well to recheck all of these accounts from first to last, and after thorough investigation, to pass this summary on to you, [b]to reassure you of the truth of all that we were taught."**

The legend goes on to describe, [a/b]"From verse 3. Literally, most excellent Theophilus. The name means **"One who loves God."**

In this particular case, Theophilus is used as a general greeting, but other scholars contend that Theophilus was an individual, "the person to whom the books of Luke and Acts were written **(Luke 1:3; Acts 1:1).** However, his exact identity is unknown. That is to say, if Theophilus can be identified, it might take us a long way as far as identifying Luke since it was Theophilus to whom the epistles of Acts and Luke were seemingly written. I repeat that unless otherwise stated, in this text the quoted version of the Bible will be the King James Version, unless otherwise specified, as in the previous case. As far as the notion that either Luke or Acts was written to a wealthy Greek by the name of Theophilus, who was "unsaved," would seemingly go out the window after reviewing the very first verses of Luke. **Luke (1:1-3):**

> **"Forasmuch as many have taken in hand to set forth in order a declaration of those things which are most surely believed among us,**
>
> **Even as they delivered them unto us, which from the beginning were eyewitnesses, and ministers of the word;**
>
> **It seemed good to me also, having had perfect understanding of all things from the very first, to write unto thee in order, most excellent Theophilus,"**

These passages make a couple of things very clear indeed, Theophilus was a person; and secondly, they all shared the same belief.

You will recall that given the politics of the time, there was great animosity between the Greeks and the Hebrews, making it all the less likely that a Greek would be asked to write the history of the Hebrew, John the Baptist, or the Messiah. The book of Luke served as an excellent summary which showed the relationship between

John the Baptist and Christ, and followed the life of Christ until his death and resurrection. Especially following the crucifixion, given the feelings of many of the disciples that redemption was not possible for the Gentiles, it was still all the more unlikely that Paul would have been needed to write the account in Greek. Needless to say, if he was, indeed, Greek, there would be no reason to ask him to write in Hebrew since the Hebrews had done a good job of recording their own history up until this time. It is more likely that Luke was a Hebrew and perhaps an Essene whose areas of expertise included the application of therapeutic modalities.

While Christ foretold of the coming wars to be necessary, his own ministry was largely one of peace, in that he taught.

**Matthew (5:38-39):**

> **"Ye have heard that it hath been said, An eye for an eye, and a tooth for a tooth:**
>
> **But I say unto you, That ye resist not evil: but whosoever shall smite the on they right cheek, turn to him the other also."**

**Matthew 5:43-44:**

> **"Ye have heard that it hath been said, Thou shalt love thy neighbour, and hate thine enemy.**
>
> **But I say unto you, Love your enemies, bless them that curse you, do good to them that hate you, and pray for them which despitefully use you, and persecute you;"**

The Hebrews, from the very beginning, had suffered many insults as their nation was decimated again and again. Perhaps the most devastating of all was foretold by Christ in **Luke 21:20-24:**

> **"And when ye shall see Jerusalem compassed with armies, then know that the desolation thereof is nigh.**
>
> **Then let them which are in Judaea flee to the**

**mountains; and let them which are in the midst**

**of it depart out; and let not them that are in the countries enter thereinto.**

**For these be the days of vengeance, that all things which are written may be fulfilled.**

**But woe unto them that are with child, and to them that give suck, in those days! for there shall be great distress in the land, and wrath upon this people.**

**And they shall fall by the edge of the sword, and shall be led away captive into all nations: and Jerusalem shall be trodden down of the Gentiles, until the times of the Gentiles be fulfilled."**

These passages seem to foretell of the coming "Jewish Wars." He goes on to say in Luke (21:32):

**"Verily I say unto you, This generation shall not pass away, till all be fulfilled."**

The ministry of Christ himself was a ministry of peace; however, as previously discussed, there were a couple of incidents, one was related to the turning over of the tables in the temple; and still another involving a call to purchase swords, culminating with Peter actually using his against the servant of the high priest, cutting off his ear, as they attempted to arrest Jesus.

The term "Jewish Wars" in itself is somewhat of a misnomer, in that this was a revolt which was spearheaded by the Zealots, certainly assisted by the Essenes, as well as the other masses of the Hebrew people. Other allies included Greek mercenaries who also were fed up with Roman oppression, as well as some of the Greek-inspired Pharisees who opposed Roman rule. Through all that followed, the Sadducees remained loyal to Rome, as was the case from the very beginning. In the end, it was the Sadducees who were to be the only sect to survive the Jewish Wars, and it was from the Sadducees that modern day Rabbinic Judaism sprang.

The term "Jewish Wars" does not fit very well in another sense, since it was the "Zealots" who became the Christians, and this was to become largely a battle of Christians against the Romans since the Zealots or Christians were to evolve into a specific and separate entity from Judaism, which has since been verified by the Dead Sea Scrolls.

"Sadducees installed by Herod were, however, very different. They were firmly aligned with the usurping monarch. They enjoyed an easy and comfortable life of prestige and privilege. They exercised a lucrative monopoly over the temple and everything associated with the temple. And they had no concept whatever of zeal for the law. Israel found itself under the yoke of a corrupt, illegitimate monarchy, and a corrupt, illegitimate priesthood, both of which were ultimately instruments of pagan Rome."[23]

"To recapitulate, then, there emerged from the confusing welter of Sobriquets and nomenclature, the configurations of a broad movement in which Essenes, Zadokites, Nazarenes, Zealots, and other such supposed factions affectively fused. The names prove to be merely designations or, at most, different manifestations, of the same religious and political impetus, diffused throughout the holy land and beyond, from the second century B.C. on."[24]

The Hebrews fought gallantly against the Romans, using hit-and-run tactics. They were successful, however, in the end. The revolt which began in 66 A.D. ended with the destruction of Jerusalem and Qumran between 66 A.D. and 70 A.D. There was one final holdout, the Mountain of Masada that deserves special mention, for which, once again, we turn to Josephus. Masada was a fortress built on top of a mountain. According to Josephus:

"Upon this top of the hill, Jonathan, the high priest, first of all, built a fortress and called it Masada; after which the rebuilding of this place employed the care of King Herod to a great degree; he also built a wall round about the entire top of the hill, 7 furlongs long; it was composed of white stone; its height was 12, and its breadth 8 cubits; there was also erected upon that wall 38 towers, each of them 50 cubits high; out of which you might pass into lesser edifices, which were built on the inside, round the entire wall; for the king reserved the top of the hill, which was a fat soil and better mold than any valley for agriculture, that such as committed themselves to this fortress for their preservation, might not even there be quite destitute of food, in case they should ever be in want of it from abroad."[25]

Long after the resistance had collapsed elsewhere, Masada continued to hold out. Jerusalem, for example, was occupied and raised within two years of the insurrection's outbreak - in A.D. 68. Masada remained impregnable, however, until A.D. 74. From within its walls, some 960 defenders withstood repeated assaults in a full-scale seige by a Roman army estimated to have numbered 15,000. They remained surrounded, however, at the foot of the mountain by the Romans, who on April 15, mounted an assault which is described as follows:

"The besieging Romans, after bombarding the fortress with heavy siege machinery, had constructed an immense ramp running up the mountainside and, on the night of April 15th, prepared their final onslaught. The garrison, under the command of Eleazar ben Jair, came to their own decision. This is an excerpt of Eleazar's speech to them, as was recorded by Josephus from one of the surviving widows. 'It is true, the power of the soul is great, even when it is imprisoned in a mortal body; For by moving it after a way that is invisible, it makes the body a sensible instrument, and causes it to advance further in its actions than mortal nature could otherwise do. However, when it is free from that weight which draws it down to the earth, and is connected with it, it obtains its own proper place, and does then become a partaker of that blessed power, and those abilities which are then in every way incapable of being hindered in their operations. It continues invisible, indeed, to the eyes of men, as does God himself; for certainly it is not itself seen while it is in the body; for it is thereafter an invisible matter, and when it is freed from it, it is not seen..."[26]

"It is extraordinary that no scholar, to our knowledge, has ever commented on these speeches before, for they raise a multitude of provocative questions. At no point, for example, does orthodox Judaism ever speak of a 'soul' - still less of its 'immortal' or 'perishable' nature. Indeed, the very concept of a soul and of immortality are alien to the mainstream of Judaic tradition and thought."[27]

Stated another way, modern Judaism and its predecessors, the Sadducees had little to do with those that waged the "Jewish Wars", in their attempt to restore the priesthood and "Yahwism". As had been previously stated by Josephus in no uncertain terms, the Pharisees and Sadducees had no connection to the Hebrews by birth. As has been shown, the seed of Abraham which wore phylacteries (leather forehead strips) and were enslaved in Egypt nearly four-thousand years ago, had a distinct appearance as Hebrews. The evidence would seem to support the fact that those that have laid claim to modern day Israel as "God's chosen people" are not genetically linked to the ancient Hebrews.

---

## Part VII Notes:

[1]The Holman Bible Dictionary, Thomas Nelson Publishers, p.753

[2]Ibid, p. 59

[3]The Complete Works of Josephus, p. 476

[4]The Complete Works of Josephus, p.333

[5]The Bible as History, Warner Keller, p. 362

[6]The Bible as History, Warner Keller, p.363

[7]Who's Who in the Bible, Comay & Brownrigg, p. 277

[8]Ibid.

[9]Asimov's Guide to the Bible, Isaac Asimov, p. 798

[11]The Berlin Egyptian Museum's Greek "Urkundn."

[11]Ibid.

[12]Who's Who in the Bible, Comay & Brownrigg, p. 144.

[13]Bible Dictionary and Concordance, p. 927.

[14]Bible Dictionary and Concordance, p. 973.

[15]Holman Bible Dictionary, p. 81.

[16]The Catholic Living Bible, Tyndale House Publishers, Inc.

[17]Ibid.

[18]The Holman Bible Dictionary, p. 1110.

[19]The Dead Sea Scrolls Deception, Michael Baigent and Richard Leigh, p. 206.

[20]Ibid. p. 207

[21]The Holman Bible Dictionary

[22]The Catholic Living Bible, Tyndale House Publishers.

[23]The Dead Sea Scrolls Deception, Michael Paget, page 203.

[24]Ibid, p. 207

[25]The Complete Works of Josephus, p. 599.

[26]Ibid, p. 601.

[27]Holy Blood, Holy Grail, Michael Baigent, Richard Leigh and Harry Lincoln, p. 376

## PART VIII

## MODERN DAY IMPLICATIONS

The African presence in South America was recorded in the logs of Christopher Columbus during his maiden and subsequent voyages to that area. The Africans made significant contributions to the culture of the South American natives, relics of which can be seen until this time. Such include the Mayan pyramids which were smaller than many of those on the continent of Africa, but they were found to have a similar relationship in comparing the area of the base to the height, as well as the orientation to the sun. The South Americas were a part of the established trade route long before the Gentile invasion of North Africa. The geographical information and maps of the world which came to them through the spoils of war led them to believe that the world was flat and that if they were to venture to the edge, they would fall off, a notion that they retained until the time of Columbus, an explorer who was led to believe otherwise by natives of Africa.

Hans Koning writes, "It has been said that the great explorers of Africa were simply the first white men carried around that continent by blacks; likewise, those famous captains were the first men sailed across the oceans by their crews."[1] Although Christopher Columbus had befriended Queen Isabella of Spain years prior to his 1492 voyage, his petition for funding had been denied over the years due to wars with the Moors who had controlled a large portion of southern Spain for hundreds of years. It was only after the defeat of the Moors by Spain toward the end of 1491 that Columbus was commissioned to undertake the voyage.

The three approaching ships are described as having been "harbingers of death" for the natives of South America. "During those

two years of the administration of the brothers of Columbus, an estimated one-half of the entire population of Hispaniola was killed, or killed themselves. The estimates run from 125 thousand to 1-1/2 million."[2] The natives were literally worked to death in the gold fields" or mercilessly killed when they did not meet their quota. "Columbus' log of the month of sailing that took him to the Caribbean has disappeared, but a digest of it, made by Bartolome De Las Casas, tells us everything we might want to know. (De Las Casas was that famous friar, later bishop, who came to the Indies and wrote their classical history. He was one of the very few churchmen to protest the treatment of the local population by the Spaniards, a protest to which he devoted his entire life" ...)[3]
It was this same friar, De Las Casas, who made the observation that the shy South American natives were not suited for such work, and that the stronger, larger Africans would be better suited for such work. As a result, the wholesale business dealing in African flesh was born, and interestingly enough, was to endure for a period of 400 years. The impact in terms of loss of human life and suffering was incalculable. "Legally (in medieval church terms), all newly discovered land "belonged" to the pope and was his to give in fief to those kings who would then have the duty to lead the inhabitants to the true faith."[4]

The voyages of Columbus took place during the reign of Pope Alexander VI. The birth of slavery seemed to create another problem for those who were involved in the church, in that up until that time, in spite of the iconoclast movement, there were shrines and icons still all over the world depicting the Virgin and child's physical appearance as being very similar to those that were now being enslaved. It was about that same time that Michelangelo was commissioned, along with Leonardo Da Vinci to forever change that image, by the pope.

Michelangelo's work on the Sistine Chapel ceiling began in 1509, using the 8,070 sq. ft. surface as his canvas. He went on to create what some regarded as the greatest work of art in Western history. There are over 350 figures created in all, including the twelve prophets and forty ancestors of Christ, none of whom bore the

Hebrew features that could be readily seen in earlier works and icons The fact that many shrines and statues of the Madonna bearing African features, although centuries old, are still with us today has created somewhat of an enigma for the church.

It has been estimated that there were approximately 1500 shrines in place, as well as a countless number of icons spread around the world at the time of the commission of Leonardo da Vinci, as well as Michelangelo's work on the Sistine Chapel. "The great age of the Black Virgin is the twelfth century, but legends about her hark back to the dawn of Christianity, the dynasty of the Merovingians and the age of Charlemagne. Like the sleepers of Ephesus, ideas go underground for a few centuries to re-emerge when times are more propitious." [5]

It has been expressed by some biblical scholars that during the ministry, as well as the epistles written by Paul, he deliberately failed to allude to the genealogy of Jesus Christ, in that it was felt that the reaction of his Gentile Greco-Roman audience would be less than favorable since, as indicated by the papyri of the time, race was clearly an issue ingrained in Roman life by decree. On the other hand, it could be argued that perhaps Paul or Saul did not see the need to discuss the genealogy of Christ since he never seemed to conceal that he himself was a Hebrew. Perhaps more times than not, Paul was accompanied by Luke, who through speculation, was said to be a former slave. "He was possibly a slave, educated, and trained in medicine within some Greco-Roman household and Eastern Mediterranean country." [6] While there is no evidence to support any claim that Luke was Greek, to the contrary, evidence supported by ancient writings points to the fact that Luke was, indeed, a Hebrew. "Some recent scholarship has suggested, however, that Luke was a Jew, whose writings were translated from a Semitic language" not Greek. [7]

In addition to being a disciple, physician and writer, it is believed by many that this same Luke is the St. Luke who late in life became obsessed with artistic pursuits which focused on the Virgin Mary and Child. It is believed by many that they are one and the same, but I am not aware of any direct evidence to confirm this claim. In any case, the artist, St. Luke, would have been a contemporary of the disciple,.and certainly, he came to be known as a prolific artist whose works became world renowned at the time.

"In A. D. 438, the Empress Eudoxia sent her sister-in-law, the Empress Pulcheria, an icon of the Virgin painted by St. Luke, which, with the possible exception of a second century mural from the catacomb of Priscilla in Rome, is the first recorded image of Our Lady. Pulcheria became an enthusiastic collector of relics pertaining to the Virgin and helped to set the fashion for holy images which flourished wherever Byzantine held sway, until the iconoclastic controversy of the 7th and 8th centuries caused a temporary backset.[8] Many of the Byzantine or Eastern block country icons have survived to this day. Interestingly enough, when Russian immigrants come to this country, even today, they will usually be carrying with them their icon of the blessed Virgin. As an antique dealer in such works explained, "It is their fondest treasure and usually the last item that they will part with, even if they are hungry, but under such conditions as dire poverty, they have been known to part with them."

The icon displayed of the blessed Virgin and Child, from Russia, and dated in the mid 1800s is to be looked upon as no more than a work of art presenting the artist's conception of the appearance of the holy Mother and Child. While it is believed that St. Luke never met Jesus, he did meet the Virgin Mary. It is therefore perhaps realistic to consider his paintings and carvings to be accurate representations. Few, if any exist outside the Vatican today. Meanwhile, it is believed by some that the Vatican is in possession of several of St. Luke's original works which continue to be protected from public view.

Although there is no biblical parallel, an extra-biblical source attributes the following statement to Paul: "For I could wish that I myself were cursed and cut off from Christ for (their) sake ...to them belong the patriarchs, and of their race, according to the flesh, is the Christ."

Just as it was the thrust of the iconoclast movement during the sixth and seventh centuries to destroy the images that some had started to worship, it was the object of the artists that followed to create an acceptable or suitable replacement, as the papal hierarchy sought to relieve its conscience. Now any semblance of spirituality that might have been associated with the Hebrews' physical form was now effectively obliterated as the image of Jesus eventually evolved to blond hair and blue eyes and an appearance that was the antithesis of those that were being enslaved.

The Dead Sea Scrolls serve to magnify the paradoxical relationships between the Hebrews and modern day Judaism via the Sadducees, as well as the Zealots - forerunners of the Christians, who fought against Rome only to have Rome surface as the center of the Christian movement. In both cases with the image of the ancient Hebrews being dissociated, and for all practical purposes, completely lost in time. At the time of the writing of the final chapter of this text, in late 1994, the interpretation of less than 20 percent of the contents of the Dead Sea Scrolls has been released to the public. Meanwhile, books have begun to surface such as "Dead Sea Scrolls Deception." The accuracy of the Dead Sea Scrolls interpretations is in question since some scholars have admitted that there is an "orthodox version of scroll interpretation" as opposed to what has been implied as a more accurate translation. Additionally, it has been said that the release of the contents of the scrolls would be embarrassing to both Rome and Israel, the latter of which has had control over the scrolls for nearly forty years. Even the manner in which Israel finally gained control of the scrolls is quite interesting and has been the subject matter in several books.

Just as the Hebrews had waged war against Rome prior to the time of Christ, there continued to be rumors of still another impending war during and following the life of Christ, which did, indeed, manifest the year 66 A.D. Mention of the coming wars by Christ carried such an impact that the subject was mentioned by Matthew, Mark and Luke in their epistles.

**Matthew (24:6):**

**"And ye shall hear of wars and rumours of war:**

**see that ye be not troubled: for all these things must come to pass, but the end is not yet.**

Mark (13:7):

**"And when ye shall hear of wars and rumours of wars, be ye not troubled: for such things must need be; but the end shall not yet."**

Luke (21:9):

**"But when ye shall hear of wars and commotions, be not terrified: for these things must first come to pass; but the end is not by and by."**

The animosity between the Romans and the Hebrews, who continued to see themselves as a nation, continued to grow as Rome launched and all out campaign to obliterate the Hebrews from the face of the earth. By 70 A.D., even the holy temple was reduced to rubble. The Romans were out to destroy all that the Hebrews stood for and certainly, their scriptures which were in scroll form were fair game. The warehousing of such scrolls by the hundreds, if not thousands, in isolated caves of Qumran were seemingly, at least partially the purpose of protecting them from the Romans. As we have previously discussed, the process of destroying the original Hebrew texts had already begun with the Greeks. It was to continue with the Romans right down to the time of Constantine, who in the fourth century A.D. called for the destruction of certain Hebrew texts which were not considered to be canonical.

It is the stockpiling of the scrolls at Qumran during the period of these wars that has made it possible for us to have a glimpse of the ancient past, at the same time, allowing us the opportunity to compare the texts of today to some of those that existed at the time of Christ. One such example is the entire text of Isaiah which was found intact on 23-foot long leather scroll, was found to agree almost word for word with our text of today. It is thought that this particular scroll dates back to 100 B.C.

There is a reasonable assumption that it was the combination of the Greek desire to destroy the Hebrew scrolls once the conversions had been made to their language, and the Jewish Wars which followed that led to the stockpiling of the scrolls. Such stockpiling approached an almost warehouse level, thus protecting them from harm. Thus, it was the combination of these circumstances which created the hostile environment that led to the storage and preservation of the ancient scrolls that are now available for us today.

Sigmund Freud wrote, "An objective proof of the period into which the life of Moses, and with it the Exodus from Egypt, fall would perhaps have sufficed, but this has not been forthcoming, and therefore it will be better to suppress any inferences that might follow our view that Moses was an Egyptian."[9]

We have demonstrated in Chapter I the time period of Moses and of the Exodus can be established using the Bible itself.

**Kings (6:1):**

> **"And it came to pass in the four hundred and**
> **eightieth year after the children of Israel**
> **were come out of the land of Egypt, in the**
> **fourth year of Solomon's reign over Israel,**
> **in the month of Zif, which is the second month,**
> **that he began to build the house of the Lord."**

As we know from even extra-biblical sources, the reign of Solomon extended for a forty-year period from 971 B.C. to 931 B.C. According to the Book of Kings, the temple work was started in 967 B.C. From that point, going back in time, 480 years, we can establish the period of the Exodus or the year in which "Israel were come out of the land of Egypt," as 1447 B.C. We know from biblical references that Moses was forty at the time in which he left the palace after killing an overseer of the Hebrew slaves and he remained in a self-imposed exile for another forty years before returning to Egypt just prior to the beginning of the Exodus. As previously discussed, this would place the birth of Moses at the year 1527 B.C., which would have been just as Freud has postulated, the period of Ahmoses.

"It might have been expected that one of the many authors who recognize Moses to be an Egyptian name would have drawn a conclusion, or at least considered the possibility, that the bearer of an Egyptian name was himself an Egyptian."[10]

It was the daughter of Ahmoses - who was at that time in the last two years of his reign as Pharaoh, which extended from 1550 to 1525 B.C. - who discovered the infant Moses lying in a basket by the Nile River, as described in the second book of Moses (Exodus 2:1-10). Queen Ahmoses Merit-Amon is the most likely candidate for being the adopted mother of Moses. Indeed, she was a princess at the time of the birth of Moses. Her father, Ahmoses (1550-1525 B.C.) was in the last two years of his reign at the time of the birth of Moses. Following the death of Ahmoses, when Moses was two years old, Ahmoses Merit-Amon became queen as she had married her brother, Amenophis I (Amenhotep), who became Pharaoh (1525-1504 B.C.) As a youngman, Moses was raised as the son of Pharaoh with all the benefits that life in the palace had to offer...

**Acts (7:22):**

> **"And Moses was learned in all the wisdom of the Egyptians, and was mighty in words and in deeds."**

"While Amenhotep I probably had several children by one or more of his sister-wives, none of them survived. The Pharaoh was therefore forced to designate his brother-in-law, Thutmoses to succeed him." The son of Thutmoses II and his half-sister, Hatseput, would have been the reigning Pharaoh and Queen of Egypt in 1487, when at the age of forty, Moses rebelled by killing the overseer of the Hebrew slaves. He would not return to Egypt for forty years, that is, until 1447 B.C. at the age of 80 years old, at which time he led the Exodus, or the release of the Hebrews from bondage in Egypt. The time of the Exodus was in the period of the New Kingdom during the reign of the fifth Pharaoh of the eighteenth dynasty, Thutmoses III, who reigned from the period 1479 to 1425 B.C., a fact which was confirmed by the extra-biblical source, Josephus. We have earlier discussed this cross-reference.

Another cross-reference can be found in the writings of the ancient Egyptian historian Manetho, who wrote, "After the departure of the tribe of shepherds from Egypt into Jerusalem, Tethmosis, the king who drove them out of Egypt..."[11]

All of this has been said and we can now view Freud's comments in somewhat of a different light, that is, there is absolutely no reason to further suppress the fact that clearly the nationality of Moses was Egyptian while his genealogy extended back to the Hebrew patriarchs. It seems as though the confusion amongst the scholars concerning the dating of the Exodus which has caused some to question the validity of the Bible as a historical text stems from Exodus (1:8-11):

> **"Now there arose up a new king over Egypt, which knew not Joseph.**
>
> **And he said unto his people, Behold, the people of the children of Israel are more and mightier than we:**
>
> **Come on, let us deal wisely with them; lest they multiply, and it come to pass that, when there falleth out any war, they join also unto our enemies, and fight against us, and so get them up and out of the land.**
>
> **Therefore, they did set over them taskmasters to afflict them with their burdens. And they built for Pharaoh treasure cities, Pithom and Raamses."**

Numbers (33:3, 5) continues:

> **"And they departed from Rameses in the first month, on the fifteenth day of the first month; on the morrow after the passover the children of Israel went out with an high hand in the sight of all the Egyptians."**

**"And the children of Israel removed from Rameses, and pitched in Succoth."**

In spite of what the ancient historians, both Mantho and Josephus had to say concerning the Pharaoh Thutmoses, and his releasing the "shepherds" (an Egyptian reference to the Hebrews), some scholars have attributed the biblical account of their leaving Rameses to their leaving the Pharaoh, by that name, rather than the city. In actuality, a Pharaoh, whose Egyptian name was Menpehtier and assigned the name Rameses I, reigned for only a one-year period 1307 to 1306 B.C., and that was nearly a hundred and forty years after the Exodus. The reign of Rameses II began more than a hundred and fifty years after the exodus and it followed that nine out of ten of the Pharaohs of the twentieth dynasty, which dated from 1196 to 1070 B.C., were all assigned the name Rameses in addition to their Egyptian names, that is Rameses followed by a Roman numeral which extended from III to XI. The book of Exodus made it clear that Rameses was a city and interestingly enough, in spite of the fact that there were eleven pharaohs assigned that name, there was never a single reference to one of them by name in the Bible. Stated another way, there is not a single reference or mention of the name Rameses as being applied to a person. In the Bible, it is only applied to a city in Goshen.

Per-ramesses-meri-imen was, indeed, discovered in 1930, approximately thirty years after the discovery of Pithom. Immediately, the experts had concern and perhaps reservation over the number of temples and public buildings which bore the crest of the Egyptian Pharaoh referred to as "Ramesses II." "The experts could hardly grasp at how first it came about that on so many temples, public buildings and in other places they came upon the cipher 'Ramesses II.' But when they examined the buildings a little more closely, the explanation was plain. Many of these buildings must have been built centuries before Ramesses II. To pander his own vanity, however, Ramesses II decided to have his monogram carved on them all."[12] Thus it has been made clear that the city was not named after the pharaoh, but that instead, the converse is true. The praenomen "Ramesses" was assigned to the pharaohs of the nineteenth dynasty centuries after the city was built and perhaps even centuries after these pharaohs had actually reigned. The conclusion of the archeologists that the city existed long before Rameses I or II serves to further validate the date of the Exodus as defined in the book of Kings, and hopefully, forevermore the issue of chronology and the reliability of the Bible as an accurate historical text can now be laid to rest.

Let it be pointed out once again that the Bible places the date of the Exodus at 1447 B.C., a fact which is cross-referenced by both ancient Egyptian and ancient Hebrew scholars, Manetho and Josephus, respectively.

Contrary to popular belief, the word "slave" is only used once in the King James version of the Bible and that is in Jeremiah 2:14; and the word "slaves" also appears once, in Revelations 18:13. In neither case does the Bible condone slavery or suggest that a slave should be loyal to his slave master, as some very liberal interpretations have laid claim. To the contrary, the words "slave master" cannot be found anywhere in the King James version of the Bible. This can be confirmed by looking at any concordance of the Bible. Frequently, the word "slave" is substituted for the word "servant" in some liberal interpretations of the King James Verison, even though the obvious difference in most cases is that one receives no wages while the other is usually paid. Needless to say, that is a big difference, thus rendering the two words far from being synonyms.

Modern historians tell us that Amenhotpe, who later changed his name to Akhnenaten, was the first of the Egyptian Pharaohs to embrace monotheism, though his focus was directed upon sun worship. The historian Josephus tells us, however that one of the reasons that Abraham visited Egypt was to discuss the concept of mono-theism. Therefore, the concept was present long before Moses or Akhnenaten was born. Freud seems to stray as he indicates that Moses was trained in Akhnenaten's school, thereby being introduced to the concept and forced his religion on the Hebrew people.

"Moses trained in Ikhnaton's school, employed the same

methods as the king; he gave commands and forced his religion on the people."[13]

One problem that we can see right off is the chronology, in that the Exodus itself began more than a hundred years before the reign of Akhnenaten IV which was from 1353 to 1335 B.C. Furthermore, sun worship was not a part of the Hebrew religion which was handed down by the patriarchs. There is no question as to Freud's sincerity or conviction to the truth, as he risked everything in publishing parts I and II of his book which sent forth radical views at that time in the German periodical, "Imago" in 1937. Some comments pertaining to this conviction remain elusive even to this day, in that he stated, "No consideration, however, will move me to set aside truth in favor of supposed national interest." The statement seems to be displaced in the context of time since the modern nation of Israel was not formed until 1947, and it can be only assumed that he was using the term loosely to describe the collective body of the Jews with no intended reference to sovereignty.

The wave of invasions of the Indo-European tribes which had earlier held the Persians at bay, rendering them impotent to afford the promised reinforcements to the Hebrews during the last of the Jewish wars, continued upon the biblical lands wave upon wave. The prophet Mohammed was not to be born for still another five centuries following the last of the Jewish Wars which ended with decimation of the Hebrews in the final diaspora in the year 135 A.D. Thereafter it came to be known that the present day Palestinians occupied the land until being colonized by the British through a mandate which was due to expire in 1948. While the British continued to take large quantities of oil and other resources out of Palestine with the Palestinians receiving little in return. The British explored methods of extending their mandate, meanwhile hostilities grew to a feverish height by 1947, with frequent battles between Arabs, Jews and the British militia that were occupying the Middle East.

Then on November 29, 1947, through what some felt to be a manipulation of the body of the United Nations, it was voted to partition Jerusalem for the purpose of creating a state of Israel, the creation of a homeland for those who had none since the final diaspora in the second century. In light of the circumstances, the timing was rather curious, especially when coupled with the fact that it was deemed that such a creation would be the fulfillment of God's promise to the seed of Abraham. The establishment of the United Nations' mandate was followed by an influx of Europeans that infused into the new nation of Israel. The paradox arises when it is recalled that modern day Rabbinic Judaism evolved from the Sadducees, who as the supporters of Roman authority were in opposition to the Hebrews. They had no genetic link with the Hebrews and were the only sect that was associated with the religion of the Hebrews to survive the final diaspora which ended with the last Jewish War of 135 A.D.

The first of the Dead Sea Scrolls was found in a cave in Qumran in the latter part of 1946. Later, in 1952, in cave number four, fragments of eight hundred manuscripts were discovered, some dating back to the second century B.C., by far the largest find at that time. As they were found in an area under Jordanian control, the scrolls found their way to the Palestinian Archeologic Museum and there were no Jewish scholars on the team that was established to decipher the contents of the scrolls. John D. Rockefeller pro-vided funding for a six-year period, beginning in 1954 until the time of his death in 1960, thus the museum was renamed the Rocke-feller Museum.

"On 14 May 1948 - the day before the British mandate was scheduled to expire - the Jewish Peoples Council met in the Tel Aviv Museum and declared their own independent state of Israel."6 As might be expected, heavy fighting followed with all the Middle Eastern nations which lasted until a cease fire took place on January 7, 1949. As was prophesied, it was not to be a lasting peace, as there has been no lasting peace even until this day.

In the interim, there were many attempts by Israel to gain control of the Dead Sea Scrolls, one of the most notorious of which was when "Former Major General Ariel Sharon reported that, in the late fifties, he and Moshe Dayan devised a plan for an underground raid on the Rockefeller, to be conducted through Jerusalem's sewer system."[15] This plan to gain control of the scrolls, was never fully implemented, but a war that was only to last six days, finally accomplished this end, as the scrolls which were considered to be "the spoils of the Six Day War," entered into the hands of the Israelis.

The scroll work proved to be quite tedious and time consuming, in that some of the fragments found were less than a centimeter square with subsequent scroll findings bringing the total number of pieces which had to be reassembled into the hundreds of thousands. It is this tedious reconstruction which the scroll scholars point to as the cause for such a protracted delay in revealing their contents to the public. Meanwhile, very close knit control was extended as a shroud of secrecy has continued to envelope the Dead Sea Scrolls. Some scholars contend that such delays were planned, as the contents, if ever revealed, would prove to be embarrassing for both the Vatican and modern day Israel.

John Strugnell was ultimately fired as the project's chief when in 1990, it was reported that "In an interview given to an Israeli journalist last October and published this week in the 'Biblical Archeology Review,' Strugnell dismissed Judaism as a horrible religion and a Christian heresy which has survived when it should have disappeared." "The only cure for Judaism," he added, "is mass conversion."[16]

Within the next couple of years, there was to be still another sharp turn of events when the Huntington Library, which had a microfilmed copy of all scroll segments tucked safely away from the turmoil of the Middle East in a vault in the library in Pasadena, decided to release the material to scholars. Although a lawsuit was threatened by Israel against the Huntington Library, it never materialized, as the Israeli group pushed for "interpretive rights," not just the right to translate. MMT is one of the most important documents found and it is believed to be a letter written to the head of one of the Jewish sects in opposition to twenty-two matters of Jewish law which the writers disagreed with as not being based on the scriptures.

It is now believed by many scholars that it was the zealots, not the Essenes that held the greatest involvement in stockpiling and generating the scroll documents of Qumran. While the Hebrews, the Essenes and the Zealots were all genetically linked to the patriarchs, there were no such links with the Greek-inspired Sadducees and Pharisees. Even still, once the "Jewish Wars" began, the fact that many Greeks were willing to fight against Roman oppression, became their common bond to the movement of the Zealots, especially given the impetus towards establishing a new religion based upon a new covenant with God, the foundation for which was provided by the ministry of Christ himself. While there were many Greeks and Pharisees who were caught up in this movement with the Hebrews, causing many of them eventually to fight and perish side by side, it was the Sadducees who remained loyal to the oppressive Romans, and they were the only sect to survive the period of the final Jewish Wars as an intact entity. While it is most likely that the Zealots were the authors of MMT Scroll, its intended recipients most likely were the Sadducees, as the split was thereby pronounced and made official.

It should be noted that the strongly traditional Hebrew sect labeled as the Essenes, never referred to themselves as such in the scrolls. The scroll's authors, whether they were "Essenes" or most probably the "Zealots," in the scrolls refer to themselves as... "the saints," "the brethren," "the elect," "they that believe," "they that are in Messiah (Christos)," "they that are of the Lord," "the sons of light," "the disciples," "the Poor," "they that are of the Way," and other similar appellations."[17] They were later to adopt the name "Christians," but interestingly, Christian(s) is used only on three occasions in the Bible: **"(Acts 26:28),**
**(I Peter 4:16), (Acts 11:26)."**[18] Worship of one God was to further evolve to the worship of the single "God Head" or "Trinity" as it is sometimes called, which is comprised of the Father, the Son and the Holy Spirit, while separate, in religious philosophy are considered to be one.

In the new covenant with God, the ultimate price had been paid through the shedding of the blood of Christ, the only begotten Son of God, the sacrificial lamb for the salvation of mankind.

**Hebrews (8:11-15), Hebrews (8:22), Hebrews (10:8-18).** The new covenant seemingly broadened the scope of acceptability, in food, as well as its preparation as Christ informed his disciples that when in some-one's home, they should eat the meal that was placed before them. **Luke (10:15-17).**

There was fierce fighting in Jerusalem as the Hebrews and their allies attempted to recapture Jerusalem which by the time of the last war had already been largely destroyed, including the temple itself. The movement of the Zealots had already started to take a new form outside the area of Palestine with the center being the church in Alexandria, Egypt that was established by St. Mark. "From churches within the Roman Empire, missionaries carried the word at first to the East, into Persia and India, then to the barbarian peoples of Western Europe. By the second century, Lyons, France was an important Christian community, where St. Irenaeus (c. 130-202), a disciple of St. Polycarp from Smyrna, became one of the most important teachers of the period."[19] **Revelation (2:8-11):**

> **"And unto the angel of the church of Smyrna write; These things saith the first and the last, which was dead, and is alive;**
>
> **I know thy works, and tribulation, and poverty, (but thou art rich) and I know the blasphemy of them which say they are Jews, and are not, but are the synagogue of Satan.**
>
> **Fear none of those things which thou shalt suffer: behold, the devil shall cast some of you into prison, that ye may be tried; and ye shall have tribulation ten days: be thou faithful unto death, and I will give thee a crown of life.**
>
> **He that hath an ear, let him hear what the Spirit sayeth unto the churches; he that overcometh shall not be hurt of the second death."**

Those who were fighting what was to be a losing battle in Palestine believed that the end of the world was near and perhaps even the words of Christ came to mind for some. Luke (21:20):

> **"And when ye shall see Jerusalem compassed with armies, then know that the desolation thereof is nay."**

But of course, the desolation in this case was limited to the land of Palestine and the Hebrews as a body of people. Christ made it clear that even he did not know when the end of the world would come, and that the scriptures must first be fulfilled, but the day and hour was known only to the heavenly Father. Matthew (24:3):

> **"And as he set up upon the Mount of Olives, the disciples came unto him privately, saying, Tell us, when shall these things be? and what shall be the sign of they coming, and of the end of the world?"**

Matthew 24:35-36:

> **"Heaven and earth shall pass away, but my words shall not pass away.**
>
> **But of that day and hour knoweth no man, no, not the angels of heaven, but my Father only."**

The means of the destruction has been foretold in the book of Revelation. At least a part of the destruction of the world would come from a falling heavenly body, a star which bears the name **"Wormwood."**

Revelation (8:10-11):

> **"And the third angel sounded, and there fell a great star from heaven, burning as it were a lamp, and it fell upon the third part of the rivers, and upon the fountains of waters;**
>
> **And the name of the star is called Wormwood:**

**and the third part of the waters became wormwood; and many men died of the waters, because they were made bitter."**

The power of such an impact was demonstrated in July 1994 with the falling comet, Shoemaker-Levy 9, landing upon Jupiter with such a force that it would have completely destroyed the earth. The net effect was many times greater than that expected if all the nuclear warheads which are presently on earth were to be simultaneously detonated.

"The twenty-one cometary fragments will pelt the solar system's largest planet during six days, starting July16, 1994."[20] "Each chunk will explode with a force greater than all the nuclear weapons on earth, and together, they will pack a million megaton punch - fifty million times more powerful than the atomic bomb dropped on Hiroshima."[21]

The comet landed upon the planet Jupiter, which is approximately nine times the mass of earth. The planet's landscape was altered significantly, as might be expected, but the damage was minuscule as compared to what would have happened if the same comet had, instead, struck the earth, in that it has been speculated that the latter would have literally exploded. Fortunately, our atmosphere provides a protective envelope around the planet earth, whereby so much friction is generated from entering bodies, which happens quite frequently, that they are usually destroyed during entry with relatively few striking the earth. The largest body to enter the atmosphere within the past hundred years which had impact on the earth was in 1908.

"Europe had a similar period of white nights in 1908, after an extra-terrestrial object exploded above Tunguska in Siberia. The atmosphere blast kicked up dust that was carried west by prevailing winds."[22]

Even though this celestial body exploded as it entered the atmosphere, the fragments scattered over a wide area, leveling a large part of the Siberian Forest, an area of several square miles.

As was discussed in the beginning, it was the Hebrews that gave us the calendar, but this was only possible through their vast knowledge of astronomy from their native land of Chaldea and Babylon. Another associated field that they developed was the knowledge of which has largely been lost, that is, the area of astrology. At one time astrology was seemingly a very highly developed field. It was through such knowledge that they were able to predict significant events, such as the birth of the Messiah.

"Assyriologists deciphered on the astronomical tables of the Babylonians the exact dates on which the star of Bethlehem was observed."[23]

This work was very arduous, and tedious, but necessary to establish the basic laws of nature, and the heavens. Josephus explains, "God afforded them a longer time of life on account of their virtue, and the good use they made of it, in astronomical and geometrical discoveries, which would not have afforded the time of foretelling [the periods of the stars] unless they had lived six hundred years; for the Great Year is completed at that interval."[24]

Out of necessity, the ancients concealed the methodology which may have made it possible to make predictions based upon celestial events.

Just as was the case in ancient Egypt and in what was perhaps the highest school of learning, known as "The Mysteries," at this critical level of knowledge written notes may have been forbidden since if such knowledge fell into the wrong hands, it would be possible to alter the course of history.

It is known that the ministry of Paul took him to Arabia for reasons which are not clear as the question is still being asked today, "What was Paul doing in Arabia?"[25] Could it have been to personally inspect the most powerful object ever to exist on the face of the earth, the account of which had been lost in the Bible, during the days of Solomon. The significance of the resurfacing of the Ark of the Covenant in the Arabian country of Ethiopia at this time is not known. It is known that there has been a temporal relationship formed by the Ark itself and at least one major significant event in time, and that was the coming of the Messiah. As we have previously discussed, the book of Nicodemus records in chapter 21, verses 11-14:

> **"And we found in the first of the seventy books, where Michael the archangel is speaking to the third son of Adam, the first man, an account that**
>
> **after five thousand five hundred years, Christ, the most beloved son of God, was to come on earth,**
>
> **And we further considered that perhaps he was the very God of Israel who spoke to Moses, two cubits and a half shall be the length thereof, and a cubit and a half toe breadth thereof, and a cubit and a half the breadth thereof, and a cubit and a half the height thereof (as taken from Exodus 25:10).**
>
> **By these five cubits and a half for the building of the ark of the Old Testament, we perceived and knew that in five thousand and a half (one thousand) years, Jesus Christ would come in the ark or tabernacle of a body;**
>
> **And so our scriptures testify that he is the Son of God."**

Nicodemus (22:16-20):

> **"And we found the account of the creation, and at what time he made the heaven and the earth and the first man Adam, and that from thence to the flood, were two thousand, two hundred and twelve years.**
>
> **And from the flood of Abraham, nine hundred and twelve. And from Abraham to Moses, four hundred and thirty. And from Moses to David the king,**

**five hundred and ten.**

**And from David to the Babylonish captivity five hundred years. And from the Babylonish captivity to the incarnation of Christ, four hundred years.**

**The sum of all of which amounts to five thousand and a half (a thousand).**

**And so it appears that Jesus Christ whom we crucified is Jesus Christ the Son of God, and true and almighty God. Amen."**

It is of interest to note that in the religious services of the Hebrew remnant in Ethiopia, once a year the Ark of the Covenant is the centerpiece of their worship. The rituals of the service remain unchanged from as they were in the days of Solomon, while at the same time, Ethiopia has the distinction of being perhaps the first nation to convert to Christianity following the conversion of the king.

"Frumentius, accordingly went back to Axum as Ethiopia's first Christian bishop and there he continued his missionary endeavors which were rewarded, in the year A.D. 331, by the conversion of the king himself. The surviving coins of Ezana's reign record the transition: The earlier ones bear crescent and disk images of the new and full moon; later examples are stamped uncompromisingly with the cross - amongst the earliest coins of any country to carry this Christian symbol."[26]

The third and greatest secret that was withheld from the conquering Gentiles has remained a secret until this time. Even now a shroud of mystery remains around the object which has quietly rested in Ethiopia for the past three thousand years. As it has been described as the most beautiful and most powerful object on earth, it is without question the holiest of objects that has been entrusted to man. While its existence is no longer a secret, having been the central subject matter for both a widely distributed book and film, it would be prudent for all nations to observe and respect the Ethiopian traditions that has provided safe protection for the centerpiece of the Hebrew religion.

Ethiopia has continued to "extend its hand" as the remnant has survived even until this day. David, Solomon and Menolik were all of the tribe of Judah. However, just as was the case of the other tribes, Judah also was to be dispersed ultimately amongst all nations as result of the diaspora, existing as no more than a residue of their former glorious nation, but the prophet Zechariah has foretold in chapter 8, verses 11-13:

> **"But now I will not be unto the residue of this people as in the former days, saith the Lord of hosts.**
>
> **For the seed shall be prosperous; the vine shall give her fruit, and the ground shall give her increase, and the heavens shall give their dew; and I will cause the remnant of this people to possess all these things.**
>
> **And it shall come to pass, that as ye were a curse among the heathen, O house of Judah, and house of Israel; so will I save you, and ye shall be a blessing: fear not, but let your hands be strong."**

Amos (9:7-9):

> **"Are ye not as children of the Ethiopians unto me, O children of Israel? saith the Lord. Have not I brought up Israel out of the land of Egypt? and the Philistines from Caphtor, and the Syrians from Kir?**
>
> **Behold, the eyes of the Lord God are upon the sinful kingdom, and I will destroy it from off the face of the earth; saving that I will not utterly destroy the house of Jacob, saith the Lord.**

**For, lo, I will command, and I will sift the house of Israel among all nations, like as corn is sifted in a sieve, yet shall not the least grain fall upon the earth."**

Amos (9:13-15):

**"Behold, the days come, saith the Lord, that the plowman shall overtake the reaper, and the treader of grapes him that soweth the seed; and the mountains shall drop sweet wine, and all the hills shall melt.**

**And I will bring again the captivity of my people of Israel, and they shall build the waste cities, and inhabit them; and they shall plant vineyards, and drink the wine thereof; they shall also make gardens, and eat the fruit of them.**

**And I will plant them upon their land, and they shall no more be pulled up out of their land which I have given them, saith the Lord thy God."**

II Chronicles (7:14):

**"If my people, which are called by my name, shall humble themselves, and pray, and seek my face, and turn from their wicked ways; then will I hear from heaven, and will forgive their sin, and will heal their land."**

Zechariah (8:16-17) continues:

**"These are the things that ye shall do; speak ye every man the truth to his neighbour; execute the judgment of truth and peace in yourgates:**

**And let none of you imagine evil in your hearts**

**against his neighbour; and love no false oath: for these are things that I hate, saith the Lord."**

---

## Part VIII Notes:

[1] Columbus: His Enterprise, Hans Koning, p. 44.

[2] Columbus: His Enterprise, Hans Koning, p. 84.

[3] Ibid., p. 48.

[4] Columbus: His Enterprise, Hans Koning, p. 66.

[5] Ibid. p. 133.

[6] Who's Who in the Bible, Comay and Brownrigg, p.252.

[7] Who's Who in the Bible, Comay and Brownrigg, p. 52.

New Testament

[8] The Cult of the Black Virgin, Ean Begg, p. 19.

[9] Moses and Monotheism, Sigmund Freud, p. 15.

[10] Ibid. p.6.

[11] Manetho, translated by W.G. Waddell, p. 101.

[12] The Bible as History Warner Keller, p. 112.

[13] Moses and Monotheism, Sigmund Freud, p. 57

[14] The Dead Sea Scrolls Deception, p. 15.

[15] The Times, March 16, 1956, p. 11.

[16] Newsweek, December 24, 1990.

[17] The Meaning of the Dead Sea Scrolls, A. Powell Davies, p. 116.

[18] Strong's Concordance of the Bible, James Strong, p. 110.

[19] Biblical Times, Amanda O'Neal, p. 90.

[20] Popular Science, July 1994.

[21] Ibid. p. 45.

[22] Ibid. p. 45.

[23] The Bible as History, Introduction, p. XXIII.

[24] The Complete Works of Josephus, p. 29.

[25] Bible Review, October 1994, p. 47, Jerome Murphy O'Connor

[26] The Sign and Seal* reported by Richard Pankhurst, writing in Hancock, Pankhurst & Willetts, Under Ethiopian

Skies, op. cit.

# PART IX

## MONOTHEOLOGISM

The Triangle, which is the religious symbol of Christians, representing the "Trinity" or "Godhead," is comprised of the Father, the Son and the Holy Spirit (Holy Ghost), was known also to the ancients as a religious symbol. The concept of the Trinity was seemingly known at the time of David, who looked to the coming of the Messiah. The Star of David, which was to become the symbol of the Hebrew religion, was made by superimposing the triangular symbol of the Trinity on itself, as shown. Stated another way, the "Trinity" or "Godhead" of Christians represents God, the Son of God, and the Holy Spirit.

The Hebrew religion worshipped the Father and looked to the coming of the Messiah. The "Holy Spirit" or more specifically, the "Spirit of God" or "Spirit of the Lord" is mentioned numerous times throughout the Old Testament, beginning with the book of Genesis. As we have discussed, while Christ was said to have been the seed of David, he was paradoxically also the root of David, in that he existed ages before any of the patriarchs. Once again, David himself referred to Christ as his Lord and Savior, as Christ asked the question, how could he be both the Lord and seed of David?

**Matthew (22:41-46):**

> **"While the Pharisees were gathered together, Jesus asked them,**
>
> **Saying, What think ye of Christ? whose son is he? They say unto him, The son of David.**
>
> **He saith unto them, How then doth David in spirit call him Lord, saying,**
>
> **The Lord said unto my Lord, Sit thou on my**

**right hand, till I make thine enemies thy footstool?**

**If David then call him Lord, how is he his son?**

**And no man was able to answer him a word, neither durst any man from that day forth ask him any more questions."**

In Revelation we are told that Christ is, indeed, the root and offspring of David. Revelation (22:16):

**"I Jesus have sent mine angel to testify unto you these things in the churches. I am the root and the offspring of David, and the bright and morning star."**

Ancient extra-biblical sources, including the Protevangelion, indeed confirm that the mother of Jesus, Mary, was genetically linked to David. Protevangelion IX verse IV:

**"Then the high priest knew Mary, that she was of the tribe of David; and he called her, and the true purple fell to her lot to spin, and she went away to her own house."**

John (8:56-58):

**"Your father Abraham rejoiced to see my day: and he saw it, and was glad.**

**Then said the Jews unto him, Thou art not yet fifty years old, and hast thou seen Abraham?**

**Jesus said unto them, Verily, verily, I say unto you, Before Abraham was, I am."**

While the Trinity or triangle is symbolic of the three entities of the Godhead, there is, in actuality, only one God, in that the Father is in the Son, and the Son is in the Father, as is the Holy Spirit. Thus Christians are said to have a "three-in-one God," which would seemingly explain Genesis.

Genesis (1:26-27):

> **"And God said, Let us make man in our image, after our likeness: and let them have dominion over the fish of the sea, and over the fowl of the air, and over the cattle, and over all the earth, and over every creeping thing that creepeth upon the earth.**
>
> **So God created man in his own image, in the image of God created he him; male and female created he them."**

Just as the entities of the Trinity are as one God, the superimposed triangles, symbolic of the Trinity, yield one star which is symbolic of one God and is commonly referred to as the Star of David. The Star of David was symbolic for the religion of the ancient Hebrews which, as we have stated, was in actuality a Judeo-Christian religion whose laws were handed down by God. Thus, it would seem to follow that there can be only one true religion whose teachings should encompass the Bible from Genesis to the book of Revelation, giving full recognition to the fact that the death and resurrection of Christ marked the beginning of a new covenant. If it is, indeed, true that the religion of the Hebrews was the one true religion based upon the laws handed down by God himself, the question becomes, how did it become so fractured or splintered, as we have multiple offshoots today? It is this fracture or break in continuity in the one true religion that was handed down by the Hebrews which has made it impossible for men to follow the path of reason which would seem to dictate out of necessity that if there is but one God, and but one set of laws handed down by God, there can be but one true worship of God and that should be according to the scriptures. It is the failure to recognize what is seemingly a basic truth that has led to millions of deaths over the centuries, untold suffering and loss of souls to satan.

Thus, of the Dead Sea Scrolls, MMT is perhaps the most important document of all, since interpretations released to date suggest that it outlines the reasons for the split between the Hebrews and what had become the establishment of the temple, otherwise known as the Sadducees. The interjection of paganism and foreign gods into the temple was certainly a major factor, especially when coupled with the disruption of the godly appointed priesthood, as we have already discussed earlier in this text. Though the necessity of the split is clearly seen, the damage to mankind has been incalculable and ultimately served only one benefactor.

Pergamum is an ancient kingdom of Western Asia Minor, later a Roman province, its capitol, a Greek city on the site of modern Bergama.[1] Pergamos was the site of the first temple in Asia Minor to be dedicated to a Roman emperor, Augustus, in the year 29 B.C. Just as the Greeks before them, the Romans also were pagan worshippers with a large area of the temple being dedicated to the altar of Zeus, and according to the book of Revelation, the city was said to be the "throne of Satan." **Revelation (2:12-13):**

> **"And to the angel of the church in Pergamos write: These things saith he which hath the sharp sword with two edges;**
>
> **I know thy works, and where thou dwellest, even where Satan's seat is: and thou holdest fast my name, and hast not denied my faith, even in those days wherein Antipas was my faithful martyr, who was slain among you, where Satan dwelleth."**

While men all over the world have come to recognize that there is one true God, the failure to grasp the totality, yet singularity of the one true religion handed down by the Hebrews, has led to continuous "religious wars." Some Christian religions teach their congregations to only focus on the New Testament, and ignore the Old Testament, which in essence teaches them to divorce themselves of the history of the patriarchs and God's relationship with them. Without the Old Testament and the old covenant, there could be no New Testament or new covenant, since the coming of the Messiah was contingent upon the fulfillment of certain prophecies, one of which was the return of the Prophet Elijah, the Greek form of which is Elias. The original prophecy apparently appeared in one of the books that has been lost to the Old Testament, but the disciples of Christ alluded to the prophecy. **Matthew (17:10-13):**

> **"And his disciples asked him, saying, Why then say the scribes that Elias must first come?**
>
> **And Jesus answered and said unto them, Elias truly shall first come, and restore all things.**
>
> **But I say unto you, That Elias is come already, and they knew him not, but have done unto him whatsoever they listed. Likewise shall also the Son of man suffer of them.**
>
> **Then the disciples understood that he spake unto them of John the Baptist."**

As stated earlier, Christ came in fulfillment of the Old Testament scriptures. **Matthew (5:17):**

> **"Think not that I am come to destroy the law, or the prophets: I am not come to destroy, but to fulfill."**

The New Testament focuses on Christ, the Son of God, as it should be, in that he is our Lord and Savior, but Christ reminds us to remember God the Father, and accordingly our prayers should be directed to the Father. **Matthew (6:9-13):**

> **"After this manner therefore pray ye: Our Father which art in heaven, Hallowed be thy name.**
>
> **Thy kingdom come. They will be done in earth as it is in heaven.**
>
> **Give us this day our daily bread.**
>
> **And forgive us our debts, as we forgive our debtors.**
>
> **And lead us not into temptation, but deliver**

**us from evil: For thine is the kingdom, and the power, and the glory, for ever. Amen."**

Christ goes on to tell us that while it is appropriate to address our prayers to the Father, we can ask that they be fulfilled in the name of the Son. John (14:13-18):

**"And whatsoever ye shall ask in my name, that will I do, that the Father may be glorified in the Son.**

**If ye shall ask any thing in my name, I will do it.**

**If ye love me, keep my commandments.**

**And I will pray the Father, and he shall give you another Comforter, that he may abide with you for ever;**

**Even the Spirit of the truth; whom the world cannot receive, because it seeth him not, neither knoweth him: but ye know him; for he dwelleth with you, and shall be in you.**

**I will not leave you comfortless: I will come to you."**

Christ has reminded us that he holds the keys of hell and death, and is the way to truth and life. Revelation (1:18):

**"I am he that liveth, and was dead; and, behold, I am alive for evermore, Amen; and have the keys of hell and of death."**

John (14:6-7):

**"Jesus saith unto him, I am the way, the truth, and the life: no man cometh unto the Father, but by me.**

**If ye had known me, ye should have known my Father also: and from henceforth ye know him, and have seen him."**

John (14:9)

**"...he that hath seen me hath seen the Father..."**

The apostle John, who wrote Revelation, as well as several other books in the New Testament, clearly felt a sense of urgency and felt that the end of the world was near. This was made clear from **I John (2:17-18):**

**"And the world passeth away, and the lust thereof: but he that doeth the will of God abideth for ever.**

**Little children, it is the last time: and as ye have heard that antichrist shall come, even now are there many antichrists; whereby we know that it is the last time."**

If the outlook of Johanan (John) seems unusually dismal or bleak, it is because the period of time in which I John was written has been estimated to be between the years 85 and 96 A.D. In other words, shortly after the first Jewish War of 70 A.D., in which the temple was destroyed, and not long before the second Jewish War which he probably did not live to see. Therefore, in the case of his contemporaries, John was, indeed, correct, the end was near.

Meanwhile, Christ has told us that no one knows the final hour but the Father himself. Many ministers today teach that before the second coming of Christ, the antichrist must first emerge. The thought that there is an intermediate step prior to the coming of Christ has left some with the feeling that there is, indeed, plenty of time. They may be stunned to learn that according to John's definition, the antichrist is already amongst us.

II John (1:7):

**"For many deceivers are entered into the world,**

**who confess not that Jesus Christ is come in the flesh. This is a deceiver and an anti-christ."**

Many of the few that have gone to the edge of death and returned, frequently report having seen Jesus. Their testimonials support Revelation (22:12-13):

**"And, behold, I come quickly; and my reward is with me, to give every man according as his work shall be.**

**I am Alpha and Omega, the beginning and the end, the first and the last."**

I Thessalonians (4:16-17):

**"For the Lord himself shall descend from heaven with a shout, with the voice of the archangel, and with the trump of God: and the dead in Christ shall rise first:**

**Then we which are alive and remain shall be caught up together with them in the**

**clouds, to meet the Lord in the air: and so shall we ever be with the Lord."**

As this text opened with a discussion of the concept of monotheism, which is the doctrine and belief in one living and true God, it will end with the discussion of a close relative of monotheism which I have chosen to refer to as "monotheology." "Theology is a body of doctrines concerning God, including his attributes and relation with man."[2] Monotheology is, therefore, one body of doctrines concerning God, including his attributes and relation with man. More specifically, as the ending "ology" means "the study of"... monotheology is the study of the one body of doctrines concerning God, including his attributes and relation with man. Accordingly, the more precise definition of theology is the study of a body of doctrines concerning God, including his attributes and relation with man. The doctrines do not come from man, but were handed down to inspired men from God who were to be the caretakers then of the law. It has been shown that in both the Old Testament and New Testament, the inspiration came from one source, to one people, the latter of which were the ancient Hebrews.

Man has been admonished not to add or take away from the doctrine of God. The doctrine of God is in the Bible, and cannot be created, or destroyed by men, nor should it be manipulated. The doctrine of God encompasses the scriptures from Genesis to Revelation. Just as there is but one God, one source and one conduit (Hebrews), from the book of Genesis, written by Moses; to the book of Revelation, written by the apostle Johanan (John), there can be but one true theology. Derivations from the one true theology, which we have termed "monotheology," would by definition constitute a manipulation. Such manipulations or derivations from monotheology, or the doctrines presented "in totality" in the scriptures, man has come to call "religion," a term which has come to be quite generic and with wide applications that can be stretched so thin that it almost loses meaning beyond "a belief." One of the best examples, is that when a "religious organization" was sued in Superior Court in Los Angeles in 1990 for fraud, one of the local leaders testified as follows to the following question:

Q: "Are the Ten Commandments, as they are commonly known, considered concepts or teaching of the Baha'i religion?"

A: "Would you like to repeat the Ten Commandments?"

Q: "Are you familiar with what is commonly referred to as the Ten Commandments?"

A: "Yes, but I don't remember them one to ten; so if you can give them to me, I could..."

Q: "My deposition is not being taken. I will rely on whatever your understanding is"

A: "Perhaps I can shorten this by saying that we certainly believe that the Ten Commandments...the spiritual basis of the Ten

Commandments is still applicable. Social teachings contained therein may not apply to this age necessarily. Is that a sufficient answer?"

Q: "Is there an adoption by the Baha'is of what is...of the Ten Commandments that is formally adopted, their wholesale adoption into the Baha'i faith?"

A: "No [3]

Needless to say, for a religious organization's leadership to fail to see the relevance in the social teachings" of God's law in "this age," would certainly raise questions concerning the origin of the doctrine upon which they have based "their teachings for this age." In this particular case, which had little to do with religion, aside from "Thou shalt not steal" and "fraud," the Baha'is quietly settled out of court for an amount in excess of two-hundred-thousand dollars. It should be pointed out that in spite of social changes which may occur throughout the ages, a basic cornerstone of religion is the fact that God's law does not change. The Ten Commandments are just as applicable today as social teachings as they were in the day of Moses, and they will be just as applicable in the future.

Religion in its purest form would be the belief in monotheism and the monotheologic application of the scriptures. The continued failure to recognize the continuum and monotheologic nature of the scriptures will cause man to continue to struggle with the man made derivations thereof until such time "that he will see the light."

The "oneness" in thought, as it pertains to the scriptures, was so strong in the writings of the Old Testament, that the authors found no room for compromise or derivation from the doctrine handed down by God, and therefore, there was no need to use the word "religion," as it was understood that there was only one true belief. In the epistle of the apostle Saul (Paul) to the Thessalonians, he advised them to stand firm in their belief in the Old Testament, as it was the gospel. The year was approximately 51-52 A.D., and therefore, the New Testament had not yet been compiled as we know it today. **(II Thessalonians 13-15).**

We are forever indebted to the Hebrews of the past who stood fast, and did not yield that we might have the scriptures today, as they were handed down through the ages by God himself. The "Holy One" of Israel in the Old Testament **(Isaiah 1:4),** and the "Holy One" of the New Testament are one and the same, as Jesus has told us that he is in the Father and that no man shall come to the Father except through him **(John 14:6, 9, 20),** just as we have shown that the sign of the Trinity when superimposed on itself is the sign of David and they are as one.

The fracture in the continuity of the belief (religion) of the ancient Hebrews as a Judeo-Christian people, was engineered by the "Great Benefactor" whose throne was at Pergamos and it was he who was to benefit the most. "One would not earn the title 'Benefactor' from the service rendered in the kingdom of God."[4] Interestingly, it should be pointed out also that the Greek version of "benefactor" is "euergetes," a title held by the first self-appointed Hellenistic kings in Egypt.

Just as Satan is the "Father of Perdition," Judas Iscariot, the betrayer of Christ, has been referred to as the "Son of Perdition" (John 17:12). A second major fracture in Christianity which is the portion of the Judeo-Christian belief that was retained by the Hebrews, occurred during the Reformation with "purgatory" being a central issue, as it had become the doctrine of the church, though the concept was foreign to the scriptures. This concept of purgatory, especially when coupled with the concept of the payment of penance or payments to the church to keep one out of purgatory, was a major cause of the Reformation and the split of Christianity into its catholic and protestant denominations. Any denominations that followed thereafter required a subtle difference in order to justify its formation and existence, and such differences, perhaps more times than not, were not based on the scriptures. Thus, we have a wide diversity of religions today, nearly all of which are offshoots of the original Hebrew religion and its worship of Yahweh (Jehovah), Yahwism, "the ancient Hebrew religion centered on the monotheistic worship of Yahweh."[5]

Monotheologism and Yahwism are one and the same.

The interjection of "celibacy" into the priesthood is not scripturally based and the word "celibacy" cannot be found in the Old Testament or New Testament. To the contrary, the God-appointed priesthood of Aaron, the Levites, which later became even more specific to the lineage of Zadok, depended heavily upon the sacred institution of marriage, particularly in the days of David, when the high priest designation was limited to the progeny of Zadok. Accordingly, the son of Zadok became the high priest, and it would follow that it would be handed down from one son to the next, as had been described in the scriptures.

The issue of celibacy and the priests in the Catholic church has caused problems for centuries, the tip of an iceberg that is only now coming to light. There is no scriptural support for the abnormal state of celibacy, or the continued denial of marriage which is an underlying, smoldering issue within the Catholic Church, that is threatening its very foundation, as the church is having difficulty filling existing positions with young priests.

The Apostle Paul advised that abstaining from women was good, but for those who were not able to adhere to such a discipline, it was much better to marry.

**I Corinthians (7:1,2):**

> **"Now concerning the things whereof ye wrote unto me: It is good for a man not to touch a woman.**
>
> **Nevertheless, to avoid fornication, let every man have his own wife, and let every woman have her own husband."**

Fornication is condemned by the scriptures as the body is described as the temple of the Holy Spirit which dwells within us. Fornication is identified as the one sin that is against one's own body.

**I Corinthians (6:18-20):**

> **"Flee fornication. Every sin that a man**

**doeth is without the body: but he that committeth fornication sinneth against his own body.**

**What? Know ye not that your body is the temple of the Holy Ghost which is in you, which ye have of God, and ye are not your own?**

**For ye are bought with a price: therefore glorify God in your body, and in your spirit which are God's."**

Meanwhile, devastating lawsuits, which are the result of aberrant sexual activity involving priests, has been a growing concern, that threatens the solvency of the church today. It is a medical fact that sexual tensions of young adults, when denied the natural channel of release through the heterosexual, holy institution of marriage, may become manifest in other ways that are less acceptable by society and intolerable by the church.

If the God-appointed high priesthood of Zadok had been faced with the issue of forced celibacy, needless to say, it would have been very short-lived, and would have ended with the first priest, Aaron, himself. Celibacy is a concept that is foreign to the doctrine of the law of God, that directs men to be fruitful and multiply, thus for the obvious reason, the validity of any such policy should be reassessed in the light of God's law.

The issues of purgatory, the payment of penance, celibacy of priests, confession and prayer to priests and "saints," were all directly contributory to the movement which became known as the "Reformation," that ultimately gave rise to the "Protestant Churches." The Protestant Churches continue to divide, each with its own "derivations" that have come to be known as "denominations." The multitude of "denominations" understandably is confusing to anyone that is new in the faith of Christ, and in many cases, "fatally" complicate the law and the basic teachings of Christ at the expense of the faithful. Given the dynamics as have been described, it should come as little surprise that for the first time in history the number of Muslims in the world reportedly exceeds the number of Catholics, but remains far outnumbered by the number of Christians. Further divisions and denominations may serve to weaken the church, while on the other hand, unification as striving toward singularity in teaching and in purpose will serve to strengthen the Christian church.

God's law does not change, but religious teachings, when they veer from the gospel of the Bible, can change drastically in a relatively short period of time. One such example I can cite from my own preadolescent years, during which time I was raised in the Catholic Church and taught that sex was a sin, even in marriage unless it was for the purpose of "procreation." At the age of thirteen years old, I was confirmed as a Lutheran, but went on to graduate from two Catholic Jesuit colleges. At the first college, I was taught that sex, within the context of marriage, without procreation in mind was no longer considered to be a sin by the church. Much to my surprise, in teaching ethics, the priest went on to say that sex between a married couple should be made "as luscious as possible" and that almost anything was acceptable, as long as both parties consented and it did not bring physical harm to either partner. Five years later, in a sexual dysfunction class in medical school at a catholic university, X-rated movies were shown to young medical students, including myself, as it was anticipated that some students might not have had any sexual experience, and this was to be their introduction to sexual intercourse. The subject of procreation as a prerequisite was not raised as an issue, as the church had already reversed itself on this matter.

Unfortunately, some catholics today still have a guilt complex when having sex in marriage, for reasons that they don't necessarily recognize, which in many cases may stem from the teachings of the church in their youth.

Meanwhile, a large segment of modern-day "Judaism" fails to recognize the concept of an after-life or Jesus Christ as the Messiah. To deny either is to continue to deny those that gave us the scriptures from Genesis to Revelation, namely, the ancient Hebrews, who in many cases, died defending such a belief. The book of Revelation, beginning with the second chapter, issues a strong admonishment.

Until man comes to recognize the concept of one God, one purpose for worship, utilizing the one doctrine handed down by God in its totality, he will fall short of attaining the "true belief" of the Hebrews referred to as Yahwism. It seems as though to date, the only ones on the face of the earth that have come to recognize the totality of this concept and to hold fast to it, as they have done for the past three-thousand years, are those who are the caretakers of the Ark of the Covenant of God. The remnant of the children of Jacob who dwell in Ethiopia today as the caretakers of the pure Judeo-Christian religion are, indeed, a legacy of the ancient Hebrews, as are their cousins who have been spread around the world as grains of sand, whose identity and knowledge of their, at times glorious past was effectively eclipsed for nearly 2,000 years. Their legacy continues to be the "celebration" of the Messiah that the world has come to call Christianity, and the joyful noise of the "Holy singers"....some call gospel.

As we have been told " **Luke (12:2,3):**

> **For there is nothing, covered, that shall**
> **not be revealed: neither hid, that shall not be known.**
>
> **Therefore, whichsoever ye have spoken in darkness**
> **shall be heard in the light; and that**
> **which ye spoken in the ear in closets**
> **shall be proclaimed upon the housetops."**

---

## Part IX Notes:

[1]Funk & Wagnall's New Comprehensive International Dictionary, 1973 edition, p. 937.

[2]Funk & Wagnall's Encyclopedic Dictionary, 1973 edition,

p. 1302.

[3]Deposition of Lois Hall Willows, Thursday, December 6, 1990, Vol. II, No. C753523,

Superior Court Public Record.

[4]Holloman Bible Dictionary, p. 165.

[5]Funk & Wagnall's New International Dictionary, 1973,

p. 1456.

# INDEX

## A



## B



## C

## D



## E

## F



## G



## H

## I



## J

## K



## L



## M

## N



## P

## Q



## R



## S

## T

## U

## W



## Y



## Z

# NOTES